The Challenge
of Post-Zionism

Postcolonial Encounters

A Zed Books series in association with the International Centre for Contemporary Cultural Research (ICCCR), Universities of Manchester and Keele.

Series editors: Richard Werbner and Pnina Werbner

This series debates the making of contemporary culture and politics in a postcolonial world. Volumes explore the impact of colonial legacies, precolonial traditions and current global and imperial forces on the everyday lives of citizens. Reaching beyond postcolonial countries to the formation of external ethnic and migrant diasporas, the series critically theorises:

- the active engagement of people themselves in the creation of their own political and cultural agendas;
- the emerging predicaments of local, national and transnational identities and subjectivities;
- the indigenous roots of nationalism, communalism, state violence and political terror;
- the cultural and religious counter-movements for or against emancipation and modernity;
- the social struggles over the imperative of human and citizenship rights within the moral and political economy.

Arising from the analysis of decolonization and recolonization, the series opens out a significant space in a growing interdisciplinary literature. The convergence of interest is very broad, from anthropology, cultural studies, social history, comparative literature, development, sociology, law and political theory. No single theoretical orientation provides the dominant thrust. Instead the series responds to the challenge of a commitment to empirical, in-depth research as the motivation for critical theory.

Titles in the series:

Richard Werbner and Terence Ranger, eds., *Postcolonial Identities in Africa* (1996)

Pnina Werbner and Tariq Modood, eds., *Debating Cultural Hybridity: Multicultural Identities and the Politics of Anti-Racism* (1997)

Tariq Modood and Pnina Werbner, eds., *The Politics of Multiculturalism in the New Europe: Racism, Identity and Community* (1997)

Richard Werbner, ed., *Memory and the Postcolony: African Anthropology and the Critique of Power* (1998)

Itty Abraham, *The Making of the Indian Atomic Bomb: Science, Secrecy and the Postcolonial State* (1998)

Nira Yuval-Davis and Pnina Werbner, eds., *Women, Citizenship and Difference* (1999)

Blair Rutherford, *Working on the Margins: Plantation Workers in Zimbabwe* (2001)

Richard Werbner, ed., *Postcolonial Subjectivities in Africa* (2002)

For full details of this list and Zed's other subject and general catalogues, please write to: The Marketing Department, Zed Books, 7 Cynthia Street, London N1 9JF, UK or email Sales@zedbooks.demon.co.uk • Visit our website at: http:/www.zedbooks.demon.co.uk

The Challenge of Post-Zionism

Alternatives to Israeli Fundamentalist Politics

Edited by

Ephraim Nimni

Zed Books

LONDON & NEW YORK

The Challenge of Post-Zionism was first published in 2003 by
Zed Books Ltd, 7 Cynthia Street, London N1 9JF, UK and
Room 400, 175 Fifth Avenue, New York, NY 10010, USA

www.zedbooks.demon.co.uk

Cover design by Andrew Corbett
Designed and set in 10/12 pt Bembo
by Long House, Cumbria, UK

A catalogue record for this book
is available from the British Library

US Cataloging-in-Publication Data
is available from the Library of Congress

ISBN   Hb 1 85649 893 X
            Pb 1 85649 894 8

◎ Contents

◎ Acknowledgements

This volume could not have been completed without the support, help and advice of many people. It started as the proceedings of a very successful session on post-Zionism jointly sponsored by the Research Group on Ethnicity and the Nation State and the Thematic Group on National Movements and Imperialism at the 14th World Congress of Sociology in Montreal, Quebec in 1998. Others kindly joined the project. The project was, alas, delayed for reasons that have nothing to do with the Middle East and something to do with Oceania. I must first thank my friend Felipe Oscar (Asher) Kupchik, who from Jerusalem provided me over the years with a plethora of material and detailed updates on the changing, volatile situation in the Middle East. I must thank my first teacher in the field, Professor Baruch Kimmerling, who instilled in me a lifelong passion for the topic. I must also thank my colleague and friend Clive Kessler, a fellow traveller across the shifting sandbanks of Oceania, who, through many discussions and much material, helped me form my ideas on post-Zionism. I must also thank the editors of this series, Pnina and Richard Werbner, and Nira Yuval Davis, who, with much friendship, care and support, continuously encouraged me to work on this book. Special thanks are due to Saul Newman for his friendship, stimulating ideas and essential grammatical corrections. Joanne Pemberton also supported me with her friendship and understanding. Gavin Kitching read part of the manuscript and offered much encouragement and many useful suggestions. I am grateful to Geoff Levey for much material and for stimulating discussions on biblical exegesis. I must thank Stephen Rothman SC, who, in the best traditions of Jewish Humanism, defended me from injustice and gave me the peace of mind to complete this project. I must also thank all the contributors for their patience and understanding with the continuous delays, as well as for their generous contributions to this book.

Special thanks to Professor Edward Said, who kindly allowed us to reprint his *Al-Ahram* column, and to the journal *Israel Studies*, a leading publication in the field, which generously allowed us to reprint Henriette Dahan-Kalev's article. Thanks to Juan Pablo Uslenghi for good suggestions and very useful material, and to Helen Pringle for very useful material. Thanks to my students for their encouragement and support. A special place in the acknowledgements is left for Robert Molteno, Zed Books politics editor, the best editor one could have, gentle, encouraging, always offering good advice, and very patient with all the delays and hitches encountered on the way.

Ephraim Nimni

⊚ Notes on Contributors

Henriette Dahan-Kalev teaches at the School of Management, Ben-Gurion University of the Negev. Recent publications include: 'The Oppression of Women by Other Women: Relations and Struggle between Mizrahi and Ashkenazi Women in Israel', in *Israel Social Science Research* (1997); 'Stereotype Discourse in Israel', in *European Legacy* (1996); and 'Veterans and Immigrants in the Mass Immigration to Israel', in *Veterans and Immigrants in the Mass Immigration 1948–1953* (1996) [Hebrew].

Avishai Ehrlich teaches political sociology at the University of Tel Aviv and at the Academic College of Tel Aviv–Jaffa. He has previously taught at Middlesex University, UK and at York University, Toronto. He has recently published (with M. Johannsen) 'Folter im Dienste der Sicherheit? Terrorismus und Menschen rechte im Israel' (Torture in the service of security? Terrorism and human rights in Israel) in J. Hasse, E. Muller and P. Schnieder (eds) *Menschenrechte, Bilanz und Perspektiven* (Human Rights, Balance and Perspective) (Nomos, Baden Baden, 2001); 'Israeli Judaism and the Peace Process' in J. Bunzl (ed.) *Sacred Wrath? Islam, Judaism and the Political Roles of Religion in the Middle East* (University of Florida Press, 2002); 'Israeli Judaism and the future of Palestine' in L. Panitch and C. Leys (eds) 'Fighting Identities: Race, Religion and Ethno-Nationalism', *Socialist Register 2003* (Merlin Press, London).

As'ad Ghanem teaches Political Science at the University of Haifa. He publishes widely in the areas of ethnic relations, Palestinian politics and Israeli internal ethnic relations. He has published (with Nadim N. Rouhana) 'Citizenship and the Parliamentary Politics of Minorities in Ethnic States:

The Palestinian Citizens of Israel', in *Nationalism and Ethnic Politics*, vol. 7, no. 4 (2001), and 'State and Minority in Israel: The Case of an Ethnic State and the Predicament of its Minority', in *Ethnic and Racial Studies*, vol. 21, no. 3 (1998). His most recent books are *The Palestinian Arab Minority in Israel: A Political Study* (SUNY Press, 2001), and *The Palestinian Regime: A 'Partial Democracy* (Sussex Academic Press, 2001).

Hanna Herzog is a former chairperson of the Department of Sociology at Tel Aviv University. She has published *Political Ethnicity* (Tel Aviv, 1986); *Realistic Women* (Jerusalem, 1994) [in Hebrew]. Her recent publications in English include *Gendering Politics: Women in Israel* (University of Michigan Press, 1999); 'A Space of Their Own: Social–Civil Discourses among Palestinian Israeli women in Peace Organizations' in *Social Politics: International Studies of Gender, State and Society*, vol. 6 (1999); 'Sociology and Identity: Trends In the Development of Sociology in Israel' in *Soziologia*, vol. 2 (2000); 'Redefining Political Spaces: A Gender Perspective on the Yishuv Historiography' in *Journal of Israeli History*, vol. 21 (2002).

Ephraim Nimni teaches politics and international relations at the University of New South Wales. He has published *Marxism and Nationalism* (Pluto Press, London, second ed. 1994); 'Nationalist Multiculturalism in Late Imperial Austria as a Critique of Contemporary Liberalism: The Case of Bauer and Renner' in the *Journal of Political Ideologies*, vol. 4 (1999); and 'Marx, Engels and the National Question' in Will Kymlicka (ed.), *The Rights of Minority Cultures* (Oxford University Press, 1995); and is the volume editor of the English translation of Otto Bauer, *The Question of Nationalities and Social Democracy* (University of Minnesota Press, 2000).

Ilan Pappé teaches in the Division of International Relations in Haifa University and has published widely on the Israeli–Palestinian conflict. He is the author of *Britain and the Arab–Israeli Conflict, 1948–1951* (Macmillan, London and New York, 1988) and *The Making of the Arab–Israeli Conflict, 1947–1951* (I.B. Tauris, London and New York, 1992). He is the editor of *The Israel/Palestine Question* (Routledge, London and New York, 1999). His *Modern History of Israel and Palestine* will be published by Cambridge University Press in 2003.

Uri Ram teaches in the Behavioural Sciences Department at Ben-Gurion University, Israel. He is currently researching the impact of globalisation on Israeli economics, society, politics and culture, and publishes widely in the field of post-Zionism and neo-Zionism. He is the author of *The Changing*

Agenda of Israeli Sociology: Theory, Ideology and Identity (1995); *Israeli Society: Critical Perspectives* (1993); 'Post-Nationalist Pasts: The Case of Israel' in *Social Science History*, vol. 22, no. 4 (1998); 'The State of the Nation: Contemporary Challenges to Zionism in Israel' in *Constellations*, vol. 6, no. 3 (1999); and 'Historiosophical Foundations of the Historical Strife in Israel' in the *Journal of Israeli History*, vol. 20, nos. 2/3 (2001).

Edward Said is the chair of the Doctoral Program in Comparative Literature at Columbia University and one of the most influential thinkers of his generation. He has lectured at more than one hundred universities, is a Fellow of the American Academy of Arts and Sciences and a member of the Council on Foreign Relations. His writings have appeared in nineteen languages. He has written influential works on Palestine and the Israeli–Palestinian conflict. His numerous books include *Culture and Imperialism* (Alfred A. Knopf, 1993); *The Politics of Dispossession: Interventions (1968–91)* (Pantheon, 1993); (with Luann Walther) *Covering Islam* (Pantheon, 1981); *Orientalism* (Pantheon, 1978); *The Question of Palestine* (Routledge, 1979); *After the Last Sky* (Pantheon, 1986) and (co-edited with Christopher Hitchens) *Blaming the Victims* (Verso, 1988).

Nira Yuval-Davis is the programme director of Gender and Ethnic Studies at the University of Greenwich in the UK. She publishes widely in the area of gender and nationalism, and on settler societies. Her books include *Gender and Nation* (Sage, London, 1997); *Woman–Nation–State* (with Floya Anthias, Macmillan, London, 1989); *Racialised Boundaries* (with Floya Anthias, Routledge, London, 1994) and *Unsettling Settler Societies* (with D. Stasiulis, Sage, London, 1995)

1 ◎ Introduction

Ephraim Nimni

Post-Zionism is a term of hope, but also of abuse in contemporary Israeli politics, and it looms large in debates about the aims, character and future of the Israeli state. The debate about the importance or triviality of post-Zionism is iconoclastic, comprehensive, bitter, subversive of cherished beliefs, collective memories and emotions, and not lacking in vilification and *ad hominem* attacks.[1] It has recently spilled over to the Jewish diaspora and to pro-Israel lobbying organisations outside Israel, some of whom have, in response, launched unprecedentedly strong criticisms of Israeli dissidents and supporters of post-Zionism.[2] Ms Limor Livnat, the Education Minister in the Sharon government, decided to ban from schools a ninth-grade history textbook, *A World of Changes*, because she considers it 'post-Zionist' and insufficiently patriotic. All school copies of the book were shredded.[3] Livnat argues that from her position in the Education ministry she intends to embark on a crusade to return post-Zionist thought 'to its rightful place'.[4] Considering that self-declared 'post-Zionists' are a small (and some say dwindling) minority in Israel, it is astonishing that this debate has created such an acrimonious controversy. The continuing heat of this controversy is a clear indication that the debate is not about a trivial matter of policy, and not even about a significant change in ideological direction, but about a crucial reassessment of the status and character of the Israeli polity. While the term post-Zionism is itself far from consensual or clear among its users and detractors, and while this vagueness generates an interpretive ambiguity that sometimes borders on confusion, the debate around post-Zionism paradoxically tackles, with unusual clarity and

1

vigour, the tensions and difficulties in the question whether Israel should be a Jewish or a democratic state, and the actual and potential contradictions in pursuing these two goals at once. In doing so, the debate undermines and denounces what it calls *soziologia meguyeset*, sociology (and by extension, political science) drafted into providing intellectual and academic support to the official narrative of the Zionist movement. While the Zionist movement has some unusual characteristics in the well-rehearsed pattern of development of nationalist movements, namely dedicated organic intellectuals that act as a transmission belt of its hegemonic ideology,[5] it has also shown a most remarkable ability to cover its own weaknesses by recourse to *hasbarah*, a sophisticated mechanism of lobbying and public relations capable of mobilising significant sections of the Jewish intelligentsia in the service of the nationalist cause at home and abroad.

Post-Zionists do not simply assert that Israelis are a specific and *sui generis* type of Jewish community; most secular Zionists do not dispute that. Neither do they merely claim that Israel operates with a different set of political norms from the ones practised by diaspora Jews. That, too, seems to be obvious. The controversial claim at the heart of post-Zionist arguments is that Israel should develop a type of civic identity and an institutional framework oriented to the universal values of liberal democracy. No ethnicity must be ontologically or institutionally privileged over any other. This is the claim that Zionists reject, arguing, on the contrary, that Israel is a Jewish (ethnic) State that came into being to resolve the national abnormality of the Jewish people, and that it will lose its existential goal and *raison d'être* if it abandons this mission. Post-Zionists respond to this argument by challenging their opponents to show how this goal can be made compatible with liberal democracy, and contend that, sooner rather than later, Israel must choose whether to be democratic or to be Jewish, as, they claim, it cannot be both. In reply, Zionists concede that Jews will have a privileged position in a Jewish state, but argue that this state can nevertheless be democratic and fair to its ethnic minorities. Secular Zionists further argue that the Jewish state does and must make concessions to the national rights of its Arab minority. The standard Zionist objection to post-Zionism is therefore that all nation-states have an ethnic component to their national identity and that the Zionist movement's goal is to 'normalize' the Jewish people so that they too have a state in which to invest their ethnic identity. The rejoinder of post-Zionists to this objection is that while most nineteenth-century democratic nation-states had a distinguishable ethnic element in their national identity and that, moreover, the circumstances that led to the creation of Zionism in nineteenth-century Europe dramatically illustrate the incapacity of territorially dispersed minorities to partake in the ethos and identity of these nation-states, on the threshold of the twenty-first century, with the emergence of multiculturalism and the politics of recognition,[6] the demand and clamour is to *rectify* this glaring and conspicuous injustice. In this regard, post-Zionists contend that most liberal democracies have moved considerably towards more 'civic' and 'post-national'[7] forms of state identity, and that, notwithstanding the debacle of former Yugoslavia, multi-ethnic states are the norm rather than the exception. Jews and Israelis should know from their own history that attempts to create nation-states from multi-ethnic societies are usually conflict-ridden or worse. In these circumstances, and because of the impossibility of reconciling the existence of an ethnic state in a multicultural society with liberal democracy, post-Zionists argue that the choice for Israel is between a neo-Zionist, messianic ethnocracy[8] and a post-Zionist liberal democracy. It can also be plausibly argued that post-Zionism finds its intellectual roots in the devaluation of the role that ethnic and national identities play in the reform of the state in Western liberal democracies.[9] But even if this is the case, the post-Zionist debate addresses issues of identity and policy that are endogenous to the Israeli state, such as the Israeli–Palestinian conflict and Israel's relation to the Jewish diaspora.[10]

As argued earlier, the debate sometimes appears vague and confusing to the uninitiated reader. Definitions of post-Zionism are hard to find, and when they appear they are often not consensual. Supporters and detractors attribute to it different and sometimes conflicting meanings. Chaim Waxman[11] identifies three contrasting contributions to the term. The first is the anti-colonial argument sustained by old radical 'anti-Zionist' groups in Israel. The second results from a generational change in Israeli universities, as the generation of the 'founding fathers' retires and a new more 'eclectic' generation takes over. The third contribution results from an 'a-Zionist'[12] interrogation of fundamental questions of Jewish nationalism, Judaism and ethnicity – questions that, according to Waxman, accompanied the Zionist enterprise from its origins. From a different perspective and opposing point of view, detractors use 'post-Zionism' simply as a term of abuse that encompasses any critique of Zionism that is not to their liking.[13] None of the above is, however, fully satisfactory, for none can account for the wider use of the term beyond the limited audiences identified in Waxman's categories. The widespread use of the term indicates that the phenomenon goes beyond these limited audiences. From a different perspective, Kevin Avruch[14] differentiates between a descriptive and normative use of 'post-Zionism', but this again raises fundamental epistemological questions as to the relation between descriptive and normative categories.

As argued earlier, one influential ingredient in the development of the post-Zionist paradigm is the devaluation of the role that nationhood and ethnicity play in the analysis of the nation-state in Western liberal democracies. This influence does not, however, come from the debate on multiculturalism and the politics of recognition initiated by Charles Taylor, but from a more economic-oriented and macro-social approach related to the process of globalisation. While the politics of recognition aims at recognising cultural and ethnic diversity as a key ingredient in the transformation of nation-states into multi-nation states, the 'post-national' argument[15] devalues and underplays ethnic diversity into more 'civic' forms of state identity, and pushes towards more civic, non-ethnic forms of citizenship.[16] The argument here is that the cohesive identity of the nation-state is being subverted and diluted by massive transformations that result from that broad process fashionably called 'globalisation'. In this equation, the emergence of post-Zionism results from the impact of globalisation on the parochial Israeli scene. It is one important manifestation of the transformation of Zionism from an ethnically homogeneous nation-state project into a more heterogeneous, post-modern civic and liberal democratic project. If globalising changes subvert the relationship between territory, community and membership, then a 'liberal' post-Zionist tendency emerges to give voice and expression to these momentous changes. The collectivist–voluntarist ethos of Israeli society is transformed by the values of post-modern capitalism into a more individualistically oriented, hedonist consumer society. According to this view, this process acts as an important catalyst for a peaceful resolution of the Israeli-Palestinian conflict. In a recent work, Gershon Shafir and Yoav Peled have put forward the argument that globalisation and economic liberalisation have gradually transformed Israel from a warlike welfare society to one oriented towards peace and private profit.[17] The slogans 'peace and privatisation', 'peace and profits' and 'peace and prosperity' express the idea that globalisation and peace are causally connected.[18] In light of the events that resulted in the *Al Aqsa intifada*, and the policies of the Bush Administration in the US, this explanation seems implausible. However, the suggestion that post-Zionism becomes the ideological expression of cosmopolitan elites, while 'neo-Zionism' becomes the reaction of those left behind by the changes impelled by neo-liberal policies, has merit and requires further discussion.

Perhaps a more hopeful line of enquiry is to reflect on the origin of post-Zionism as part of a major transitional period in Israeli social sciences, and tentatively, in the wider Israeli society. In the last decade or so, there was a considerable shift in paradigms influencing Israeli academia, and this shift provided the intellectual backdrop for the development of post-Zionism.[19] One of the most important consequences of this rupture or epistemological break[20] was a noticeable move away from a conceptual paradigm designed to sustain intellectually the Zionist enterprise. A new generation of researchers and scholars felt that their commitment to academic research and argument was more important than sustaining Zionist truisms at all costs; they took a more distant and openly critical view of the established 'truths' of Zionism and a more detached and balanced view of its intellectual role, even if, as individuals, they were unwilling to break with Zionism *in toto*. Perhaps one of the finest products of this shift of paradigms, and one that accounts in its main arguments for this significant break with the older style of Israeli social analysis, is Baruch Kimmerling's recent discussion of the demise of the hegemony of secular Zionism and its profound impact in contemporary Israeli politics.[21] As Kimmerling argues in what will no doubt become a seminal work on Israeli society at the threshold of the twenty-first century, collective memory is considered in Israel to be objective history. In such a reified atmosphere of continuous and pervasive devotional imagining of history, historical arguments are not only the subject of interrogation and debate within ivory towers. They crucially and inevitably become powerful ideological and political weapons to be used as markers of the collective not only in domestic debates, but more crucially in external struggles such as the Arab-Israeli conflict and the conquest of the hearts and minds of Diaspora Jews. They are also consensus builders for loyal citizens.[22] If *hasbarah* is a crucial element in the Zionist endeavour, appealing and consensual historical arguments sanctioned by the high priests of Israeli academia must be deployed to legitimise the enterprise. When in the last decade and half, a group of historians, sociologists, and political scientists attempted to challenge crucial tenets of this incontestable history-as-memory, it became clear to the guardians of the status quo that the argument was not only about a new interpretation of history. The argument was, in their view, moving towards a new subversive genealogy of Israel as a colonial-settler state and thereby undermining its legitimacy and *raison d'être*. These so-called 'new historians', as they were pejoratively branded by their opponents, attempted from a diversity of perspectives, in a string of publications in some the most prestigious publishing houses in the English reading world, to challenge and question some of the grounding myths of the official Israeli history-as-memory.[23]

While prominent 'new historians' such as Benny Morris and Zeev Sternhell do not challenge the ideological premises of Zionism, nor the inevitability of the Zionist settlement given the European Jewish condition in the first part of the twentieth century, their well-documented criticism of the official Israeli history-as-memory certainly weakens the premises of Zionist historiography in favour of a more balanced and detached interpretation of the Zionist settlement in Palestine. It is in particular the partial and hesitant Israeli discovery of the 'nakba'[24] through the works of the 'new historians', and the inevitable parallels with visions of Jewish displacement that the Israeli discovery of the *nakba* evokes, that the umbilical cord that nourishes post-Zionist arguments for civic equality between Jews and Arabs comes into being. While the 'new historians' are not exactly forerunners of post-Zionism − because other factors such as the emergence of multiculturalism and the contemporary challenge to the idea of the nation-state are weighty ingredients in the post-Zionist problematic − there is no doubt that the redefinition of Israeli–Palestinian history advanced by the 'new historians' has significant and immediate impact in the reconceptualisation of contemporary and future Israeli–Palestinian relations. In much the same way, the *intifada* in its different stages is not only a challenge to Zionist ideology and the supremacy of an ethnic state, but also more generally to Western conceptions of the nation-state,[25] and, in particular, the unreasonable linkage between state, sovereignty, territory and nation. Here the inability of the Israeli state to come to terms with the Palestinian question is one further example, although a more violent, extreme and salient one, of the general difficulty of the nation-state to come to terms with multi-ethnic populations. In this way, post-Zionism turns the Zionist problematic of Jewish displacement on its head by questioning the point of departure of Zionism: that security for persecuted minorities can be provided only by nation-states in which these minorities become majorities. The challenge of post-Zionism subverts this foundational Zionist axiom. The Jewish nation-state is no longer an adequate solution for the security of displaced Jews. At the outset of the twenty-first century, Jews *qua* Jews are more physically endangered in Israel than in any other part of the world.[26]

International observers, justifiably impatient with the continuous and unending Israeli–Palestinian tragedy, find post-Zionism wanting in terms of the prescriptive recommendations that result from its analysis. While confusing post-Zionists with 'new historians', Perry Anderson claims that the emergence of post-Zionist scholarship and of the small sector of post-Zionist public opinion is the most welcome development in recent years, and he recognizes the outstanding intellectual achievements of Benny Morris, Avi Shlaim, Gershon Shafir, Baruch Kimmerling, Tom Segev and others. However, Anderson claims that the fearless research and uncompromising judgement that have been typical marks of their investigations of the past stop suddenly short of the present. He further argues that post-Zionism carries a mixture of courage and pusillanimity, and claims that most post-Zionists are analytical lions and prescriptive lambs.[27] At a personal, *ad hominem* level, the accusation is reminiscent of old armchair new leftism, for, unlike most of their counterparts in the English-speaking world, these individuals are assiduous contributors to the mass media and public debate in Israel and are regularly vituperated and reviled for this. Besides, as the cases of Pappé and others show, it takes somewhat more courage to articulate and defend these arguments in Israeli universities and Israeli political and legal battles than at the University of California, Los Angeles. The general conceptual point is not, however, entirely wrong, and it shows a visible weakness in the post-Zionist paradigm. The argument is more convincingly discussed by Edward Said in his account of an encounter with 'new historians'.[28] In his description of a public meeting between himself and two other Palestinian intellectuals, Elie Sambar and Nur Masalha, and Benny Morris, Ilan Pappé, and Zeev Sternhell in Paris in 1998, he finds Pappé brilliant and iconoclastic, and shows considerable admiration for the findings of both Sternhell and Morris. He criticises his fellow Palestinians and Arabs for not paying sufficient attention to the way in which Morris[29] provides meticulous and formidable evidence for the *nakba* and the destitution of Palestinians, and shows great admiration for Sternhell's scholarly and equally meticulous demolition of the constitutive myths of socialist Zionism,[30] calling for the translation of these books into

Arabic. Following on from the new historians' demolition of the Zionist grand narrative about settlement in Palestine, Said argues that it is necessary for Palestinians to engage in a similar critical exploration of their own myths and national ideas, and urges fellow Arabs and Palestinians to do so. But Said expresses considerable surprise and consternation that, in view of their important findings, Morris and Sternhell both seem reluctant to draw conclusions from their own evidence and condemn the Zionist settlement of Palestine. While, according to Said, Sternhell admits that a Jewish state could not have come into being without getting rid of Palestinians and has expressed that it was wrong to expel Palestinians, Said is puzzled by Sternhell's claim that there was no other choice. In the case of Benny Morris, Said argues that, notwithstanding the evidence he so meticulously and painstakingly collected, Morris is still reluctant to draw the inevitable conclusions about Zionism that emerge from his own evidence. Said claims that a 'profound contradiction bordering on schizophrenia' informs the work of Sternhell and Morris. He then concludes that a change of perception can occur only in an atmosphere where intellectuals are freer to reflect and ponder on the unsettling realities of present-day Israel. The great virtue of the new historians and, by implication, of post-Zionism, is the discovery of the conceptual limits of the Zionist paradigm in ways that are not apparent to most Israelis and many Palestinians, and Said calls for a relentless, continuous Palestinian dialogue with post-Zionists and new historians.[31]

It is necessary to admit that the tensions and inconsistencies identified by Said and Anderson are present in the writings of most (but not all) post-Zionists. Post-Zionist inconsistencies must, as Said argues, be addressed in the confidence of honest Israeli–Palestinian dialogue and, equally, in Israeli reflection on the immorality of actions that resulted from the Zionist settlement in Palestine. But this reflection must be accompanied by an understanding of the complexity of the situation that led to the Zionist settlement in Palestine. It is also important to see how these questionable and disastrous actions were in part forced upon Palestinian Jews and some Jewish holocaust survivors by the cruel and cold logic of the model of the European nation-state. The Zionist argument that there was no place for Jews but in a Jewish state in Palestine may have been conceptually born out of the seductive influence of European nationalism and colonialism, but its concrete mass application resulted directly from the refusal of Western democracies to accept more Jews while there was still time.[32]

Without such refusal, the Zionist dream would have remained for ever in the realm of utopia. It is in this bi-directional, dialogical and reflective path that what Said calls the 'schizophrenia' of the post-Zionist transition can be progressively ameliorated.

However, it is in the very novelty of the post-Zionist paradigm that one can find an explanation for Said's riddle. The model is still tentative and partly confused, even as it is iconoclastic and path-breaking. It is trapped in the defence of some Zionist principles while rejecting others, caught in what Gramsci calls 'the throes of a dying social order and the birth pangs of a new one'.[33] In the transitional situation, many forms of contradictory and discontinuous thought emerge. This dislocation and transition is not only ideological, but intellectual and demographic,[34] as old models no longer provide persuasive explanations of contemporary Israeli riddles and dilemmas. Baruch Kimmerling shows this momentous transition in his account of the collapse of the old Ashkenazi, 'socialist', established, secular hegemony (encapsulated in the Hebrew acronym 'ahuselim', a term close to the US acronym WASP).[35] Kimmerling has also convincingly demonstrated, in his path-breaking book on Israeli society,[36] that Israel has become a plural and multicultural society, contrary to the monoculturalism envisaged in the early Zionist dream.

In a recent fascinating study, Yehouda Shenhav discusses the official Zionist attempt to utilise the demands for restitution of Jewish refugees from the Arab world (*Mizrahim*) as a counter-claim to the Palestinian demand for compensation. These attempts, however, repeatedly backfired, precisely because Zionist discourse demands a common national Jewish identity, which limits the claim of a separate Arab-Jewish identity that could have given substance to the demands for equal status with Palestinian refugees. Zionism perceived the Mizrahi ethnic discourse as an 'intra-Jewish' element, carefully circumscribed by the 'pan-Jewish' doctrine of Zionism. It continuously insisted on the acculturation of Arab Jews, but in the process the Mizrahim introduced an alienated, separate Arab-Jewish dimension into the Israeli collective,[37] one that in recent years has made a more assertive definition of itself within Israeli society. Likewise, the large community of recent immigrants from the former Soviet Union seeks to participate in the Israeli political and social arena not as individuals, but as a distinct group that maintains a separate identity through the medium of the Russian language.[38]

These facts are not in themselves subversive of the Zionist identity of the state, for, as occurred in European liberal democracies, the plural, multicultural character of the society can remain submerged under the official nationalist ideology of one state under the tutelage of the official ethnicity. However, in much the same way as multiculturalism and the politics of difference – the ideologies that ascribe normative value to cultural diversity and demand the recognition of ethnic minorities in the public domain – undermine the certainties of the old European nationalisms that required cultural homogeneity for the nation-state, so the Israeli state is undergoing a similar process of uncovering the plural and multicultural cracks papered over by the doctrine of a monocultural nationalism (Zionism), which advocated as its main discursive motif the idea of a single Jewish nation returning to the land of its ancestors. In sharp contrast, Kimmerling argues that one of the most dramatic changes to have occurred in Israel is the evaporation of the image of a single unified society and the significant decline of a unique Israeli identity. He further identifies seven cultures and counter-cultures, which includes Israeli Arabs, while he acknowledges that none of these groups is homogeneous. This is complemented by a continuous subdivision of collective memory and nationalism into many conflicting versions.[39]

From the mounting evidence presented in a significant number of publications from a variety of perspectives, it is clear that significant changes are taking place in Israel, and that these changes cannot be accounted for by the traditional analytical tools and ideological frameworks that accompanied the development of Zionism. At the same time, diverse voices from sometimes conflicting perspectives and situations are attempting to account for these weighty changes with analytical and conceptual frameworks that are not compatible with the traditional Zionist model. The weight and diversity of evidence presented point toward paradigmatic and epistemological changes. However, as in the circumstances discussed by Said, the alternative models are not yet clear and the analysis in some cases remains paradoxical and indecisive. Scholars who have provided penetrating discussion and compelling evidence of these major paradigmatic changes remain unconvinced by, and, in many cases, hostile to, the idea of post-Zionism. Kimmerling, perhaps more than anyone else, has produced a brilliant tour de force in his account of the momentous changes taking place in Israel. Against his will, Kimmerling is often identified by supporters and detractors with the post-Zionist argument. He remains, however, a critic of the term.

Many contemporary observers have been so impressed by these rapid changes in the relative power of various groups within the Israeli state, and its transformation from a monocultural system to plurality, that they have proclaimed the start of a 'post-Zionist era.' This term is problematic and unhelpful, however, because such fashionable 'endism' is overloaded with strong negative or positive sentiments (depending on ideological bias) and lacks explanatory power.[40]

Yehouda Shenhav argued recently that 'we have to stop using this category of post-Zionism because people invoke it confusingly'.[41] Yet he is not only perceived as a 'post-Zionist' by detractors, but has convincingly shown the limitations, ambiguities and patronising attitude of Zionism towards Arab Jews in Israel.

Neri Livneh further quotes a debate that took place in the 'Mizrahi Democratic Rainbow' (*Keshet Hademokratit Hamizrahit*), an organisation that aims to show to the wider Israeli public the harm done to Arab Jews and Palestinians. The strongest opponent of post-Zionism argued that the organisation was 'conducting a trenchant dialogue with Israeli society and trying to tell the history of Israeli society from the viewpoint of the Mizrahim, and not only as was customary in the past, from the point of view of male Ashkenazim. In my view, though, we are not post-Zionists because we are absolutely not people who want to dismantle the state'.[42]

It seems to me that it is *precisely* for the reasons indicated above that it is necessary to continue to use the term post-Zionism, while incorporating it into a democratic hegemonic project that will slowly infuse it with unambiguous meaning. In the transitional period that results from the shift in values taking place in Israel, the term post-Zionism is an 'empty signifier',[43] a concept not characterised by density of meaning, but by an emptiness of content that allows supporters and detractors to articulate it easily into conflicting discourses. In other words, 'post-Zionism' is an abstraction arising from a disparate set of antagonisms, and it has not yet anchored in any clear hegemonic project. It has been propelled to notoriety by discomfort with existing terminology (for example, the Zionist narrative cannot explain the proliferation of ethnicities in Israel), and by its abusive deployment by defenders of the old order as a term of invective, creating a purely negative chain of signification: post-Zionism (bad) is everything that is not Zionism (good). As Professor David Newman explains,

> There is a concerted campaign to completely discredit anyone who thinks differently about Israeli society – especially if these ideas touch upon contemporary Israel as a multicultural, civil society or the legitimacy of a Palestinian state – in short, anything which can be labeled as being 'post-Zionist' despite the fact that this term is nothing more than a bad piece of packaging for anyone who wants to think differently.[44]

Some critics of the old order who are unable or unwilling to partake in a wider counter-hegemonic movement also use the term in a negative way. These people use the term to signify the specificity of their demands and to signal an indifference to wider issues (for example, 'we wish only to advance the position of Mizrahim and not to address the Palestinian question; this is why we are not post-Zionists'). In the hegemonic tussle that ensues from the transitional period, the task is to provide the term with the explanatory power it currently lacks by articulating a set of clear alternatives to the Zionist paradigm, and attempting to mobilise the various constituencies disaffected by the old order. Consequently, the best way to dispel the confused usage of the term is to engage in a vigorous debate over the issues that such confusion continuously suggests are problematic (democracy, Palestinian Israelis, Arab Jews, multiculturalism, and the role of ethnicity in public life), and to try in this way to create chains of signification that will supplant the term's negative use while anchoring the argument in a more general emancipatory project.[45]

In the present Israeli circumstances, it is perhaps the debate on multi-culturalism that is the most promising. Until recently, the topic has been hardly touched upon in Israel, but the visibility of the problem goes well beyond the issue of Palestinian Israeli citizens. It also relates to the visibility of Mizrahim and Russian immigrants, all of whom are demanding some kind of collective recognition that is ultimately incompatible with the boundaries of Zionism. But the idea of civic nationhood also has its dangers and paradoxes,[46] often returning ethnicity by the back door as a disguised state criterion. A serious and comprehensive debate on multi-culturalism and democratic community rights[47] will protect post-Zionism from the seductive and self-defeating danger of defining the identity of the state in purely unitary national–civic or secular terms. No unitary nation-state identity can be purely secular or 'non-ethnic'. If post-Zionism insists on advocating civic–secular nationalism, it will leave the door open to the two accusations identified by William Connolly:[48] its identity will be empty because the civic image of the nation will be drained from the 'thick', palpably 'Israeli' cultural experiences that give it vitality, and it will be hypocritical because it will secretly draw sustenance from Israeli (ethnic) culture, or from what Kimmerling defines as the discredited '*ahusel*' culture. The goal should be to build instead a multi-nation state with constitutionally enshrined collective rights for each constituent community.

However, the debate has hardly begun, and this book does not claim to provide a model for anchoring post-Zionist discourse. The aim here is more modest: it is to describe to the English-reading public the challenge that post-Zionist debate presents, from different and often contradictory perspectives, to the old Zionist order. The goal is to show the raw argument at source and the disagreement it generates from the perspective of Israeli radical and democratic politics. Some of the contributors are supporters of post-Zionism, some are critical, and some are ambivalent.

Uri Ram argues that while almost the entire population of Jewish descent in Israel is Zionist, the boundaries of Zionism have been significantly transgressed between the 1970s and the 1990s by neo-Zionism and post-Zionism. Neo-Zionism is an exclusionary, messianic and fundamentalist movement that regards the land of Israel and the sacredness of the territory as its essential source of identity. From a diametrically opposite perspective, post-Zionism emerged among the middle classes of the coastal plains and it is more individualistically oriented, less concerned about historical myths and more committed to civil rights than to ethnic nationalism. Ram argues that both trends, neo-Zionism and post-Zionism, co-existed in an embryonic form in classical Zionism. The novelty is the accentuation of one dimension to the detriment of the other.

Ilan Pappé describes the clash between the three main ideological streams within Zionism. The leading stream, traditional Zionism, to which both Labour and Likud belong, is presented as the chief rationale behind government policy since the inception of the state. Neo-Zionism is an extreme interpretation of Zionism and is an uneasy alliance between ortho-dox rabbis and ultra-nationalist settlers, with the support of the spiritual leaders of the Mizrahi Jews. Post-Zionism is a Jewish phenomenon which, according to Pappé, is a transitional phase out of Zionism – but it is not clear into what, because it is necessary to define that future in a joint debate with Palestinians. Thus far, the neo-Zionists have the upper hand, but this can be changed by a bolder definition of objectives by those in the democratic camp, by the willingness of the Palestinian side to engage in open and sincere debate about a solution on a civic and democratic basis, and by the willingness of the US and its European allies to put pressure on the Israeli government.

Avishai Ehrlich contends that the Zionist project is still evolving, and that post-Zionism, as a liberal critique of Zionism, can be understood in parallel with socialist and orthodox religious critiques of Zionism. Post-Zionism appears at the end of the cold war in tandem with theories of globalisation, thus becoming the local Israeli version of globalisation. One of the consequences for the Middle East of the end of the cold war was the Oslo process. Here post-Zionists falsely believed that the Israeli–Palestinian conflict would be resolved mainly as a result of Israel's greater integration into world markets. Contrary to this, Ehrlich argues that, as a result of the failure of the Oslo process, Israel will become more particularistic and oriented towards 'political Judaism' (Jewish 'fundamentalism') to the detriment of secular Zionism.

As'ad Ghanem argues that the general positions held by both components of the Israeli population, the Jewish majority and the Palestinian minority, are significantly different from the common civic identity expected in the post-Zionist context. Jews hold traditional Zionist values and Palestinians hold anti-Zionist positions, even if the two groups formally agree that they are citizens of the same state. This formal aspect of their existence has, in itself, no meaning for the development of a shared 'Israeli' identity, of the kind that exists in democratic countries. After discussing the findings of a survey carried out among Israeli Jews and Palestinian citizens of Israel, Ghanem concludes that the distance between the two positions remains large, and it will require significant changes on the part of the ethnocentric majority to accommodate the Palestinian minority on an equal footing.

Ephraim Nimni looks at post-Zionism from the perspective of the Jewish diaspora, and argues that the post-Zionist debate in Israel will have a beneficial effect on the ethos, identity, and lifestyle of Jewish communities in the diaspora. Instead of devoting precious energies and resources to supporting the Israeli government in its conflict with the Palestinian people – a faraway conflict not connected to their immediate circumstances – Jewish communities should instead concentrate their efforts on building vibrant diaspora Jewish institutions and making a decisive contribution to the institutionalisation of multiculturalism, an essential condition for Jewish diasporic survival and continuity.

Hanna Herzog understands post-Zionism not as a break with Zionism nor as a form of anti-Zionism, but as a search for a more equitable society in Israel, much in the same way as post-modernity strives to correct and improve modernity. She further argues that it is important to differentiate between post-Zionism as a social condition and post-Zionism as a political demand. As a social condition, post-Zionism gave rise to a debate over the definition of social boundaries and the significance of the collective and the state. Post-Zionism as a political tool adopted two central ideas from the post-modernist discourse: the end of the grand narrative and the subversive logic of the genealogical argument. In confronting the dominant Zionist discourse, various viewpoints of the women's problematic are making themselves heard. While the post-Zionist discourse does speak of a change in the place of the individual in relation to the collective, it is only feminist post-Zionist discourse that translates this abstract demand into a concrete language.

Following the theme of the challenge of gender and ethnicity to the dominant Zionist discourse, Henriette Dahan-Kalev presents a moving and heartfelt autobiographical account of the frustrations, pains and tribulations of a Mizrahi girl growing up in a society scornful of her background. This society saw her non-European background as a handicap and tried to acculturate her into dominant Ashkenazi values through its sexist idea of good looks. She concludes that her story is one primarily of oppression: of patriarchal, European, colonial, Western, Zionist oppression. Like many non-religious Mizrahim, she feels doubly alienated by the impossibility of a return to her roots, and by the steamroller that squashed everything in her outside the distorting Ashkenazi, Zionist, Israeli, European hegemony.

The reader will now be in a position to judge post-Zionism in its novelty, vagueness, promise, and contradiction. The issues raised by the challenge of post-Zionism will not fade away easily, and the key questions it raises for contemporary Israel will make sure it remains crucial to the future of the Israeli polity. Even if, at the time of writing, the violent repression of Palestinian society has reached levels of intensity not known in recent years, the issues raised by post-Zionism are not entirely absent from public debate. Dialogue with Palestinians will have to resume, preferably sooner rather than later, and opinion polls show that the overwhelming majority of Palestinians and Israelis think so. At that point the issues that such dialogue will inevitably address will reinvigorate the challenge of post-Zionism. In war or peace, the last word on post-Zionism has not been said.

NOTES

1. For example, under a spurious allegation of unprofessional behaviour, there was an attempt to dismiss one of our contributors, Professor Ilan Pappé, one of the best-known advocates of post-Zionism, from Haifa University. For the background to the case, see John Pilger's column in the *New Statesman*, 3 June 2002, pp. 11–12. As Neri Livneh argued in an interesting series of articles on post-Zionism in the Israeli newspaper *Ha'aretz* ('Post-Zionism only rings once', *Ha'aretz*, 22 September 2001) '...the fact is that Pappé and others (post-Zionists) have the effect of unsettling ideological rivals, both in and out of academia, and making them take a hostile attitude not only toward different opinions, but also toward those who espouse them'.

2. See Solomon Socrates, 'Israel's Academic Extremists' in *Middle East Quarterly*, Fall 2001, a quasi-conspiratorial rant whose favourite subject is the destructive effect of the 'Israeli tenured left'.

3. See 'Classwar', Suzanne Goldenberg's report in the *Education Guardian*, 31 July 2001. Ms Livnat further argued in a recent meeting of the Jewish Agency that post-Zionist or anti-Zionist elements are inventing lies and distorting history: 'Freedom of speech allows them to have their say, but we will not let this become part of our textbooks. Moreover, only those who support Zionism will have a part in the education system'. See http://www.jafi.org.il/agenda/2001/english/wk23/4.asp. I am grateful to Pnina Werbner for alerting me to this.

4. Limor Livnat, 'A World of Falsehood', in *Jerusalem Post*, 19 March 2001, p. 8. I am grateful to Helen Pringle for this reference.

5. Antonio Gramsci, *Selections from the Prison Notebooks*, ed. and trans. Quintin Hoare and G. Nowell Smith, Lawrence and Wishart, London, 1976, pp. 12–17.

6. See Charles Taylor, 'The Politics of Recognition', in C. Taylor and Amy Guttman (eds), *Multiculturalism: Examining the Politics of Recognition*, Princeton University Press, 1994.

7. These terms are in themselves problematic. For a critical discussion see the Introduction to: J. Couture, K. Nielsen, S. Seymour (eds), *Rethinking Nationalism*, University of Calgary Press, 1996; W. Connolly 'Pluralism, Multiculturalism and the Nation-State: Rethinking the Connections', *Journal of Political Ideologies*, vol. 1, no. 1, 1996. pp. 53–73 and Taras Kuzio, 'Nationalising states or Nation-Building? A Critical Review of the Theoretical Literature and Empirical Evidence', in *Nations and Nationalism*, vol. 7 (20), April 2001, pp. 135–54. See also the concluding remarks of this introduction.

8. Oren Yiftachel (1998) 'Nation-Building and the Division of Space: Ashkenazi Domination in the Israeli "Ethnocracy"',' in *Nationalism and Ethnic Politics*, vol. 4, no. 3, pp. 33–58. Ethnocracy is a political regime instituted on the basis of *qualified rights to citizenship* and with *ethnic affiliation* as the distinguishing principle, to ensure that the most important instruments of state power are controlled on behalf of an ethnic collectivity (www.statsvitenskap.uio.no/ansatte/serie/notat/fulltekst/0193/Ethnocr-2.html).

9. This theoretically complex discussion cannot be addressed here. See W. Kymlicka and C. Straehle (1999) 'Cosmopolitanism, Nation-States and Minority Nationalism: A Critical Review of Recent Literature', in the *European Journal of Philosophy*, vol. 7, no. 1, April, pp. 65–88; Sasja Tempelman (1999) 'Constructions of Cultural Identity: Multiculturalism and Exclusion', in *Political Studies*, vol. 47, no. 1, March, pp. 17–31; E. Nimni (1999) 'Nationalist Multiculturalism in late Imperial Austria as a Critique of Contemporary Liberalism: the case of Bauer and Renner', in the *Journal of Political Ideologies*, vol. 4, no. 3, October, pp. 289–314.

10. On post-Zionism and the Jewish diaspora see David M. Gordis, 'Toward a post-Zionist Model of Jewish Life', in Raphael Patai and Emanuel Goldsmith (eds) (1995) *Events and Movements in Modern Judaism*, New York, Paragon House, pp. 197–218. Here, without breaking with Zionist premises, Gordis castigates Zionism's inability to come to terms with the affirmative character of Jewish diaspora relationships by understanding the unwillingness of Western diaspora Jews to emigrate to Israel as *shlilat hamedinah* (negation of the [Jewish] state). Gordis claims that this feeds directly from the Zionist *shlilat hagolah*, the Zionist negation of the legitimacy of Jewish diaspora life. See p. 208.

11. Chaim Waxman (1997) 'Critical Sociology and the end of Ideology in Israel', in *Israel Studies*, vol. 2, no. 1, pp. 194–210.

12. The distinction between 'anti-Zionism' and 'a-Zionism' is an old and curious peculiarity of Israeli radical politics. The first rejects the legitimacy of the Israeli state at least as it is presently constituted, and the second accepts the legitimacy of the existence of Israel as a nation-state, while questioning the idea that Israel should be a Jewish state. The positions crystallise around the debate about the validity of the 'law of return', the legal instrument that grants citizenship to every agreeing Jew on arrival in Israel. The argument is of course more involved, but this is not the place to dissect it.

13. For a case in point, see the example of the noted liberal political philosopher Yael (Yuli) Tamir in an article in an Israeli newspaper ('Divide the Land or Divide Democracy', in *Ha'aretz*, 14 May 2002). To highlight the 'moderate' and 'territorially modest' position for a Jewish nation state, which she advocates, she presents it as being half way between the 'post-Zionism [sic] of Azmi Bishara' (a victimized Israeli Arab member of parliament) and the Zionism of General Effi Eitan, an extremist minister of the ultra-Zionist National Religious Party in the Sharon government, whom Tamir accuses of doublespeak. However, Professor Tamir claims, in her celebrated book *Liberal Nationalism* (Princeton, Princeton University Press, 1993, p. 3), that 'the era of homogeneous and viable nation states is over'. It would assist the cause of Tamir's campaign against the doublespeak of minister Eitan if she could explain how she reconciles her support for a 'modest' Jewish nation-state with the quote above.

14. Kevin Avruch (1998) 'Political Judaism and the Post-Zionist Era', in *Judaism*, vol. 47, no. 2, Spring, pp. 146–59.

15. See Yasemin Soysal (1994) *Limits of citizenship: Migrants and Postnational Membership in Europe*, Chicago, University of Chicago Press.

16. On the debate between the post-national argument and the politics of recognition approach, see the debate between Charles Taylor and Jurgen Habermas in Charles Taylor (1994) *Multiculturalism: Examining the Politics of Recognition*, edited and introduced by Amy Gutman, Princeton, Princeton University Press.

17. In its year of publication, this argument sounds like an unfortunate misjudgement of the situation by two first-rate, serious scholars. See Gershon Shafir and Yoav Peled (2002) *Being Israeli: The Dynamics of Multiple Citizenship*, Cambridge, Cambridge University Press.

18. See Uri Ram, 'The Promised Land of Business Opportunities: Liberal Post-Zionism in the Glocal Age', in Gershon Shafir and Yoav Peled (eds) (2000) *The New Israel: Peace Making and Liberalization*, Boulder, Colo., Westview.

19. This shift in paradigm has been comprehensively discussed in Uri Ram (1995) *The Changing Agenda of Israeli Sociology*, New York, State University of New York Press. It seems to me that this changing agenda goes much beyond Israeli sociology to engulf Israeli social sciences as a whole.

20. Étienne Balibar (1978) 'From Bachelard to Althusser: The Concept of "Epistemological Break",' in *Economy and Society*, vol. 7, no. 3, August, pp. 207–37.

21. Baruch Kimmerling (2001) *The Invention and Decline of Israeliness*, Berkeley, University of California Press.

22. For an elaboration of this argument, see the pioneering work of Lawrence J. Silberstein (1999) *The Postzionism Debates*, London, Routledge, pp. 110–11.

23. There have been many versions of these iconoclastic works and some have been extensively discussed and reviewed. It will be sufficient to mention, among many others, Simha Flapan (1987) *The Birth of Israel: Myths and Realities*, New York, Pantheon; Benny Morris (1987) *The Birth of the Palestinian Refugee Problem, 1947–1949*, Cambridge, Cambridge University Press; Benni Morris (1999) *Righteous Victims: a History of the Zionist–Arab Conflict, 1881–1999*, New York, Knopf; Ilan Pappé (1992) *The Making of the Arab–Israeli Conflict, 1947–51*, New York, St. Martin's Press; Ilan Pappé (1999) *The Israel/Palestine Question*, London and New York, Routledge; Michael Shalev (1992) *Labour and The Political Economy In Israel*, Oxford, Oxford University Press; Zeev Sternhell (1998) *The Founding Myths of Israel: Nationalism, Socialism, and the Making of the Jewish State*, Princeton, Princeton University Press; Avi Shlaim (2000) *The Iron Wall: Israel and the Arab World*, New York, W.W. Norton; Eugene Rogan and Avi Shlaim (2001) *The War for Palestine, Rewriting the History of 1948*, with an afterword by Edward Said, Cambridge, Cambridge University Press. For a caricature of the new historians' argument from a Zionist perspective, see Efraim Karsh (1997) *Fabricating Israeli History: The 'New Historians'*, London, Frank Cass.

24. The year 1948 is known in Arabic as *A'm al-Nakba* (the year of the catastrophe), a term deeper than 'military defeat'; it signifies the anguish and suffering that resulted from the displacement of the Palestinian population and the disappearance, from everywhere except Palestinian memory, of hundreds of villages and thousands of homes.

25. Jonathan Boyarin (1992) *Storm from Paradise, The Politics of Jewish Memory*, Minneapolis, University of Minnesota Press, p. 116.

26. The issue becomes a macabre irony in the conversation between the noted liberal political philosopher Professor Yael (Yuli) Tamir and the syndicated *New York Times* journalist Thomas Friedman. According to Friedman: 'Israel's former absorption minister, Yuli Tamir, told me this story: After a recent suicide bombing in Jerusalem in which three Israelis were killed, a friend called to ask whether her teenage daughter was safe because the suicide bomb had gone off next to a youth group office her daughter frequented. "I told my friend: 'Thank God, she's safe. She's in Auschwitz'," Yuli said. Yuli's daughter was in Poland at the time visiting the Nazi death camp with her youth group, but the irony of her words of relief was not lost on her.' Thomas L. Friedman (2002) 'Reeling, But Ready', in the *New York Times*, section 4, p. 15, 28 April. Thanks to Avishai Ehrlich, who alerted me to the story.

27. Perry Anderson (2001) 'Scurrying towards Bethlehem', in *New Left Review*, second series, no. 10, July–August, pp. 22–5.

28. Edward Said (1998) 'New History, Old Ideas', in *Al-Ahram* weekly, 21–27 May. See Appendix to this volume.

29. Morris (1987) *The Birth of the Palestinian Refugee Problem*.

30. Sternhell (1998) *The Founding Myths*.

31. Said (1998) 'New History, Old Ideas'.

32. Boyarin (1992) *Storm from Paradise*, p. 120.

33. Gramsci (1976) *Prison Notebooks*.

34. Consider that Israel will, in the next decade, be the largest concentration of Jews in the world, and in the next generation Israel will have the absolute majority of world Jews without the need for any further Jewish immigration. Paradoxically, however, the non-Jewish component in the Israeli population is increasing, as a significant number of migrants from the former Soviet Union is non-Jewish, according to the Israeli legal definition of who is a Jew. There are also a significant number of foreign workers. According to the Rappaport Centre for the Study of Assimilation at Bar Ilan University, 28 per cent of Israelis are non-Jewish according to the Israeli legal definition. See David Weinberg (2002) 'A Jewish State?', in the *Jerusalem Post*, 23 June.

35. Baruch Kimmerling (2001b) *Ketz shilton ha-Ahuselim* (translated as 'The End of Ashkenazi Hegemony'), Tel Aviv, Keter, [Hebrew]. '*Ahuselim*' is the Hebrew acronym for secular, established, socialist, nationalist Ashkenazim. The English translation of the title is somewhat imprecise, for the reference is not to Ashkenazim as an ethnic community, but to the '*Ahuselim*' (something like Israeli WASPs).

36. Kimmerling (2001a) *The Invention*.

37. Yehouda Shenhav (2002) 'Ethnicity and National Memory: The World Organization of Jews from Arab Countries (WOJA) in the Context of the Palestinian National Struggle', in the *British Journal of Middle Eastern Studies*, vol. 29, no. 1, pp. 27–56.

38. M. Al-Haj (2002) 'Ethnic mobilization in an ethno-national state: the case of immigrants from the Former Soviet Union in Israel', in *Ethnic and Racial Studies*, vol. 25, no. 2, March, pp. 238–57.

39. Kimmerling (2001a) *The Invention*, pp. 1–2.

40. Ibid., p. 7.

41. Quoted in Livneh (2001) 'Post-Zionism only rings once'.

42. Ibid.

43. Ernesto Laclau and Chantal Mouffe (1985) *Hegemony and Socialist Strategy*, London, Verso, p. 112. Yanis Stavrakakis (1999) *Lacan and the Political*, London, Routledge, pp. 77–8. See, in particular, Ernesto Laclau (1996) 'Why do empty signifiers matter to politics?', in *Emancipation(s)*, London, Verso.

44. David Newman (2001) 'Zionist McCarthyism', opinion column in the *Jerusalem Post*, 14 March, p. 8. I am very grateful to Helen Pringle for this reference.

45. For an example of the way in which an emancipatory political discourse can be reconfigured in non-essentialist terms through hegemonic articulation, see the discussion of 'post-anarchism' in Saul Newman (2001) *From Bakunin to Lacan: Anti-authoritarianism and the Dislocation of Power*, Lanham, Md., Lexington, pp. 173–4.

46. For a discussion on the problematic distinction between civic and ethnic nationalism, see Taras Kuzio (2002) 'The Myth of the Civic State: A Critical Survey of Hans Kohn's Framework for Understanding Nationalism', in *Ethnic and Racial Studies*, vol. 25, no. 1, 20–29 January.

47. On this topic, see Alain Gagnon and James Tully (eds) (2001) *Multinational Democracies*, with a foreword by Charles Taylor, Cambridge, Cambridge University Press, 2001; Nimni (1999) 'Nationalist Multiculturalism'.

48. William Connolly (1999) *Why I am not a Secularist*, Minneapolis, University of Minnesota Press, p. 91.

2 ◎ From Nation-State to Nation-----State

Nation, History and Identity Struggles in Jewish Israel*

Uri Ram

Nationality and historicity

For the last two centuries, nationalism has been to modernity what Christianity had been in the preceding centuries to feudalism, i.e., it furnished the polity of the era with a pertinent cosmology. In the rapidly disenchanting, capitalising and bureaucratising world, where 'all that is solid melts into air', where on the one hand the market adjourns all ties and meanings, and on the other hand the state commands all affiliations, nationalism had become a substitute 'religion for the masses', giving them a sense of collective cohesion and existential purpose.

As Anthony Smith put it so well, nationalism assumed the role of 'a "surrogate" religion which aims to overcome the sense of futility engendered by the removal of any vision of an existence after death, by linking individuals to persisting communities whose generations form indissoluble links in a chain of memories and identities'.[1] Yet, nationalism by itself could not cope with the expansion of secularism and its anxieties. All that was left to fill the existential void was 'memory and hope, history and destiny'.[2] 'History' has been the worldly counterpart of the divine 'Providence'.

Nationalism has thus purchased the warrant for its lower-case (mundane) history in an upper-case (teleological) History. In the modern world, asserts Smith, 'history has become both a moral teacher and a temporal and terrestrial drama of salvation'.[3] Historians, in particular, have assumed the role of the nation's teachers and preachers. Their task has been 'to fit the many pieces of [the historical] jigsaw together into a clear and harmonious pattern', and to 'translate the idealised images of the ethnic past into tactile realities, according to modern canons of knowledge'.[4] Scholars and

20

historians bent on rediscovering or reconstituting a national past, as Smith so tellingly put it, 'have felt no compunction about pressing the latest techniques or scientific methods into the service of an unashamedly romantic venture. They have used "science" to systematize and "verify" poetic metaphors of collective life, and construct images and mythologies of a dramatic and inspiring past'.[5]

Thus upper-case 'History' has extracted from 'history' national origins and ancestry, legendary heroes and exemplary figures, dramatic events and golden epochs, immemorial lineages and durable traditions.[6] National memories and historiographies had been quintessentially *historicist* in the sense of having 'a predilection for interpreting individual and social phenomena as the product of sequences of events which unfold the identity of laws of growth of those phenomena' and in the sense of aiming towards 'establish[ing], through detailed historical investigation, the origins, growth and purpose of particular entities, or classes of entity'.[7]

In the 1980s and 1990s, historical revisions and debates resounded in many countries around the globe. Historical controversies made headway in Germany, France and the United States, to mention just some of the more publicised cases. In fact, historical revisions, often borrowing theoretical novelties from neighbouring disciplines or adopting artistic and literary sensitivities, have become worldwide phenomena, exciting public opinion in Japan, Australia, India, Africa, Europe, Latin America and Canada. Questions of collective memory and of historiography have emerged in the 1980s and 1990s as a major preoccupation of literary and intellectuals worldwide, especially – though not exclusively – following the lead of 'minority' scholars, who challenge mainstream identities and narratives.[8]

It seems that 'History' has a history of its own, and that this history is closely knitted with that of the 'Nation' and of nationalism. The current crisis of memory in historiography derives from the atmosphere of crisis which surrounds 'national identities' almost everywhere nowadays. What one witnesses in the recent period, in the form of manifold historical revisions and controversies, is an ebbing of the nationality tide. This is manifested in the transition from one dominant mode of memory and historicity to another, namely, a transition from an historicist to a post-historicist notion of the itinerary of the collectivity. In the era of the ascendancy of nationalism, historicist memory functioned as a major progenitor of constructed collective identities, or of the uniting of nations. In the era of the ascendancy of the global social formation and post-modern culture, post-historicist memory functions as a progenitor of the decon-struction, the dissolution and the fragmentation of collective identities, or of the disuniting of nations (to follow the title of Arthur Schlesinger's book, which laments this).[9]

The emerging post-historicist mode may be defined by contrasting it with the historicist one, as cited above. The post-historicist paradigm is suspicious of the predilection of historicism to compress individual and social phenomena into 'identities' and 'laws of growth'. From its perspective, such compression forces a cascade of dispersed and blurred events into unified, fixed, essential entities. Post-historicism deconstructs historical 'identities', exposing them as artifacts, and deconstructs historical 'laws', exposing the contingencies underlying them. Rather than positing historical laws, it aims to decipher the historical practices by which ostensible 'origins, growth and purpose' camouflage actual manipulations, exploitations and exclusions. Thus while historicist memory constructs nations, post-historicist memory deconstructs them. They thus strip collectivities and states of their transcendental, upper-case History signification, 'disenchant' their ostensible primordialities, and open them up for democratic communication and negotiation based on modern associational membership.[10]

Construction and deconstruction of collective identities are not entirely separable, of course. Just as in the past the construction of modern national identities involved the deconstruction, or outright destruction, of former traditional identities – tribal, regional, ethnic, religious – so the decon-struction of national identities today involves the reconstruction of lost identities, or the outright invention of new ones. 'History', in other words, is a major cultural arena where national 'stories' are contrived in one period (typically from the last decades of the nineteenth century to the 1950s, with some predecessors such as the English, French and German), and dis-entangled in another (typically in the last decades of the twentieth century).

Current historical revisions and controversies should thus be interpreted against the backdrop of specific crises of national identities, and accumu-latively as indications of the crisis of national identity as such in the era of globalisation. On these occasions the constructed past transforms from a unifying fold into a contested terrain, in which social categories hitherto subsisting on the margins of the grand national narrative, or entirely outcast from it, gain a voice and launch a struggle for the acceptability of their own bigger (globalist), or smaller (localist) narratives, and through it for their cultural legitimacy and social status. This is why historical revisions and debates shed light on the present no less, if not more, than on the past, paradoxical as it may sound. In the past, national identities served as vehicles for political and economic modernisation. Today they are in a decline induced by the pressures of globalisation, the vehicle of which are post-modern identities. As Lash and Urrey put it succinctly, 'mobile objects and reflexive subjects produce disorganised capitalism which involves the dissipation of the national fate community'.[11]

Globality and locality

Yet globalisation should not be conflated with homogenization. As Robertson put it, globalisation may lead towards 'global valorisation of particular identities'[12]. One of the offshoots of globalisation, and dialectically one of its potential obstructions, is the backlash, or defensive reaction, of what may be termed local identities. The formerly 'united' nations are today 'disunited' by forces that undermine them simultaneously from 'above' and from 'below'. Two trends work in parallel: on the one hand, a trend towards supranational political and economic globalisation, and, on the other, towards infranational culture and identity localisation[13]. In their combination, globalisation and localisation emanate what was recently labelled 'glocalisation'.[14] In this process formerly solidified nations do fragment, but some of their components consolidate separately in an attempt to arrest the threatening flood of universal facelessness, or what some term consumerist cultural imperialism. The thaw of nationalist cores facilitates a consolidation of the peripheral components. It spurs the surfacing of formerly suppressed 'minorities' (sometimes demographic majorities) and it licenses the formula-tion of new 'local politics' and new identities centred around distinctive ideal interests (human rights, environmental concerns), life-styles (sexual orientations), and so forth. At the other end of the spectrum, the dissolution of the centre provokes socially marginal groups (usually from the declining lower middle class) to mobilise for the 'protection' of the nation (white nativity and Christian fundamentalism in the US, neo-fascist and extreme nationalist right-wing groups in France and Germany and so on).

The scissor movement of globalisation and localisation – the afore-mentioned glocalisation – undermines the sovereignty and autonomy of nation-states both from 'above' and from 'below'. From above, nation-states are worn by supranational vibrant financial and communicative networks, immense continent-wide commercial and monetary blocs, and potent multinational corporations. From below, nation-states are worn by regional, ethnic, popular and individually activated fragments.[15]

What happens to the nation-state can perhaps be illustrated by the analogy of the neighbourhood grocery. In the 1950s, this was still the major retail outlet for foodstuffs. It was later surpassed (in advanced industrial societies) by big supermarket chains ('Fordist standardisation', in neo-Marxist analysis of globalisation);[16] still later, the supermarkets were supplemented by 'delicatessen' and 'gourmet' stores, catering for particular tastes, based on ethnic foods, special staples or qualities, or distinct orientations (vegetarian, organic etc – 'post-Fordist specialisation'). Now all this does not mean that the grocery disappears overnight, certainly not in impoverished neighbourhoods and peripheries, but it does mean that it is no longer the major retail outlet of foodstuffs, and certainly not the cutting edge. Its role has been eroded due to pressures from above – the supermarket chain stores, and from below – the delicatessen and gourmet stores. Something of this sort is happening to the romantic cafes of Paris, where reportedly for every fast-food joint opening in a certain street, three cafes are closed, and something of this sort is also happening to the cosy bookstores of Manhattan, where bookselling is taken over by 'megastore' and 'superstore' chains, and the only viability left for small bookstores is specialisation.

Not surprisingly, something like this happened to the nation-state in the last decades of the twentieth century, the era of globalisation, localisation and post-modernisation. Like the grocers', the romantic cafes, and the bookstores, nationhood and the nation-state are not about to disappear overnight. Yet as Hobsbawm[17] and Gellner[18] maintain, they cannot be considered any more as the actors who shape the era (but see the counter-arguments of Smith).[19] The issue is not of the outright disappearance of the nation-state and of national identities, but rather of the proliferation of other identities alongside the national. Thus the age is characterised as one of boundary-crossing and hybridity. As Pieterse put it, 'state power remains extremely strategic, but it is no longer the only game in town'.[20] Bodnar has sealed his study of collective memory in the United States on an appropriate note: 'In this postmodern era various interests and cultures mix more freely in the public sphere – nationalism, internationalism, consumerism, ethnicity, race, gender, private feelings, and official concerns'.[21]

Something of this sort is happening to the nation-state in Israel, though this case, like any other, has its historical particularities and non-structural contingencies. In Israel, in the pace and the circumstances particular to it, one can detect in the last fifteen years or so of the twentieth century the decline of a homogeneous national narrative, and the emergence of a plurality of alternative or complementary narratives (including an ultra-nationalist backlash, which is not the focus of this study).[22]

In Israel, as in so many other places – at least in those social circles exposed to the global tradition-shredding and meaning-evaporating post-modern culture – no simple 'story' can be accepted innocently any more, not the story of scientific objectivity nor the story of national unity. As in the United States and elsewhere, in Israel too 'the idea of historical objectivity is perceived as problematic more than at any time in the past'[23] and 'certainty has been replaced by doubt and the present is no longer seen as something that emerged neatly and purposefully from the past, a view that was implicit in the story of nation building'.[24] As argued and demonstrated in this study, a challenge to the stories of objective history and national unity is widespread and is vigorously pronounced by critical sociologists and new historians.[25] Let us turn now to the case of Israel.

Neo-Zionism and post-Zionism

What are the socio-historical circumstances that have recently brought about the crisis of national identity and the transformation of historical consciousness in Israel? The high tide of nationalist identity came in the wake of the establishment of the state in 1948. In the pre-state Jewish community this identity was primarily expressed by the 'pioneering' 'civil religion' of the Labour movement. In the era of the state the ethos of 'pioneering' (*haluziyut*) was transmuted into that 'statism' (*mamlachtiut*). Throughout there also persisted secondary versions of national identity: the religious–national, the liberal–civic, and the rightist–nationalist.[26] In the late 1960s, nationalist identification subsided somewhat, but a series of un-predictable turns, which started with the 1967 War, mixed the cards again and again.

The occupation of the West Bank and other territories in that war re-animated the old creed (predominantly of the right wing) of Greater Israel; a new social stratum, hitherto marginalised, of religious–national Yeshiva graduates, mobilised since 1974 by the Block of Faithful (*Gush Emunim*), exploited the opportunity to appropriate and renew the earlier part of the century's pioneering ethos. In addition, this territorial expansion spurred unprecedented economic growth and with it the emergence of newly acquired riches; simultaneously, however, this development incited an outburst of protest by the second generation of the impoverished Mizrahi population. In the 1970s, the protest was stirred by a handful of 'Black

Panthers', but by and large it channelled mass support for the Likud party. Here were planted the seeds of the future fall of the labour movement and its ethos. The fall came ten years after the 1967 war, and so after the 1973 October war. In that war Israel barely survived a massive Egyptian–Syrian surprise attack. The governing party suffered widespread denunciation and in 1977 it lost the election for the first time in decades.

The rise to power of the right-wing Likud party accelerated the three processes mentioned above: the expansion and deepening of the Jewish settlement in the occupied territories, and the general strengthening of religious-national influence upon Israeli politics; augmentation of the Mizrahi protest and elevation of the status of Mizrahi culture and its symbols; and the expansion of the range of activity of business corporations and of the neo-liberal, market-oriented stratum of entrepreneurs and managers. The year 1979 saw a major boost for the Likud government and its leader, Menachem Begin, following the first peace treaty signed between Israel and an Arab state – Egypt. In 1981 Likud won the elections again, in one of the most malicious ethnic electoral campaigns. Yet the 1980s proceeded to a different tune. In the first half of the decade Israel was forced to its knees in triple-digit inflation generated by uncontrolled monetary liberalisation, and in a life-costly entanglement in Lebanon (following its 1982 invasion there). This war bears extraordinary importance in the development of Israeli political culture. It was the first war deeply contested in Israeli public opinion.[27] All previous wars were widely perceived as 'no choice', defensive wars; this one was openly declared by the prime minister to be a 'war of choice', that is, a war initiated by Israel to achieve a political end – the destruction of the Palestinian Liberation Organization, then seated in southern Lebanon. The opposition to it marks the genesis of an autonomous civil society in Israel, where state and society had usually been intimately meshed.

The entry of Labour into a 'national unity government' following the 1984 elections facilitated the curbing of inflation and the withdrawal of troops from Lebanon (though a 'security zone' and an Israeli-sponsored local militia were left behind). In the socio-economic arena, the liberalisation policy continued to intensify with every successive government. Since the mid-1980s, Israel has witnessed its first 'bourgeois revolution', in which the collectivist institutions founded by the labour movement fell like a house of cards, and the 'privatization' ethos, led by a now robust bourgeois class, took total precedence. This process reached a symbolic peak in 1994, when the Labour movement lost its historic command over the Histadrut, the large Federation of Labour. In 1987 another deeply contested war began, this time a Palestinian popular resistance to the Israeli occupation – the *intifada*, and it augmented the 'Vietnam effect' of the Lebanese war. In 1991, Israeli self-confidence was dealt another blow when its soft civilian underbelly was exposed to ballistic threat, and its dependence on the US clearly underscored. In 1992 Labour won the elections (by a meagre majority) and in September 1993 the Oslo accord was signed between Israel and the PLO. A peace treaty with Jordan was signed later, and negotiations with Syria were conducted.

In November 1995 the prime minister of Israel, Yitzhak Rabin, was assassinated. His murderer, a student at Bar Ilan, a religious–nationalist university, was a neo-Zionist zealot. This event consummated two decades of growing malevolence between the two major political blocs that had emerged in Israel since the 1970s. The immediate consequence was – surprisingly – the return of the right wing to power; yet overall the 1990s were marked by the growing dismantling of Oslo and by the paralysis of the big parties and the political system as a whole. The governments of Israel became reactive rather than initiative, and more reluctant to reach territorial compromise with the Palestinians. The short episode of the Barak government in the end of the 1990s generated much hope initially in the Israeli peace camp, but turned out later to be inconsequential, or even disastrous, in its (non)achievements. The premiership of Ariel Sharon in the early 2000s signalled a new upsurge of neo-Zionist militancy. Yet underneath the political turmoil, the large structural changes continue to reshape Israeli political culture, and to this we now turn.

Though almost the entire population of Jewish descent in Israel confesses allegiance to Zionism, the boundaries of Zionist discourse have been significantly transgressed between the 1970s and the 1990s. They were transgressed from both right and left. I label 'neo-Zionism' and 'post-Zionism' the respective right-wing and left-wing transgressions of classical Zionism. Arguably, while neither one is a majoritarian trend, both re-define the contours of Israeli collective identity in a very significant way. The historical revision and debate in Israel is a manifestation of the decline of the classical Zionist ethos and the renewed contest over Israeli identity. Through the debate the lines of public discourse are re-delineated.

Neo-Zionism emerged in the 1970s. Its constituency consists largely of the Jewish settlers in the occupied territories and their many supporters in the so-called 'national camp' throughout the country. It is represented by a variety of extreme right-wing parties, including core parts of the national–religious party (Mafdal) and Likud.[28] This trend regards 'the Biblical Land of Israel' (identified as all areas under Israeli military control) as more fundamental to Israeli identity than the state of Israel (a smaller territory defined by the 1948 'green-line' borders). The motherland is conceived as a superior end, the state as an instrument for its control. The culture of neo-Zionism is an admixture of Zionist and Jewish ingredients, where secular nationalism is conceived not as reflecting discord between the two, which characterized classical Zionism, but as a stage in an immanent religious revival.[29] The political allegiance of neo-Zionism is to an ostensible 'Jewish people', conceived as a unique spiritual-ethnic community, rather than to Israeli nationality, in its down-to-earth sense of a political community defined by common citizenship. Legal (and practical) affiliation to the collectivity is considered secondary to the ostensible ascriptive national brotherhood. Neo-Zionism is thus an exclusionary, nationalist, even racist, anti-democratic political–cultural trend, striving to heighten the fence surrounding Israeli identity. It is fed by, and in turn feeds, a high level of regional conflict and a low level of global integration. Conflict vindicates its alarming messages, while global integration loosens its grip on the national mind.

The second Palestinian *intifada*, which erupted in September 2000, re-oiled the wheels of neo-Zionism, which had cracked after the Oslo agreement. The short-term impact upon the Jewish population in Israel was to throw it again into nationalistic solidarity. Yet one may doubt whether this will be the long-term effect – as we shall argue below.

Post-Zionism started to emerge in the 1980s. Its constituency is composed mainly of the extensive 'new' middle class, typically concentrated in the country's coastal area, especially in the city of Tel Aviv and its vicinity (where a quarter of the population resides). This trend grants more esteem to individual rights than to collective glory. In blunt contrast to neo-Zionism, it considers the collectivity as a tool for the welfare of the individual. In its historical horizon, the present ('quality of life') is much more important than the past ('History'), and the near future (the children) is more meaningful than the remote past (ancestors). One political avant-garde of it is the *Yesh Gvul* (literally 'there is a border/limit') movement, which surfaced in response to the 1982 war. It consists of reserve soldiers and officers who refuse to serve in the occupation forces in Lebanon and the Palestinian territories, arguing that the role of the military is defence, not repression. Though the movement is quite small, the principles of civil disobedience that it represents have gained recognition by a larger sector of the population, which is committed to civil rights rather than to ethnic nationalism. Post-Zionism is, then, a trend of libertarian openness, which strives to lower the boundaries of Israeli identity, and to include in it all relevant 'others'. It is fed by, and in turn it feeds, a lower level of regional conflict and a higher level of global integration. Conflict mobilises nationalistic feelings, and thus disables post-Zionism; global integration draws people to cosmopolitan consumerism, and thus is suitable to it. Though in the short run the effect of the second Palestinian *intifada* was to re-empower neo-Zionism, it seems that the re-emergence of a relatively large movement of 'refuseniks', reminiscent of *Yesh Gvul* of the 1980s, and the growing public support it gains, are harbingers of a new resurgence of the post-Zionist spirit in Israel.

It should be emphasised that the traits of both neo-Zionism and post-Zionism are not entirely foreign to 'classical' Zionism. In fact, these are two contrasting accentuations of Zionist traits. Their novelty consists precisely in their one-sided accentuation: neo-Zionism accentuates the messianic and particularistic dimensions of Zionism, while post-Zionism accentuates the normalising and universalist dimensions of it. In their opposing ways, both trends indicate the transition towards a post-nationalist Israeli collective identity. The nationalist stage was an imperative of the era of territorial colonisation, nation-building and state formation. Decades later, a variety of internal and external pressures erodes nationalism and enhances the emergence of post-national alternatives. Neo-Zionism and post-Zionism are labels for these dawning alternatives. Neo-Zionism elevates to an exclusive (and exclusionary) status the ethnic dimension of Israeli nationalism; post-Zionism elevates to an exclusive (and in this case inclusive) status the civic dimension of Israeli statehood.

This ground-shaking of the dominant nationalist ethos, Zionism, is amply demonstrated in the historical revisions and debates that took place in Israel in the 1990s. The unilinear and teleological national meta-narrative is scrambled by a variety of supra-narratives (post-Zionist cosmopolitanism); sub-narratives (empowered marginalised or excluded groups: women, Palestinians, Mizrahi Jews, orthodox Jews); backlash narratives (neo-Zionist ethnicity); and subsidiary narratives (bourgeois-liberal). Diverse social categories whose voices had been until recently silenced take a stand in the public arena, articulate their own versions of history, and retell it. Their 'truths' diverge naturally, or more correctly, historically, from the hegemonic 'truth'.

The new politics of identity and memory refurbishes drastically the tissue of collective identity in Israel. In place of a unilinear, teleological national identity, there is now a variety of contesting identities. All of them are critical of the nationalist and socialist master-narrative, some highlighting the nationalist dimension, others the socialist dimension. Let us focus now on the scene of collective identities and historical narratives in Israel.

Identities and narratives

National identity has been hegemonic among the population of Jewish descent in Israel. Zionism, modern Jewish nationalism, originated in Eastern Europe in the last quarter of the nineteenth century. Being a national movement without a territory, Zionism adopted naturally the ethnic, or integrative, type of nationalism which prevailed in the region.[30] In Palestine, diasporic Jewish nationalism turned into a settler-colonial nationalism. The state of Israel inherited the ethnic principle of membership, and never adopted the alternative liberal–territorial principle. To this day the dominant ethos of the state is Zionist, i.e., Jewish nationalist. Though citizenship is de jure equal to Jews and Arabs in Israel, a de facto distinction is easily discernible between the dominated minority and the dominant majority and its state.[31]

The Zionist movement, the Jewish community in Palestine, and later the state of Israel had been most successful in the dissemination and internalisation of national faith among the population of Jewish descent. Two historical experiences have had formative impact upon contemporary Israeli Jewish identity: the annihilation of Jews in the Holocaust and the protracted state of war between Israel and the Arab states.[32] These powerful traumas have amplified and fortified the ethnic national identity.

The newly established nation of Israel, which was born out of diaspora Judaism, had to re-imagine itself,[33] re-invent a tradition,[34] and re-narrate a historical identity.[35] The social and political project of Jewish immigration to Palestine, the settlement and colonisation of the land, and the construction of a Jewish community and state there, all against Arab opposition and hostility, were rendered culturally in terms of national 'revival', territorial 'repatriation', and historical 'redemption'.

Historians, together with authors, poets, painters, sculptors, journalists, teachers, and other intellectuals, artists and persons of letters – at a later stage including also social scientists – took active and even leading parts in the composition and propagation of the national narrative. Far from being a remote academic arbiter, Israeli academia was part and parcel of the national endeavour.[36] Academic disciplines, and especially the ones we are concerned with here, history and sociology, had been shaped under the spell of national ideology. Until quite recently the dominant historical paradigm has been underpinned by premises furnished by the national revival school, led by Ben Zion Dinur and others,[37] and the dominant sociological paradigm has been underpinned by premises furnished by the nation-building school, led by S.N. Eisenstadt and others.[38] The history and sociology written in Israel until the mid–late 1980s, conferred an ostensible scientific aura and academic legitimisation upon collective memory and collective ideology required by the crystallising national identity. The affinity between power and knowledge has been indeed tight in Israel. It would not be a gross exaggeration to suggest that, until recently, 'the nation' has studied itself rather than being properly studied.

But this situation has radically changed, at least in part. The carriers of the change on the intellectual terrain are scholars labelled 'critical sociologists' and 'new historians', who charge those they deem 'mainstream sociologists' and 'old historians' with being apologetic towards their topic. The historians' debate that erupted in the late 1980s became exuberant in the mid-1990s. It gained extensive coverage in the mass media, became the axis of several academic conferences held in the country, and was the leading topic in issues of different scholarly journals. Key terms, such as the 'new history' and 'post-Zionism', have become common in cultural and even daily parlance in Israel.

What are Israeli historians and sociologists debating about? The multiplicity of issues raised may be classified into three major thematic categories: the Israeli–Arab national conflict; the social policies of the labour movement; and Hebrew–Zionist culture.

The Israeli–Arab national conflict is the special area of the core group of the new historians. These historians have challenged the conventional view of the foreign and security policy of Israel, especially (so far) with regard to the 1940s and 1950s. In the conventional view, Israel is considered to have always been peace-seeking and given to compromise, while the Arab states are portrayed as stubborn aggressors. The new historians argue, among other things, that the state of Israel declined opportunities for negotiations with Arab states,[39] but on the other hand concluded an unwritten pact with the Jordanian kingdom to parcel between the two of them the territory known as the West Bank, so as to prevent the establishment of a Palestinian state there.[40]

Furthermore, new historians argue that Israel bears a large – in certain versions, a major – responsibility for the creation of the Palestinian refugee problem, to follow a title of Benny Morris's extensive study of the topic.[41] It is argued that during Israel's War of Independence in 1948, senior Israeli military commanders, encouraged implicitly by Israel's highest authority of the time, Prime Minister David Ben Gurion, evicted hundreds of thousands of Palestinians from their villages and expelled them beyond the state's borders. On top of this, Israel exercised (and still does) a tough 'no return' policy towards the refugees. Until these revelations scandalised academia and public opinion, professional historians simply avoided these unpleasant aspects of the war, while popular histories and school textbooks tended to refer to it briefly as an Arab 'mass escape', sometimes airing the theory that this escape was ordered by an Arab leadership. Today, under the force of evidence amassed mainly by Morris, matters of facts are hardly disputed,[42] though issues of the circumstances and imperatives involved are still very hotly contested.[43]

In addition, Israel's border security policy of the 1950s – retaliation in kind for terrorist attacks on its citizens – had been discerned as overblown and adventurous. It is claimed that this policy finally provoked an unnecessary war in 1956. As a potential alternative to Prime Minister Ben Gurion's 'activist' hard line, a reconsideration is given to the relatively 'moderate' line of Moshe Sharett, foreign minister and, for a short period, Prime Minister.[44]

Critical sociologists who researched the early stages of Jewish settlement in Palestine, at the end of the nineteenth century and early decades of the twentieth century, have applied an analogous analysis, but in more structural terms. They presented the Zionist settlement as a colonising project, involving acquisition of lands, closure of labour markets, and displacement of native Arab peasants.[45] This new critical sociology challenged mainstream Israeli sociology, which offered a 'dualistic' concept of Israeli–Arab relations, according to which the two societies had developed side by side, each according to its own inherent modernising impetus.[46] Furthermore, critical sociologists determined that a military culture emerged in Israeli society, a culture which has significantly contributed to the reproduction of the national conflict.[47]

The second category of dispute is that of the social policies of the Labour movement, which had been dominant in Israeli society from the 1930s to the 1970s. Mainstream sociology and history used to depict the founders of the movement as idealist pioneers, and used to adulate their particular blend of national development and social(ist) construction, captured by the formula 'socialist constructivism'.[48] In sharp distinction, new historians argue that the Jewish labour movement had been conspicuously nationalist, modelled after the most integrative kind of East European nationalism of the time; that its ideology of equality was no more than a mobilisation ruse; and that nothing was further removed from its mind than the construction of a model socialist society.[49]

A barrage of critical sociologists had expressed coinciding views since the 1970s. They highlighted the power-driven, manipulative organisational nature of the Labour elite;[50] they exposed the discriminatory policies exercised by the movement and its governments towards the Arab citizens of Israel in areas such as housing, education, employment and welfare,[51] and they disclosed the methods of domination and control over this population by way of de facto second-class citizenship and an ethnically dominated democratic system.[52]

A particular target of harsh critique was the pattern of integration of the wave of Jewish immigration from Muslim countries during the 1950s and early 1960s, which almost doubled the population of the state and radically transformed its ethnic complexion. Mainstream sociology had analysed this issue in its 'nation-building' framework in terms of 'absorption', a process in which the newcomers are 'desocialised' from their former traditional identity and are 'resocialised' into modern Israeli culture.[53] Critical sociology, again in contradistinction, analysed the same process in terms of the construction of classes in a capitalist division of labour or in terms of an unequal distribution of power.[54] It argued that the Labour movement, and more specifically the leading party, Mapai, initiated labour-intensive industrialisation, directed the immigrants to dependent peripheral locations, and placed them in proletarian and marginal positions.[55] The other side of the same process of 'underdevelopment' of the new Mizrahi population was the 'development' of the veteran Ashkenazi population (Jews of European descent) into a 'new bourgeoisie', a state-sponsored managerial class.[56]

Still later, the second generation of these same Jewish immigrants from Muslim countries were channelled into education and military-service conduits that reproduced the initial social inequality,[57] and the Jewish–Arab culture of the immigrants had been utterly curbed and quelled.[58] Another staple of the Labour movement's self-image exposed as a myth was gender equality.[59]

In addition to what is considered a leftist–radical critique, a bourgeois–liberal version of Israeli history has also begun to emerge. In this version the role of the Labour movement in the process of nation-building is depreciated, and the role of the 'private sector' entrepreneurial class is inflated. The latter is presented as the 'real' constructor of the economic infrastructure of the Jewish community, and collectivist ideology is presented as having been a hindrance to the further investment and development of this community. In this version of history, the first and fourth waves of Jewish immigrants, petit-bourgeois farmers and urban merchants, gain a place in a narrative which had hitherto considered them as 'failures', and had hailed as a success story the second and third waves of Jewish immigrants, who formulated the collectivist ethos and established the collective institutions of the Labour movement.[60]

The third area under dispute in the historians' debate is Zionist–Hebrew culture. A major thesis in this regard is that the cornerstone for the construction of a new 'positive' Israeli identity in Eretz Israel was the contrast drawn between it and a contrived 'negative' identity of diaspora Jews.[61] In this view the major creed of Hebrew culture was the 'negation of diaspora'. The pioneers who settled in Palestine and their Sabra (native-born) descendants were depicted as physically agile and spiritually brazen Biblical peasant-fighters, and diaspora Jews were depicted as the antithetical others of the Zionist self. Furthermore, the Jewish past was condensed into a single, linear meta-narrative of 'from dispersal to redemption', in which Zionism emerged as the telos of all Jewish history.[62]

Others charge that the cultural hiatus erected between Zionist settlers and diaspora Jews was responsible for the tragic fact that during the disastrous times of the holocaust the leadership of the *Yishuv* (pre-state Jewish community in Palestine) did not go out of its way to rescue persecuted Jews from Nazi claws.[63] This charge is disavowed by mainstream historians, who allude to the frailty and helplessness that paralysed this leadership in the inconceivable circumstances of those days.[64] Still others argue that, regardless of what was actually done or could have been done to rescue Jews, the memory of the holocaust is being 'nationalised' in Israel and utilised for political purposes, while the universal lessons from it and a bare sympathy for its victims are grossly omitted.[65] Specifically ferocious in its attacks on Zionist conduct during the holocaust is the anti-Zionist religious Orthodox version.[66]

In every respect, whether the argument relates to Palestinian Arabs, to Mizrahi immigrants or to European Jewry, the conventional Zionist 'story' is shattered, and its 'truths' severely challenged. Zionist idiomatic currencies, such as 'a country with no people for a people with no country' (referring to the Jewish settlement in Palestine), or 'there is nobody to talk with' (referring to the claimed absence of Arab partners for peace), or 'all of Israel guarantee each other' (referring to Jewish solidarity), are rebuffed or questioned. Beyond specifics, such arguments thwart the Zionist objective of being considered as the sole delegate of the interests of Jews in all times and places, the genuine representative of Jewish culture in its variety, and the necessary culmination of Jewish history.[67] On a general level, claims such as those raised by the new historians and critical sociologists deconstruct the Zionist national grand narrative and expose its contradictions, instabilities, omissions and lapses, which have marginalised and repressed others.

Concluding remarks: from historicism to post-historicism

Historiographical text and historical context are closely bound. There is no 'pure identity' or 'objective memory'. In the last two decades, the recognition of the ties that bind social positions, historical consciousness and scholarly representations has gained enormous acceptance in academia. Many tend to regard the politics of knowledge and the politics of identity as closely coupled. The notion of 'pure identity' has been radically criticised. The notion of primordial, fixed, homogeneous identity is widely challenged today by concepts of identity which refer to 'otherness', 'difference', 'hybridity', 'diaspora', 'migration' and 'boundary crossing'. Identity is thought of as associative, permeable, unstable and discursive. From this perspective, signs such as 'femininity', 'nation', or 'race' are no longer considered to be direct representations of ostensibly 'real' referents such as biological sex, ethnic group or physiognomic characteristics, respectively. In this respect, the signs themselves lose their 'purity' as known identities, and their deployment becomes instead a discursive relational practice. Identity, then, is largely considered today as an unstable social construct or cultural practice, rather than as a fixed natural given.

In their conjunction, the critiques of essentialist identity and of objective memory have effected a crisis of representation, or, in other words, a crisis of national narratives, which are functionalist, consensual, teleological, linear, homogeneous and triumphal; in short, historicist. Instead there emerged narratives that are critical, complementary or alternative, narratives that allude to other identities, to the otherness of self-identity, and to the fragmentation of the nation. Such narratives connote the experience and the perspective of voices lost, silenced, marginalised, and neglected by the process of nation-formation, or even of contestant elites or declining middle classes. Such sub-narratives deconstruct the national meta-narrative; in short, as argued in this study, they propose post-historicist identities and narratives.

The new identities and narratives in Israel challenge one by one the old national myths. Though explicitly historians dispute past events, implicitly the disputation is of present sociological significance. On a larger scale, the Israeli debate is just one case within a wider phenomenon of historical revision and controversy in contemporary nation-states, events which both manifest and articulate crises of national identity related to globalisation processes and to the post-modernisation of culture.

The eruption of the crisis of identity in Israel should be understood against the background of both local social changes and global political transformations, as well as against the background of the recent emergence of multicultural voices, post-modernist sensibilities and post-structuralist methodologies. A combination of local, global and cultural influences thus accounts for a new, deconstructive critique and politics of identity which reshapes Israel's sense of collective identity in general, and its collective memory in particular. The decline of the national Zionist ethos, so vigorously manifested in the transformation of Israeli collective memory and historical consciousness, has triggered the emergence of two mutually antagonistic alternatives: a globalist, post-Zionist, liberal ethos, and a localist, ethno-religious, neo-Zionist ethos. Israel will continue, of course, to be a nation-state, but the hyphen connecting nation and state will lengthen and stretch; it will be a nation-----state: the two principles will continue to diverge, struggle and perhaps recombine.

NOTES

* This chapter was composed as a part of a broad study in progress, about Israel in the global era. The study was made possible by a research grant from the United States Institute of Peace, Washington DC, to which the author is grateful. The opinions, findings, and conclusions expressed in this study are those of the author, and do not necessarily reflect the views of the United States Institute of Peace.

1. Anthony D. Smith (1986) *The Ethnic Origins of Nation*, Oxford, Oxford University Press, pp. 179–80.
2. Ibid.
3. Ibid.
4. Ibid.
5. Ibid., p. 182.
6. Cf. ibid., pp. 191–200.
7. Anthony D. Smith (1981) *The Ethnic Revival*, Cambridge, Cambridge University Press, p. 88.
8. The literature on historical controversies is huge. The following is just a sample: Stefan

Berger (1995) 'Historians and Nation-Building in Germany after Reunification', in *Past and Present*, no. 148, pp. 187–222; Charles Maier (1988) *The Unmasterable Past: History, Holocaust and German National Identity*, Cambridge, Mass., Harvard University Press; Henry Rousso (1991) *The Vichy Syndrome: History and Memory in France Since 1944*, Cambridge, Mass., Harvard University Press; Robert Gildea (1994) *The Past in French History*, New Haven, Yale University Press; Eric Foner (ed.) (1990) *The New American History*, Philadelphia, Temple University Press; Joyce Oldham Appelby, Lynn Hunt and Margaret Jacobs (1994) *Telling the Truth About History*, New York, Norton; Ann Curthoys (1993) 'Identity Crisis: Colonialism, Nation and Gender in Australian History', in *Gender and History*, no. 5, pp. 165–76; Ross Gibson (1992) *South of the West: Postcolonialism and the Narrative Construction of Australia*, Bloomington, Indiana University Press; Sneja Gunew (1990) 'Denaturalizing Cultural Nationalisms: Multicultural Readings of "Australia",' in Homi Bhabha (ed.) *Nation and Narration*, London, Routledge, pp. 99–120; Partha Chatterjee (1993) *The Nation and its Fragments: Colonial and Post-colonial Histories*, Princeton, Princeton University Press; Ranajit Guha and Gayatri C. Spivak (eds) (1988) *Selected Subaltern Studies*, New York; Gyan Prakash (1994) 'Subaltern Studies as Postcolonial Criticism', in the *American Historical Review*, no. 99, pp 1475–90; Frederick Cooper (1994) 'Conflict and Connection: Rethinking Colonial African History', in the *American Historical Review*, no. 99, pp. 1516–45; Steven Feierman (1995) 'Africa in History: The End of Universal Narratives', edited by Gyan Prakash, pp. 40–65; Anastasia N. Karakasidou (1994) 'Sacred Scholars, Profane Advocates: Intellectuals Modeling National Consciousness in Greece', in *Identities* no. 1, pp. 35–61; David Hertzberger (1995) *Narrating the Past: Fiction and History in Post-War Spain*, Durham, NC, Duke University Press; Florencia E. Mallon (1994) 'The Promise and Dilemma of Subaltern Studies: Perspectives from Latin American History', in the *American Historical Review*, no. 99, pp. 1491–1515; Bryan Palmer (1994) 'Canadian Controversies', in *History Today*, no. 44, pp. 44–9; Keith Jenkins (1997) *The Post-Modern History Reader*, London, Routledge.

9. Arthur Schlesinger Jr (1991) *The Disuniting of America: Reflections on a Multicultural Society*, New York, Norton.

10. To put it in the terminology of Jurgen Habermas, historicist historiography may be considered a counterpart of conventional identity and morality, while post-historicist historiography may be considered a counterpart of post-conventional identity and morality. Jurgen Habermas (1984; 1987) *The Theory of Communicative Action, Vol. I* and *Vol. II*, Cambridge, Mass., MIT Press; 'Citizenship and National Identity', in Bart van Steenberg (ed.) (1994) *The Condition of Citizenship*, London, Sage, pp. 20–35.

11. Scott Lash and John Urry (1994) *Economics of Time and Space*, London, Sage, p. 313.

12. Mike Featherstone (1995) *Undoing Culture: Globalization, Postmodernism and Identity*, Berkeley, Sage; Johann P. Arnason (1990) 'Nationalism, Globalization and Modernity', in Mike Featherstone (ed.), *Global Culture*, New York, Sage; Ronald Robertson (1987) 'Globalization Theory and Civilization Analysis', in *Comparative Civilizations Review*, no. 17, p. 21.

13. Eric Hobsbawm (1990) *Nations and Nationalism Since 1780*, Cambridge, Cambridge University Press; Manuel Castells (1997) *The Power of Identity* (vol. 2 of *The Information Age*), London, Blackwell.

14. Barry Axford (1995) *The Global System: Economics, Politics and Culture*, Cambridge, Polity Press, p. 156.

15. Robert J.S. Ross (1990) 'The Relative Decline of Relative Economy: Global Capitalism and the Political Economy of State Change', in Edward S. Greenberg and Thomas M. Mayer (eds), *Changes in the State*, Berkeley, Sage, pp. 206–23; Manfred Bienefeld (1994)

'Capitalism and the Nation-State', in *Socialist Register*, no. 30, London, Merlin Press, pp. 94–129; John Dunn (ed.) (1995) *Contemporary Crisis of the Nation-State*. Oxford, Blackwell; Wolfgang C. Muller and Vincent Wright (eds) (1994) *The State in Western Europe*, London, Frank Cass; Vincent Cable (1995) 'The Diminished Nation-State: A Study in the Loss of Economic Power', in *Daedalus*, no. 124, pp. 23–53; Vivian A. Schmidt (1995) 'The New World Order, Incorporated: The Rise of Business and the Decline of the Nation-State', in *Daedalus*, no. 124, pp. 75–106; Yasmin Nuhoglu Soysal (1994) *Limits of Citizenship: Migrants and Postnational Membership in Europe*, Chicago, Chicago University Press; Crawford Young (ed.) (1993) *The Rising Tide of Cultural Pluralism: The Nation State at Bay?*, Madison, University of Wisconsin Press; Castells, *The Power of Identity*.

16. Cf. David Harvey (1989) *The Condition of Postmodernity*, Oxford, Blackwell.
17. Hobsbawm, *Nations and Nationalism Since 1780*.
18. Ernest Gellner (1983) *Nations and Nationalism*, Ithaca, NY, Cornell University Press.
19. Anthony D. Smith (1995) *Nations and Nationalism in the Global Era*, Cambridge, Polity Press.
20. Jan Nederveen Pieterse (1995) 'Globalization as Hybridization', in Mike Featherstone and Scott Lash (eds), *Global Modernities*, New York, Sage, p. 63.
21. John Bodnar (1991) *Remaking America: Public Memory, Commemoration and Patriotism in the Twentieth Century*, Princeton, Princeton University Press, p. 252.
22. cf. Ian Lustick (1988) *For the Land and the Lord*, New York, Council on Foreign Relations; Ehud Sprinzak (1991) *The Ascendance of Israel's Radical Right*, Oxford, Oxford University Press.
23. Peter Novick (1988) *That Noble Dream: the 'Objectivity' Question and the American Historical Profession*, Cambridge, Cambridge University Press, p. 17.
24. Bodnar, *Remaking America*, p. 252.
25. See also Uri Ram (ed.) (1993) *Israeli Society: Critical Perspectives*, Tel Aviv, Breirot [Hebrew]; (1998) 'Post-Nationalist Pasts: the Case of Israel', in *Social Science History*; Ilan Pappé (1993) 'The New History of the 1948 War', in *Theory and Critique*, no. 3, pp. 99–114 [Hebrew]; Yagil Levi and Yoav Peled (1993) 'The Break That Never Was: Israeli Sociology Reflected Through the Six Day War', in *Theory and Critique* no. 3, pp. 115–28; Baruch Kimmerling (1992) 'Sociology, Ideology and Nation Building: The Palestinians and Their Meaning in Israeli Sociology', in the *American Sociological Review*, no. 57, pp. 460–6; Lawrence Silberstein (ed.) (1991) *New Perspectives on Israeli History*, New York, New York University Press.
26. Charles Liebman and Don Yehiya Eliezer (1983) *Civil Religion in Israel*, Berkeley, University of California Press.
27. Sara Helman (1993) 'Conscientious Objection to Military Service as an Attempt to Redefine the Contents of Citizenship', Jerusalem, Hebrew University, p. 456 [Hebrew]; Gad Barzilai (1996) *Wars, Internal Conflict and Political Order*, Albany, NY, SUNY Press.
28. Sprinzak, *The Ascendance*, p. 328; Yoram Peri (1989) 'From Political Nationalisn to Ethno-Nationalism: The Case of Israel', in Y. Lukacs and A.M. Battah (eds) (1989) *The Arab–Israeli Conflict*, Boulder, Colo., Westview, pp. 41–53.
29. Aviezer Ravitsky (1996) *Messianism, Zionism and Jewish Religious Radicalism*, Chicago, Chicago University Press.
30. For a basic typology of nationalism see Smith, *The Ethnic Origins*, pp. 79–84.
31. Yoav Peled (1993) 'Strangers in Utopia: The Civic Status of Israel's Palestinian Citizens', in *Theory and Critique*, no. 3, pp. 21–38 [Hebrew].
32. Yair Oron (1993) *Israeli-Jewish Identity*, Tel Aviv, Siriyat Poalim [Hebrew].
33. Benedict Anderson (1991 [1983]) *Imagined Communities*, London, Verso.

34. Eric Hobsbawm and Terence Ranger (eds) (1983) *The Invention of Tradition*, Cambridge, Cambridge University Press.

35. Bhabha (ed.), *Nation and Narration*.

36. Uri Ram (1996) 'Historical Consciousness in Israel: Between Zionism and Post-Zionism', in *Gesher*, no. 132, pp. 93–7 [Hebrew].

37. Uri Ram (1995) 'Zionist Historiography and the Invention of Modern Jewish Nationhood: the Case of Ben Zion Dinur', in *History and Memory*, no. 7, pp. 91–124; Jacob Barnai (1995) *Historiography and Nationalism*, Jerusalem, Magnes [Hebrew].

38. Ram (ed.), *Israeli Society*; Ram, 'Zionist Historiography', p. 251.

39. Simha Flapan (1987) *The Birth of Israel: Myths and Realities*, London, Croom Helm; Jerome Slater (1995) 'Lost Opportunities for Peace: Reassessing the Arab–Israeli Conflict', in *Tikkun*, no. 10, pp. 59–64, 88.

40. Ilan Pappé (1992) *The Making of the Arab–Israeli Conflict*, London, I.B.Tauris; Avi Shlaim (1988) *Collusion Across the Jordan: King Abdullah, the Zionist Movement, and the Partition of Palestine*, New York, Columbia University Press.

41. Benny Morris (1991) *The Birth of the Palestinian Refugee Problem, 1947–1949*, Tel Aviv, Am Oved, 1991 [Hebrew].

42. But see Shabtai Tevet (1989) 'The New Historians', in *Ha'aretz* (4, 14 and 21 April), Tel Aviv.

43. For example, Alon Kadish (1989) 'The Refugee Problem: The History and the Accusation', in *Ha'aretz* (14 August).

44. Benny Morris (1993) *Israel's Border Wars, 1949–1956*, Oxford, Clarendon Press; Eyal Kafkafi (1994) *An Optional War: To Sinai and Back, 1956–1957*, Ramat Efal, Yad Tabenkin [Hebrew]; Ilan Pappé (1986) 'Moshe Sharett, David Ben Gurion and the "Palestinian Option", 1948–1956', in *Zionism* no. 11, pp. 361–80 [Hebrew].

45. Gershon Shafir (1989) *Land, Labor and the Origins of the Israeli–Palestinian Conflict, 1882–1914*, Cambridge, Cambridge University Press; Baruch Kimmerling (1983) *Zionism and Territory: The Socio-Territorial Dimensions of Zionist Politics*, Berkeley, Institute of International Studies, University of California Press; Gershon Shafir (1993) 'Territory, Labor and Population in Zionist Colonization', in Uri Ram (ed.). *Israeli Society: Critical Perspectives*, Tel Aviv, Breirot, pp. 104–19; Avishai Ehrlich (1987) 'Israel: Conflict, War and Social Change', in Colin Creighton and Martin Shaw (eds), *The Sociology of War and Peace*, Dobbs Ferry, NY, Sheridan House.

46. Shmuel Noah Eisenstadt (1967) *Israeli Society: Background, Development, Problems*, Jerusalem, Magnes [Hebrew]; Dan Horowitz and Moshe Lissak (1977) *The Origins of the Israeli Polity*, Tel Aviv, Am Oved [Hebrew].

47. Baruch Kimmerling (1993) 'Militarism in Israeli Society', in *Theory and Criticism*, no. 4, pp. 123–40; Uri Ben-Eliezer (1995) *The Emergence of Israeli Militarism, 1936–1956*, Tel Aviv, Dvir [Hebrew].

48. Eisenstadt, Israeli Society; Anita Shapira (1980) *Berl Katznelson: A Biography*, Tel Aviv, Am Oved [Hebrew]; Yosef Gorni (1973) *Achdut Haavoda, 1919–1930*, Tel Aviv, Hakibbutz Hameuhad [Hebrew].

49. Zeev Sternhell (1995) *Nation-Building or New Society?* Tel Aviv, Am Oved [Hebrew], translated into English (1997) as *Founding Myth of Israel: Nationalism, Socialism and the Making of the Jewish State*, Princeton, Princeton University Press.

50. Yonathan Shapiro (1975) *The Organization of Power*, Tel Aviv, Am Oved [Hebrew]; (1993) 'The Historical Origins of Israeli Democracy', in Carry Diamond and Ehud Sprinzak (eds) *Israeli Democracy Under Stress*, Boulder, Colo., Lynne Rienner; Lev Grinberg (1993) *The Histadrut Above All*, Jerusalem, Nevo [Hebrew].

51. Henry Rosenfeld (1978) 'The Class Situation of the Arab National Minority in Israel', in *Comparative Studies in Society and History*, no. 21, pp. 3–20; Zeev Rosenhak (1995) 'New Development in the Study of the Palestinian Citizens of Israel: An Analytical Survey', in *Megamot*, no. 47, pp. 167–90 [Hebrew]; Michael Shalev (1992) *Labor and the Political Economy of Israel*, Oxford, Oxford University Press; Oren Yiftachel (1992) *Planning a Mixed Region in Israel: The Political Geography of Arab-Jewish Relations in the Galilee*, Aldershot, Avebury; Majid Al-Haj (1995) *Education, Empowerment and Control: The Case of Arabs in Israel*, Albany, NY, SUNY Press.

52. Sammy Smooha (1990) 'Minority Status in Ethnic Democracy: The Status of the Arab Minority in Israel' in *Ethnic and Racial Studies* no. 13, pp. 389–413; Lustick, *For the Land and the Lord*; Peled, 'Strangers in Utopia'; Azmi Bishara (1993) 'On the Question of the Palestinian Minority in Israel', in Ram (ed.) *Israeli Society*, pp. 203–21.

53. Eisenstadt, *Israeli Society*; Rivka Bar Yosef (1980 [1969]) 'Desocialization and Resocialization: The Adjustment Process of Immigrants', in Ernest Krausz (ed.) *Studies of Israeli Society: Vol. I. Migration, Ethnicity and Community*, Brunswick, NJ, Transaction Books, pp. 19–37.

54. Sammy Smooha (1978) *Israel: Pluralism and Conflict*, Berkeley, University of California Press.

55. Shlomo Swirski (1981) *Orientals and Ashkenazim in Israel*, Haifa, Notebooks for Research and Critique [Hebrew]; (1993) 'Tomorrow', in Ram (ed.) *Israeli Society*, pp. 351–63.

56. Henry Rosenfeld and Shulamit Carmi (1976) 'The Privatization of Public Means, the State Made Middle Class, and the Realization of Family Values in Israel', in J.G. Peristiany (ed.), *Kinship and Modernization in Mediterranean Society*, Rome, The Centre for Mediterranean Studies, American University Field Staff; Shulamit Carmi and Henry Rosenfeld (1989) 'The Rise of Militaristic Nationalism in Israel', in the *International Journal of Politics, Culture and Society*, no. 3, pp. 95–149.

57. Shlomo Swirski (1990) *Education in Israel: Schooling for Inequality*, Tel Aviv, Breirot [Hebrew]; Shlomo Swirski (1995) *Seeds of Inequality*, Tel Aviv, Breirot [Hebrew]; Yaakov Nahon (1993) 'Occupational Status', in Moshe Lissak and Shmuel Noah Eisenstadt (eds) *Ethnic Communities in Israel*, Jerusalem, The Jerusalem Institute of Israel Studies [Hebrew].

58. Amiel Alkalai (1993) *After Jews and Arabs: Remaking Levantine Culture*, Minneapolis, University of Minnesota Press; Ella Shohat (1989) *Israeli Cinema: East/West and the Politics of Representation*, Austin, University of Texas Press; Gabi Piterberg (1995) 'The Nation and its Raconteurs: Orientalism and Nationalist Historiography', in *Theory and Critique*, no. 6, pp. 81–104 [Hebrew].

59. Deborah Bernstein (1987) *The Struggle for Equality: Urban Women Workers in Pre-State Israeli Society*, New York, Praeger; (1992) 'Human Being – or Housewife? The Status of Women in the Jewish Working Class Family in Palestine of the 1920s and 1930s', in Deborah Bernstein (ed.), *Pioneers and Homeworks*, Albany, NY, SUNY Press, pp. 235–60; Silviya Fogel-Bijaui (1991) 'Mothers and Revolution: the Case of Women in the Kibbutz, 1910–1948', in *Shorashim*, no. 6, pp. 143–92 [Hebrew]; Hanna Herzog (1994) 'A Forgotten Chapter in the Historiography of the Yishuv: Women's Organizations', in *Cathedra*, no. 70, pp. 111–33.

60. Dan Giladi (1973) *Jewish Palestine During the Fourth Aliya Period (1924–1929)*, Tel Aviv, Am Oved [Hebrew]; (1994) *The Return to Our Forefathers' Land: Z.D. Lavontin: A Proponent of A Free Enterprise Approach to Zionism*, Jerusalem, Friends of the Israel Center for Social and Economic Progress [Hebrew]; Yosef Katz (1989) *hyozma hapratit bebinyan eretz israel betkufat haliya hashniya*, Ramat Gan, Bar Ilan University; (1993) *The Colonization Activity in Palestine of the Zionist Private Companies and Associations*, Jerusalem, Chamul [Hebrew].

61. Amnon Raz-Krakotzkin (1994) 'Exile Within Sovereignty: Toward a Critique of the "Negation of Exile" in Israeli Culture (Parts I & II)' in *Theory and Critique*, nos. 4 and 5, pp. 6–23; 113–32 [Hebrew].

62. Ruth Firer (1985) *The Agents of Zionist Education*, Kiryat Tivon, Oranim [Hebrew]; Ram, 'Zionist Historiography'.

63. Shabtai Beit Zvi (1977) *Post-Ugandan Zionism in the Crucible of the Holocaust*, Tel Aviv, Bronfman [Hebrew]; Yosef Grodzinsky (1994) 'The Holocaust, the Yishuv, Their Leaders and Their Historians (Parts A and B)', in *Ha'aretz*, 8, 15 April; Tom Segev (1991) *The Seventh Million: The Israelis and the Holocaust*, Jerusalem, Keter [Hebrew].

64. Hava Eshkoli-Wagman (1994) *Silence: Mapai and the Holocaust, 1943–1945*, Jerusalem, Yad Yizhak Ben Zvi; Yehuda Bauer (1993) 'No "Tom" and no "Segev",' in *Iton 77*, Tel Aviv, pp. 24–8; (1994) 'That's What a Jewish State is For', in *Ha'aretz*, 27 September; Shabtai Tevet (1994a) 'The Black Hole: Ben Gurion Between Holocaust and Revival', in *Alpayim*, no. 10, pp. 111–95 [Hebrew]; (1994b) 'Shock, Ambivalence or Helplessness?', in *Ha'aretz Sfarim*, 30 March, pp. 4–5; Yehiam Weitz (1994) *Aware But Helpless: Mapai and the Holocaust, 1943–1945*, Jerusalem, Yad Yizhak Ben Zvi [Hebrew]; Dan Michman (1994) 'On History and Charlatanism', in *Ha'aretz*, 6 May; Dina Porat (1986) *An Entangled Leadership: The Yishuv and the Holocaust, 1942–1945*, Tel Aviv, Am Oved [Hebrew]; (1990) 'Contemporary Historiography of Zionist Efforts During the Holocaust Period', in *Yahadut Zemanenu*, no. 6, pp. 117–32 [Hebrew].

65. Henry Wasserman (1986) 'The Nationalization of the Memory of the Six Million', in *Politika*, pp. 7–16, 55; Dan Diner (1988) 'The Yishuv in the Face of the Holocaust of European Jewry' (review article), in *Haziyonut*, no. 13, pp. 301–8 [Hebrew]; Ruth Firer (1989) *Agents of the Holocaust Lesson*, Tel Aviv, Hakkibbutz Hameuhad [Hebrew]; Moshe Zukerman (1993) *Shoah in the Sealed Room*, Tel Aviv, The Author [Hebrew]; Idit Zertal (1994) 'The Sacrifice and the Sanctified: The Construction of Mational Martyrology', in *Zmanim*, no. 48, pp. 26–45 [Hebrew]; (1996) *From Catastrophe to Power: Jewish Illegal Immigration to Palestine, 1945–1948*, Tel Aviv, Am Oved [Hebrew].

66. See David Asaf (1995) 'The Robbers of Memory', in *Ha'aretz*, 17 February; Dina Porat (1995) 'Two Jewish Peoples', in *Ha'aretz*, 17 February.

67. Firer, *The Agents of Zionist Education*; Boaz Evron (1988) *A National Reckoning*, Tel Aviv, Dvir [Hebrew]; Barnai, *Historiography and Nationalism*; Yehuda Libes (1992) 'New Directions in Kabbala Research', in *Peamim*, no. 50, pp. 150–70 [Hebrew].

3 ◎ The Square Circle

The Struggle for Survival of Traditional Zionism

Ilan Pappé

The victory of Ehud Barak in the 1999 Israeli general election was hailed locally and internationally as the return of the Jewish state to the peace track. A sigh of relief accompanied the defeat of Binyamin Netanyahu, and an optimistic air surrounded the resumption of peace negotiations with the Palestinians. As the international media were quick to note, the final stage in the long road begun in Oslo was at hand. A year and a half later, in autumn 2000, Barak led Israel and Palestine into a new war: Oslo was gone and with it the hopes for a comprehensive peace in the torn land of Israel and Palestine. The sense of frustration and crisis was even deeper than the one accompanying the Netanyahu era, as the Barak 'peace policy' was conducted in a highly dramatic manner and was presented with the help of an extremely sanguine discourse of peace.

With the collapse of peace talks also disappeared the relatively pluralistic era in the intellectual life of the Jewish state. In quite a surprising manner, at Israel's 'moment of truth' in history, just before the final phase in the negotiations on the Palestine question had supposedly begun, the internal debate, so heated a few years before that it resulted in the assassination of Yizhak Rabin, had subsided and in fact completely disappeared. Israel entered that last stage with a consensual government, based on a large majority of Jewish members of the Knesset, and an opposition that accepted, with few reservations, the basic picture of a final settlement as depicted by the government and offered to the Palestinians. From Peace Now on the left to the settlers' community on the right, a wide consensus on the nature of the conflict's solution seemed to be accepted. These two extra-parliamentary bodies both have ministerial representation in the government.

This situation meant that the party breakdown in the Israeli parliament after the 1999 and 2001 elections, or the past dichotomy between Likud and Labour, no longer served as an appropriate indicator of the nature of the political debate within the state of Israel on all the crucial subjects on its national agenda – particularly on the solution of the Palestine question. I choose in this chapter another reification or political categorisation for characterising the present internal debate in the Israeli society and state – that of ideological streams. Contrary to many Western societies, Israel, very much like societies in the Balkans, is still very torn by ideology. The state itself is a powerful apparatus of indoctrination and those challenging it are principally motivated by what can only be called an ideological outlook – a future vision based on a particular interpretation of the past in order either to alter or preserve the present.

The chapter describes a clash between three ideological streams within Zionism, the positions of which became clear as a result of these two election campaigns, and due to the crisis the two sides were drawn to on the brink of entering the last stages in the Oslo accord. The leading stream, which I will call traditional Zionism, to which both Labour and Likud belong, is presented here as underlying the policies and plans of all Israeli governments since the creation of the state. This ideological outlook is challenged by two opposing streams, neo-Zionism and post-Zionism. It is our purpose here to try to assess the debate's sites and area, its present balance of power, and its implication for the future, not only of the state of Israel, but more importantly of the Palestine question.

These three streams seem to engage in a battle over memory, reality and vision, or over the past, present and future. There is no clear-cut victory or defeat here; there is a complicated picture which I would like to draw in this chapter, with each reaction having been successful on only one of the three ideological fronts. Needless to say, the future balance of this ideological battle will have a considerable influence on the lives not only of Israelis, but also of Palestinians and anyone else in the region who has been affected by Zionism and Israel in the last 150 years.

Traditional Zionism is mainstream Zionism or labour Zionism, definitions which refer to the hegemonic representation of Zionism since 1882 until the fall of the Labour party from power in the 1977 elections. In 1977, traditional Zionism was successfully challenged politically by an alternative, more ethnocentric and segregative variant of Zionism known as Revisionism. This variant was committed, ever since its creation in 1922, to total Zionist control and sovereignty over the whole of historical Palestine. But despite its political loss, and evidenced by its return to power for short periods, in 1992 and again in 1999 (I even argue that the 2001 Sharon government is also part of this stream, even if he himself comes from Likud), traditional Zionism has remained the principal prism through which the political centre and the professional elites in Israel view the Israel–Palestine reality. Indeed, this was the ideological basis on which the Israeli architects of Oslo constructed their peace settlement and it still underpins the present Israeli posture towards the final stages of the Israeli–Palestinian peace accord.

From the left, traditional Zionism has been challenged since the 1980s by post-Zionism, a movement of critique that I have described in recent articles in the *Journal of Palestine Studies*.[1] Post-Zionism is a term I used to describe a cultural view from within Israel which strongly criticized Zionist policy and conduct up to 1948, accepted many of the claims made by the Palestinians with regards to 1948 itself, and envisaged a non-Jewish state in Israel as the best solution for the country's internal and external predicaments. As such, it represented a point of view that can be, and is, acceptable to a large number of Palestinian citizens in Israel. In fact, its only hope of becoming a meaningful political alternative depended considerably on its ability to form a lasting political alliance with the Palestinian national minority in Israel.

This alliance has not yet been formed, and thus we cannot talk about post-Zionism as a political challenge. Its success lies elsewhere, as I will show in the first part of this chapter, in the battle over collective memory and the past. The main political challenge to traditional Zionism comes from the Right. The Right in Israel is currently occupied by a fundamentalist Zionist point of view, or more conveniently, as it was termed by Uri Ram, a neo-Zionist point of view.[2] Neo-Zionism is a violent, extreme interpretation of Zionism. It existed, as marginal variant of Zionism, both in the Labour and Revisionist camps, and was nourished in the teaching centres controlled by the religious Zionist movement Hapoel Hamizrachi (which became the national religious party, Mafdal). It burst out as an official alternative after the 1967 war, pushed forward by expansionists in the Labour movement, leaders of the newly formed Likud, and important rabbis in religious circles. In the 1980s, neo-Zionism widened its constituency by forming an alliance between the settlers in the occupied territories and deprived and marginalised sections of Jewish society in Israel. It is an uneasy alliance between expansionist nationalists, ultra-orthodox rabbis, and ethnic spiritual leaders of the Mizrahi Jews; all presenting themselves as champions of the underprivileged Mizrahi Jewish communities in Israel. The Mizrahi Jews as an electorate still supported this alliance until recently, but it has a much more complicated and sophisticated view, which disables us from defining its location on the ideological map that we are drawing. Quite probably it is divided, like the rest of the Jewish community in Israel, between the three ideological streams.

This chapter follows the fortunes of the traditional Zionist view in three stages. It describes its defeat as an interpretation of the past, its success in determining the present and its struggle to remain dominant in the future.

Traditional Zionism: the demise of an intellectual illusion

The traditional Zionist perception has undergone dramatic, substantial transformations ever since the creation of the movement in 1882. Colonialism, nationalism and socialism played a role as principal influences on the formulation of traditional Zionist ideology and practice. Several works have recently looked at these transformations with a critical eye and I am not going to add to them. I would like to provide a snapshot of its present condition. It is by default that I can sketch the boundaries of this sociological reification – traditional Zionism – through which I have chosen to describe mainstream Zionist views: it should include anyone who is not a non- or anti-Zionist Jew in Israel on the one hand, and not a fundamentalist or ultra-orthodox Jew on the other. It is easier to find the members of this socio-ideological category within the Israeli media and academia. Many, if not most, of those controlling the academic and polemical scene in Israel define themselves as Zionists who are utterly opposed to the 'extreme' margins of the Israeli political spectrum.

For a very long period there was no need for these articulators of the traditional Zionist view to clarify their positions towards the past. The appearance of 'post-Zionist' scholarship forced the gatekeepers of traditional Zionism to reassert their historiographical interpretations as well as their moral convictions. Collective memory and moral self-perception are closely linked and it is no wonder that a post-Zionist critique of the past triggered a public debate from which one can learn much about the present position of traditional Zionism on history. This position feeds the policies of the present and will affect the postures of the future. Several of the participants from the traditional Zionist camp themselves stated, albeit disparagingly, that the only merit they see in post-Zionist scholarship is that it has compelled them to redefine and update more clearly their perceptions of the Zionist and Israeli past.

Traditional Zionists are now engaged in a rescue operation, as is claimed by one of their disciples, David Ohana, in a recent book, *The Last Israelis*.[3] The operation is to salvage Zionism from its neo-Zionist enemies on the right and its post-Zionist foes on the left. This rescue operation is carried out the name of liberalism and humanism as well as Zionism. In their reconstructed view, Zionism was a national movement, humanist, liberal and socialist, which brought modernisation and progress to primitive Palestine, made the desert bloom, re-built the ruined cities of the land and introduced modern agriculture and industry to the benefit of everyone, Arab and Jew alike. Zionism was resisted by a combination of Islamic fanaticism, pro-Arab British colonialism and the local tradition and culture of political violence. Against all odds, and despite a most cruel local resistance, Zionism remained loyal to humanist precepts of individual and collective behaviour and tirelessly stretched out its hand to its Arab neighbours, who kept rejecting it. Against all odds, the Zionists also miraculously established a state in the face of a hostile Arab world. A state that, notwithstanding an objective shortage of space and means, absorbed one million Jews who had been expelled from the Arab world, and offered them progress and integration in the only democracy in the Middle East. It was a defensive state trying to contain ever-growing Arab hostility and world apathy; a state that took in Jews from more than one hundred places in the diaspora, gathered them in and made one new Jewish people out of them. It was a moral, just movement of redemption, which unfortunately found other people on its homeland, but nonetheless offered them a share in a better future, which they foolishly rejected. This idyllic picture, so runs the reconstruction, was undermined and shattered by the evil consequences of the 1967 war and the political earthquake of 1977, which brought Likud to power. After, and because of, 1967, negative features have developed, such as territorial expansionism and religious fanaticism on the right, and self-doubt and self-hatred on the extreme left. But it is a reversible development that can be stopped by returning to the traditional Zionist values of humanism, democracy and liberalism.

In thousands of boring micro-histories this narrative has been substantiated in Israeli academia and challenged only by Palestinian scholarship, which was suspected in the West and by anti-Zionist parties in Israel as mere propaganda. The doyens of the profession were allowed to indulge in macro-histories, forging all these micro-histories into a master story, providing scholarly scaffolding for the Zionist claim to Palestine and for the virtue of the modernising road Israel has taken. Now this traditional view is challenged by post-Zionist scholarship, portraying Zionism as a colonialist project, morally suspect, with inherent problems, which serve as the main explanation for Israel's internal and external predicaments today. It is no wonder that such a reconstruction was opposed, once it had been attempted from within Israeli academia.

The salvage operation is a struggle over images and perceptions. It is led by historians identified with the Zionist left within the Israeli academy. Its major thrust is directed against post-Zionist scholarship, as the right-wing neo-Zionists are less active in the field of past images and are much stronger in selling a new vision for the future. In the mid-1990s, in several books, articles and conferences, the professionalism of post-Zionist scholars was questioned, and an attempt has been made ever since to point to factual flaws in their claims – flaws which were described as part of a conscious distortion meant to serve anti-Zionist ideology. This was a shift from earlier establishment reactions to post-Zionist scholarship. In the late 1980s, the common reaction was to ignore the professionalism of the post-Zionist historians and view them simply as an ideological group. Shabtai Teveth, a journalist, was recruited then by the establishment for this task. It was beyond the dignity of historians to take part in what they deemed a purely ideological and political debate. Teveth tried, and still tries, to challenge particularly Benny Morris's claims about the role of Israel in the making of the Palestinian refugee problem. He succeeded in entering a few international venues, but failed to receive the attention that Morris has received ever since his work was published. Another recruit was the novelist Aharon Meged, who challenged the moral basis of the work of post-Zionist scholars.[4]

But in the 1990s, mainstream historians and sociologists joined the debate, initially declaring reluctance to be drawn into these 'non-academic' matters. But the attraction of 'post-Zionism' abroad and inside Israel necessitated a more systematic approach. The mixture of academic professionalism with an anti-Zionist edge turned 'post-Zionism' into a refreshing contribution to Middle East studies in Israel and in the West. It was difficult to ignore a process by which positions held in the past by marginal anti-Zionist groups turned into scholarly statements by members of Israeli academia.

These statements have been challenged recently by leading historians and sociologists such as Moshe Lissak, Anita Shapira, Yossef Gorny and Shlomo Ahronson – all full professors with high public as well as academic standing. Their reaction was far more sophisticated than that of Teveth and Meged. The counter-critiques absorbed some marginal points made by post-Zionism but rejected its major conclusions on Israel's past and present.[5]

Against the revisionist nature of post-Zionism, these scholars presented a reformist view of the origins of Zionism, the 1948 war and the early years of statehood. The most common adjective employed by these scholars has been 'exceptional', *harig*. If there had been colonialist characteristics in Zionist conduct in the late nineteenth century, goes the reformist argument, if there were atrocities and expulsions committed during the 1948 war and if there were discriminations and abuses in the early years of statehood, they were all exceptions which do not teach us about the rule, which remained what it always had been – Zionism as a national movement combining humanism and liberalism in its outlook and practice.

Their reaction, however, revealed one significant success of post-Zionist scholarship. They accepted as legitimate topics hitherto regarded as taboo in Israeli academia, such as the issue of Zionist conduct during the Second World War. The gist of the post-Zionist critique, exemplified in the essential work of Tom Segev, *The Seventh Million,* which was presented as a documentary film on Israeli TV, is that the Jewish community was interested in the fate of European Jews only when it served Zionism. This argument has been countered by Yehuda Bauer and Israel Gutman, the two leading historians of the Yad Va-Shem institute. They were supported by Haim Guri, the national poet of Zionism and Israel, who added a sentimental aspect to the debate.[6]

A second success of the post-Zionist approach was that it fitted the mood of many Israelis at their jubilee (1998), particularly on the left and on the social margins. This mood was generated by the political, cultural and social reality of Israel, a society torn by religious, ethnic, cultural and economic cleavages, which had undermined all efforts to produce a celebratory mood during the state's fiftieth anniversary. Different groups still feel deprived owing to historical injustices that persist today, and are interested to hear what scholars have to say about it, and how far academia identifies with them. Progressive educationalists in particular were captivated by the freshness of the critical debate on Israel's past and present offered by the academics.

During 1997, another array of well-known scholars who usually do not deal with Israel as academic subject matter joined the establishment in an effort to undermine the credibility of post-Zionist scholarship. Amnon Rubinstein, Hedva Ben-Israel and Immanuel Sivan led this defensive operation. These three scholars are even more closely associated with the Zionist left, and added new layers of depth to the debate. They did not attack the 'findings' or the 'facts' put forward by post-Zionism but the ideological and theoretical context of its research. Ben-Israel and Sivan in particular chose to confront the theoreticians whom they believed lay behind the work of post-Zionist scholars – Eric Hobsbawm in the case of Ben-Israel and Edward Said in the case of Sivan. Sivan deployed Arab critiques of Said to undermine Said's deconstruction of orientalism. Although this deepened the debate, it also exposed the extent to which Israeli scholars with an international reputation are committed to Zionism. When a debate is motivated by such commitment it is no wonder that the discourse used, especially against Said, is violent and personal.[7]

The climax of the scholarly counter-attack was Efraim Karsh's strange book, *Fabricating Israeli History*.[8] It is a shallow book, holding very little in the way of new evidence, and is devoted to an attack mainly on Avi Shlaim and Benny Morris. Karsh, from his seat in London, is unaware of both the extent of post-Zionist scholarship and of the level of its acceptance in Israel itself. Like Teveth before him, he picks on insignificant details of the whole picture, and is therefore unable to present an alternative narrative to the one produced by these two professional historians.

Karsh's voice is unimportant when judged against the debate going on in Israel. The effort invested by the Israeli academy was far more meaningful and serious. It involved not only a discussion on the essence of Zionism, but also on the integrity of the academicians themselves. In the 1990s it created an uneasy coexistence in the academy into which it was about to draw the political debate in Israeli society. If there ever were ivory towers in Israel, they were under threat of collapse. The polarisation in the political field entered the academic field through the front door: a dramatic entrance denied for years by the pretentious claim of traditional Zionist scholars of being able to divorce their academic work from their ideological positions.

The cartographic power of traditional Zionism: drawing the post-Oslo map

While traditional Zionism was limping unconvincingly into the following century as a scholarly interpretation of Palestine's past, it was still a major factor in shaping the Jewish perception on the present. While post-Zionism had in the 1990s impressive support in academia, and to a certain extent in the press and other cultural media, its vision of a secular, democratic non-Zionist Israel (or Israel and Palestine as a unitary state) won only a marginal following in Israeli Jewish politics (apart, of course, from Israeli Palestinians, who supported such a vision wholeheartedly).

Traditional Zionism has been represented on the political scene throughout the years by Labour Zionism. This movement, due to its dominant position in the political and social centres in Israel, still provides the major political interpretation for the Israel–Palestine reality. In the past, traditional Zionism was opposed by right-wing revisionism, represented by Likud. This party and its sister parties demanded a greater Eretz-Israel, stretching over Jordan and Palestine. While in power, however, Likud did not find the strength or courage to annex officially the Palestinian areas occupied in 1967, although it did increase settlements in those areas. In the post-Oslo reality, it seems that the two shrinking mega-parties of Israel, Likud and Labour, became closer than ever in their interpretation of the past and their vision for the future. When using the terms Labour and Likud, I mean not just the platforms and positions of the two parties – these are only part of it – but also the attitudes of their electorates as manifested in the media, polls and political discourse of those who regard themselves as belonging to the 'silent majority' or to 'mainstream' Israel.

The present traditional Zionist view was translated into practical terms in the Oslo agreement, or more precisely in the Israeli interpretation of Oslo. The first part of this position was that *pre-1967 Israel is not negotiable*; hence the future of the refugees or a discussion of Israel's role in the making of the problem were excluded from the negotiating table (not to mention a categorical refusal to include Palestinians in Israel in any Israeli–Palestinian dialogue on the future).

For the traditional Zionists, the geographical and territorial space of the Israeli–Palestinian conflict is confined to the areas occupied by Israel in 1967, apart from East Jerusalem and its environs. This is the space in which eventually the permanent, not temporary, solution of the question will be implemented. Geographically, the negotiable areas do not include most of the territory controlled today by the settlers. In the areas left, the Israelis will control the parameters while the Palestinians will have some functions. This formula is a hybrid of two old Israeli 'peace' plans: one offered by Yigal Allon, the other by Moshe Dayan. Both were presented in the 1970s. Allon sought a territorial compromise with the Jordanians, based on the demographic distribution in the territories. Dayan suggested dividing the functions of authority between Israel and Jordan – Israel holding mainly security functions in the West Bank, the Jordanians all the rest. These two approaches, with the Palestinians replacing the Hashemites as partners, are the basis of the current proposals of a *permanent settlement* offered jointly by Labour and Likud in the post-Oslo reality.

This is the shared vision. As for its realization, here too we can talk of one ideological Labour-Likud movement. The solution should be dictated to the Palestinians. We have seen this in action ever since the conclusion of the Oslo accord; a dictation which has been exercised by all previous governments of Israel. The notion of dictation enjoyed and still enjoys wide support among the Jewish population. In fact, as the elections of 1996 have shown, the majority of Jewish voters in Israel were willing to impose the Oslo reality on the Palestinians in an even harsher guise, that suggested by Binyamin Netayahu. His fall from power had nothing to do with a critique of this policy, which in many ways Barak and Sharon continued: to harden the conditions for peace suggested by Rabin. The composition of the 1999 and 2001 governments and their teams of principal negotiators (ex-generals and Omri, the son of Ariel Sharon) perpetuated the harsh approach: this was the case when Likud was out of the government in 1999, and when it led the Likud–Labour government in 2001.

This is why Oslo was so attractive for the Israelis. It appealed to the political centre. Immediately after the 1996 Israeli elections, Yossi Beilin, a leading figure on Labour's left wing, commented that he believed Labour and Likud could find common ground for peacemaking. A common platform is the best way for political parties such as Likud and Labour to avoid relying too heavily on fringe ideological parties. Scrutiny of the two parties' platforms does indeed show quite considerable overlap on the question of Oslo. Labour proposes that in the final peace agreement most of the 144 Jewish settlements in the West Bank and Gaza remain intact and under Israeli sovereignty. Labour insists that Jerusalem remain united under Israeli control. Their official positions differ on the question of Palestinian state-hood, but in reality both offer the Palestinians far from normal statehood.

The extent of the agreement within the centre of the Israeli political system can be seen in the Eitan–Beilin document, a document that sets the parameters for any future unity government in Israel. Beilin is supposedly on the left of the Labour party and Eitan on the right of Likud, and yet they found it quite easy to agree that a diktat should be presented to the Palestinians regarding the lines of a permanent settlement of the Palestine problem. In it almost all the settlements are to remain under Israeli control and sovereignty, Jerusalem is to be united under Israeli rule, and Israel is to be responsible for security on the Jordan river. There is no mention of any solution to the refugee problem, but there is agreement that a semblance of statehood should be given to the Palestinians in the areas that would remain under their control.

To sum up, for traditional Zionists the Palestinian Authority was expected to accept a scheme which would make Palestine a Bantustan on most of the West Bank and the Gaza Strip, with a mini-capital at Abu Dis, without any solution for the refugee problem and without any dismantling of Jewish settlements.

This vision has an economic dimension too, which cuts across national boundaries. Part of this vision is the introduction of a capitalist, free-market economy in both Israel and Palestine. Under the Paris agreements, which were the economic component of Oslo, signed in 1994, Israel and Palestine were to be one economic unit. This can be seen in the way the customs outfits are connected, and in the way a joint taxation policy is being exercised. Such unification is ensured by the decision to postpone any substantial negotiations over the introduction of a Palestinian currency. Furthermore, the agreement grants Israel the right to veto any development scheme put forward by the PA, ensuring that the monetary and developmental policies of Israel and its currency exchanges play a dominant role in the Palestinian economy. Other aspects of the economy, such as foreign trade and industry, are also totally dominated by the Israelis, according to the agreement of the interim report.

The introduction of the Israeli version of a capitalist society into the Palestinian areas can only have a disastrous effect. With the absence of democratic structure and a very low GNP, such an introduction and integration as offered by Oslo can only turn the areas under the Palestinian Authority into the slums of Israel. An excellent example for such a development can already be seen in Erez, the buffer zone between Israel and the Gaza Strip. There the Israelis, with the blessing of the Americans and the EU, opened an 'industrial park'. Let this name not mislead readers; it is a production line where all the workers are Palestinians on very low wages, and the employers are Israelis. Israel has similar visions for such 'parks' on the borders with Jordan and the West Bank. Industrialists in Israel therefore see themselves as belonging to the peace camp. This is only one aspect of the capitalization of the peace process; another is the support given by a limited number of Palestinians, who can benefit from such economic transactions.

While this double burden of economic misery and lack of genuine progress on the national question led to a Palestinian revolt against the post-Oslo reality, it would take more than the 2000 *intifada* to persuade Israelis to wish to change the reality emerging after Oslo. For the majority of the Jewish population in Israel this peace is based on unbeatable logic, one pronounced many times by the late prime minister Yizhak Rabin. The

Palestinians were in a very dismal situation before Oslo; they were offered an improvement – not a very impressive one, but still one that can be defined as an N+1 formula, N being the previous situation, 1 being Gaza, Jericho and Ramallah covered with Palestinian flags and guarded by Palestinian policemen. 1- is a non-democratic authority, which replaced Israeli occupation with Palestinian security services. This, for most Israelis, is peace, provided there is no terror and no bombs. For most Israelis, peace is their daily security; this was enhanced by Oslo until the second *intifada,* that of 2000, and is demanded by the Israelis as peace for the post-*intifada* period.

The neo-Zionist future: the making of an Israeli zealotocracy

With this geopolitical vision, even the ultra-Orthodox parties of Shas and Agudat Israel were willing to go along. But a vision of the future is not just a matter of defining borders or containing Palestinian national aspirations and rights; it is also a matter of the identity and essence of the society. And here we encounter the neo-Zionist vision shared by the settler community, supporters of the national religious party Mafdal, the ultra-orthodox parties and a new secular right closely associated financially and ideologically with the New Right in the USA (among its number is a new right-wing party of Russian immigrants called Israel Beiteinu – Israel Our Home).

Unlike the post-Zionists, after the 1999 elections the neo-Zionist alliance was already represented in government, and received even stronger representation in the Sharon government of February 2001. They had six ministries in 1999 and nine in 2001, although, compared to Netanyahu's government, they have of course lost power. They joined the Barak government with ease because the national agenda shifted for a short while from an interest in territory and political borders to socio-cultural questions. The mini-state offered by Barak to the Palestinians frightened the neo-Zionists, but they accepted their inability to put forward an alternative. Since 2001, it has been more difficult to hear the neo-Zionist agenda on domestic issues, as security and defence have overshadowed all else, but the illusory sense of stability during the 1990s, particularly the year of Barak's reign, disclosed quite clearly how the Jewish state is envisaged within this ideological stratum.

Post-Oslo Israel was multi-ethnic, multicultural and deeply divided on issues of culture, law, morality and education. This was not a division of clear positions but rather a confusion of insecure voices. The various groups constituting Israeli society tended to stress their particular identity at the expense of the state's identity, a tendency manifested in the way citizens accept or shun general civil duties such as taxes, and in their commitment, or lack of it, to shared causes. The voters had already in the 1996 elections showed their belief that the particular interests of Ethiopian, Russian, North African, secular Tel-Avivians and Palestinian Israelis could best be served by sectarian voting. This trend was reinforced in the 1999 elections. For many Israelis, this voting pattern constitutes a threat, and they find neo-Zionism's greatest attraction in the simple, ready-made remedy for such disintegration. Neo-Zionism conveys confidence, not confusion, about the future. Its main tactic is to present itself as having the key for unifying disintegrated, polarized Israeli society, the key being a crystal-clear version of Judaism as a national movement, something that the articulators and intellectuals of Labour Zionism never succeeded in doing. Neo-Zionists can pretend to be the unifying force bridging the wide spectrum of conflicting interpretations of Judaism both as a religion and as a national movement. While post-Zionist scholars suggest accepting the fractured reality as an indication of the need to turn Israel into a state for all its citizens and not try to identify the state with one group at the expense of others, neo-Zionists propose a Jewish religious and nationalist cement that would prevent further fragmentation and disintegration.

Four parallel processes are taking place, which forge this neo-Zionist option: the fanaticisation of the national religious groups in Israel (whose strongholds are in the settlements and in a wide network of Yeshiva centres, funded by the state); the nationalisation or Zionisation of the previously anti-Zionist ultra-Orthodox Jews; the ethnic insulation of segments of the Mizrahi Jewish community caught in the geographical and social margins of society; and the fast integration of Israel into capitalist globalisation, which adds an intellectual neo-conservative centre, à la New Right, to the alliance. The four groups share one vision: an ethnic religious theocracy as the best means of facing Israel's external and domestic problems. The dominant group among them is religious leaders, be they rabbis, magicians, healers, politicians or educators. This elite shares a most prerogative perception of secular Jews and non-Jews in Israel. According to a recent book in Israel exposing these views, this fanatic alliance sees secular Jews as the 'Messiah's Donkey'[9] – they did their job carrying Jews back to their holy land, but they are now obsolete and can be treated as non-Jews. Non-Jews are like beasts – you may utilise and exploit them, at times you may fear them, but you are always above them. As this book shows, medieval Jewish thought, constructed to balance and provide solace and revenge in the face of a most hostile gentile environment, is reused here as a basis for a modern racist ideology, constructing a clear exclusive model for the future – an Israel without secular Jews and non-Jews.

This concept is formulated and dominated by the national religious thinkers (mainly rabbis). It is presented as Zionism, not Judaism. It is connected to the old Zionist fulfilment precept, *Hagshama* – which in its old interpretation meant only one thing: settling the land. At first, neo-Zionists saw settlement of the West Bank, Gaza Strip and Golan as the ultimate act of patriotism. But settlement activity decreased, first due to the Oslo accord, second because of the al-Aqsa *intifada*. Fulfilment now curtails strict observance of Jewish law and struggle against traditional Zionism in the judicial and legislative realm; its main target is the supreme high court, due to that body's attempt to safeguard the public sphere from religious imposition. This activity did not stop even when, in February 2001, a unity government was formed under Ariel Sharon; as the negotiations over this government's budget indicated, the neo-Zionist agenda in domestic affairs did not change.

The neo-Zionist view of the past is nationalist and romantic. Israel of the Second Temple era is the glorious past, to be reconstructed. The resemblance to the BJP in India is striking. Both parties wish to demolish a past of a few hundred years old in the name of a distant past a few thousand years old. Hence, neo-Zionists take seriously the idea of rebuilding a third Temple instead of Haram al-Sharif, and prepare cadres of would-be priests to serve there when the time comes (they differ on how to achieve this goal, whether by blowing up the two mosques on the mount, or waiting for divine intervention to pave the way for their schemes).

Their greatest success, apart from having significant representation in government since 1996, is their growing impact on the educational system in Israel. They controlled the office under Netanyahu; they shared it under Barak, and retook it under Sharon. They appeal to a nationalist reconstruction of the past, free of any hesitation or criticism. They have produced teaching modules which are going to be the essential educational kit for the next generation of Israeli children in elementary and high schools, should they remain in, or return to, power. This kit can produce only one type of graduate: racist, insular and extremely ethnocentric (recent research on children only proves that, even without such an effort, quite a few are exhibiting these views).

So while Israeli academia and other cultural arenas were at least exposed to universal critique, the school system in Israel regressed into an entrenched, extreme Zionist interpretation of history and society. It is this polarised reality which produced, alongside TV programmes such as *Tekkuma* (portraying, albeit implicitly, a problematic past, and propagating the need for a more democratic and liberal future), a contrasting set of educational programmes stressing the superiority of ethnicity over any other set of values. These schemes have been developed by the Mafdal ever since occupying the ministry of education in the Netanyahu government, and implemented by Limor Livnat, the minister of education in the Sharon government since February 2001. The main effort here is to stress 'Zionist' conviction, in its neo-Zionist interpretation, among elementary and high-school children.

Even towards the end of Netanyahu's time in power, the ministry of education produced new history books for the elementary system to commemorate the country's fiftieth anniversary. One such book, titled *Israel's Jubilee*, which covers the state's chronicles ever since its foundation in 1948, appeared in three volumes. The book hardly mentions the Palestinians – not in relation to the 1948 war, not as citizens of Israel under a military regime up to 1966, and not as an occupied population in the West Bank and the Gaza Strip since 1967. The presence of Palestinian refugees is something that readers of this book will not learn about. They will be aware only of the existence of Palestinian terrorism, which emerged sometime in the 1960s for unknown reasons.[10]

The ministry claimed that this book is not an official textbook, but only recommended by the ministry as a supplementary aid to teachers and pupils alike. This cautious approach is due to the criticism voiced in the post-Zionist press. However, judging by the past, the Israeli educational system is one of the most conformist parts of the state, and so most of its members are likely to heed the ministry's recommendations. Moreover, it was recommended within a wider project sponsored by the ministry which turned the fiftieth anniversary into a 'central theme' for all schools in 1998. Asked what this meant, the ministry explained it to be a curriculum aiming at 'soul searching' on unresolved dilemmas and conflict. The way out of these dilemmas could only be 'inward' – it is to be found in the uncontested Jewish moral right to the land of Israel.

Between 1996 and 1998, and again between 1999 and 2001, the whole educational system was injected with additional neo-Zionist doses. Just before the government's fall at the end of 1998, a new plan was announced, aiming to 'link pupils more closely with the army'. This Spartan or Prussian scheme was meant to encompass children from kindergarten to the end of high school, and prepare them for 'military environment and values: coping with situations of pressure and developing leadership skills in a battlefield'. Physical fitness, as required by the army, was to be a precondition for matriculating and graduating in the future. An obligatory part of the future educational system is to be participation in army manoeuvres and military indoctrination. This is meant to be complemented by enriched lessons in Zionism and Eretz Israel studies. In the last three years of high school, a plan titled 'the scheme for increasing the motivation and preparedness for the IDF' promised to focus in the first year on 'the individual's commitment to his or her homeland', and in the second two years on 'actual participation in military life'. This was already common practice in many schools, but always as a marginal part of school life, prepared by traditional Zionists. Now, the individual pupil would learn the history of the land according to the neo-Zionist interpretation – a study bound to shape his or her vision of the future. One doubts how much a post-Zionist lecturer can do, if he or she is lucky enough to have the opportunity later on to voice different opinions.

For a very short period, 1999–2000, it seemed as if new winds were blowing in the corridors of the ministry of education. Yossi Sarid, the head of the left Zionist party, Meretz (albeit with a neo-Zionist deputy), was appointed to the office by Ehud Barak in 1999. From 1992 to 1996, Meretz had held the office, and under Shulamit Aloni oriented a different educational effort. A team of Israeli academics and teachers began in 1995 toiling over a historiographical curriculum that would examine Israel's history from a more critical angle. The aim was to present more positively the Palestinian side of the story. A member of a committee preparing this new programme, Avner Ben-Amos, told *Ha'aretz*:

> In the past the teaching of history [in Israel] was dominated by a version which claimed that we [the Israelis] had an unquestionable right to the land to which we returned after 2,000 years of exile, and we reached an empty land. Nowadays we cannot divorce the teaching of history from the debate inside the academy and the professional literature. We have to insert the Palestinian version into the story of Israel's history, so that the pupils will know that there is another group that was affected by Zionism and the Independence [1948] war.[11]

But with the election of the unity government in 2001 and the appointment of the neo-Zionist minister Livnat, these projects were put into the bottom drawer, and if any actual impact was traced it was destroyed. It is difficult to know how long this new neo-Zionist frost will continue. It would be safe to conclude that an uneasy coexistence of two contradictory approaches to Zionist history will remain while the traditional Zionists persist in their attempts to construct, or reconstruct, an ideological centre within the political system and the intellectual milieu, a centre represented by the labour movement in the past. As long as the security threats continue at the same level as in 2001, they may succeed in doing so. In less tense times, when the public would be loth to give up any social or economic discussion for the sake of security, the argument would be rejoined forcefully. The debate is between those willing to challenge fundamentally the tenets of Zionism in the name of democracy and liberalism, and those who would remain fanatically committed to those tenets at the expense of democracy and liberalism. The Labour movement wanted to square the circle and find a way of reconciling these tenets with the wish to conclude peace and turn Israel into a democratic, liberal entity. As it turns out you, cannot have both – you must choose one or the other. This realization is at the heart of the post-Zionist position, but it is also the motivating force behind neo-Zionism.

So a current balance sheet of Israel reads as follows. In the political field, the centre is dominated by two traditional Zionist parties, closely connected to the professional elites in the country, who see no need to make decisions about Israel's future development apart from the realm of Israeli–Palestinian relations. The area to decide upon is the West Bank and the Gaza Strip, and the tendency is, notwithstanding the second *intifada*, to give up at least half of it for an autonomous Palestinian entity that could be called a state, if necessary. The rest of the area will be settled by Jews and annexed to Israel, with Jerusalem remaining a united city and the capital of Israel. The refugee problem remains unsolved or at least postponed for the distant future.

The political centre's vision of the past renders it indifferent to domestic socio-economic development. As the election of the unity government in 2001 showed, the centre is blind to the correlation between the primacy of ethnic identity on the one hand, and economic poverty and social deprivation on the other. Politicians and academics in the traditional Zionist camp refuse to accept the fragmented nature of Israeli society, nor are they seriously worried by it. Their main concern is to enhance Israel's nuclear capability and high-tech prosperity as the guarantors of Israel's future survival, whereas the post-Zionist reading of the past sees a just solution to the refugee problem as a far better guarantee of security.

The domestic scene is abandoned, and this is where neo-Zionism as an option thrives. Control of the educational system, as well as the displacement of government in the realm of social services – by providing, for instance, financial aid, child care and extended school days for deprived areas and sectors – enables the neo-Zionists steadily to increase their electorate. They adopted the traditional Zionist discourse of 'one people', excluding the Palestinian citizens of Israel, but gave it new meaning so that secular Jews, foreign workers (estimated in 2000 at about 300,000) and non-Jews (estimated to be another 300,000, who came from the ex-Soviet Union and Ethiopia) may also be excluded. There are, of course, internal power struggles between the various components of the neo-Zionist coalition, but the common ground is wide, and so far this coalition has not cracked; on the contrary, it is has gained momentum and force.

Conclusion: can post-Zionism survive?

So far, post-Zionism, as a vision of the future, can be found in geo-cultural centres such as Tel Aviv, western neighbourhoods in Jerusalem, and at times around the Kibbutzim, which are turning steadily into shopping malls and holiday villages. Its stress on secularism and universalism polarises the society to the extent that a kind of 'silent majority' is posed a choice between sinful Babylon or holy Jerusalem; liberal democratic Israel or racist Israel? An ethnocentric view of the past, a nationalist interpretation of the present and a theocratic vision of the future seemed to most Israelis in the 1999 elections to be the best option. Those traditional Zionists who offered a third option were exposed as utopians at best and deceivers at worst.

With the outbreak of the second *intifada*, the narrative that Barak's traditional Zionist government provided to explain the failure of the Camp David summit in August 2000 and the eruption of violence in the occupied territories was accepted chiefly by neo-Zionists. Their interpretation, through Ariel Sharon and his entourage, became accepted in Israel as a consensus. Not surprisingly this killed for a while the buds of post-Zionism that had emerged in the media and in academia. A retreat into narrow-mindedness in both these arenas was apparent. But it is hard to tell how long this will last. A year and half into the second *intifada* and some revival of the post-Zionist left could be traced in anti-occupation movements, soldiers' refusal to serve in the occupied territories and the crystallisation of post-Zionist political cells among faculty and students in the campuses. However, these phenomena are, at the time of writing, marginal and fragile and have not undermined the hegemony of neo-Zionist attitudes and perception of the Palestinians which feed the decision-making process of the Sharon government.

This chapter is not intended to predict exactly who may gain the upper hand, but to provide socio-political categorisation which transcends parties and temporary constellations, and better explain basic attitudes towards the Palestinians and other Arabs in official educational and media policies in the near future.

Israel after fifty years is a society at several crossroads. One is obvious, well reported and immediate. Its political leadership has to decide about how much of the occupied territories it has to give up in order to move the peace process on. But this is a minor junction; if and when Israel crosses it successfully, it is going to reach a more important and complex set of problems, the most important of which is the ethnic–civic dichotomy of Israel. The post-Zionist scholars, with the help of the media, have already hinted at the options. One is an ethnic state, reconstructing the past in a way that would allow no compromise with the Palestinians, no equal rights for Israeli Arabs (and possibly their transfer), and no social justice for Israel's deprived. This ethnicity is closely associated with an inflexible interpretation of Judaism – an ethnocracy, or rather a zealotocracy. As far as we can judge, it also entails a fixation with free-market economics and capitalism, which is already widespread in Israel (a country which has the greatest disparity level in the Western world between rich and poor).

The other option is a civic society accepting the historical verdict of the post-Zionist scholars and connecting the wrongs of the past to positive possibilities in the future. These include a comprehensive peace in Palestine, a genuine democracy without discrimination of any kind, and a more egalitarian society able to offer hope to deprived groups and wronged minorities. It can be a formula not just for Israel but also, in the more distant future, for a new political entity stretching between the River Jordan and Mediterranean – a secular, democratic Palestine.

The neo-Zionists have so far had the upper hand. They have the advantage of being dissociated in the public mind from the deeds of the past. Hence, unlike the traditional Zionists, they have no qualms about describing a most unpleasant chapter in the early history of the state of Israel: discrimination against Mizrahi and orthodox Jews. They also have no moral misgivings about describing massacres and expulsions of Palestinians, as they advocate them implicitly today. And yet, unlike the traditional Zionists, they are able to offer a crystal-clear future, not a confused mix of secular democracy and ethnic theocracy, but one built on an unquestionable preference for the latter. Unlike traditional Zionism, neo-Zionists do not try to square a circle by presenting a reality based on oxymorons such as 'enlightened occupation', 'pure arms', 'liberal ethnocracy' or 'ethnic democracy'.

Neo-Zionists are helped by a confused Israeli academia still struggling to keep the illusion of a society which is far from such a crossroads. Traditional Zionists, who still control the major obligatory introductory courses in the human sciences, describe Israel as a society able to be both ethnic and civic. For some, the confusion is over because they have opted for the post-Zionist way. They accept a past in which Zionists were wrongdoers and know how this could be rectified. But they are in danger of being alienated from their own society, as their message is contradicted daily by the educational and political systems.

Three factors can change this gloomy prospect. One is a clear, bold definition of objectives by all those who count themselves as belonging to the civic and democratic camp in Israel, a clarification that should reopen the question of what substitute there should be for the Jewish nation-state so that human and civic rights might be achieved for both Israelis and Palestinians. These objectives have not been clarified as yet, and there is more confusion than determination in the post-Zionist camp. This is why I use advisedly the term post-Zionism, with all the difficulties it carries, because for good or ill, this approach is not totally liberated from Zionist ideology, with all its limitations and problematic.

The second is a willingness on the Palestinian side to engage openly on a civic and democratic basis in a search for a joint solution. Post-Zionism is a Jewish phenomenon, a transitional phase out of Zionism. But into what? There is little point in defining the destination without finding out first what Palestinian aspirations are with regards to universalism, humanism and democracy. Can a civic and democratic state serve both people? Can the present political structure be transformed into one state? Are these goals best served within a federal structure so that they could satisfy or respect national identities, or is it necessary to have two states (if at all possible given the post-Oslo reality)?

The last factor is the position taken by the USA and its European allies. Without pressure, there is little hope for change within Israel. But this pressure does not have to be in the form of sanctions or boycotts; these can be counter-productive, and create a more entrenched neo-Zionist approach. The need is for a genuine Western position in support of civic and democratic societies. The West must leave behind the approach that identified humanist societies only when they were pro-Western in the cold war, or, in the context of the Middle East, when they had the potential to become 'democracies' according to modernization theories put forward by scholars such as Huntington (who, to judge by his latest work, does not include any of the present Arab states). The Amnesty International report of 1998, in its chapters on the US and Israel, should be an eye-opener for everyone who too easily identifies certain societies as exhibiting humanist and democratic behaviour, and sees others as intrinsically undemocratic.

In short, there is a need in the West to redefine agents of progress, stability and human welfare in the region. The distorted self-image of the 'only democracy in the Middle East' has to be challenged by Europeans and Americans. A reasonable way of doing this is one which takes into account the complex motivations of Zionism at its very beginning, and the intricate web of fears, ambitions and interests which sways the Jewish majority in Israel today. There may have been an ambition for humanist behaviour or a democratic construction, but other considerations and ideological perceptions took over and dominated the Zionist and Israeli project in Palestine. A continuous Western portrayal of Israel as a democratic island in an Arab wilderness has been one of the major obstacles to those in Israel working to create a humanist, civic society for the benefit of everyone living in Israel and Palestine.

NOTES

1. Ilan Pappé (1997) 'Post-Zionist Critique of Israel and the Palestinians', parts 1–3, in *Journal of Palestine Studies*, vol. 26, no. 2, Winter, pp. 29–41; vol. 26, no. 3, Spring, pp. 37–43; vol. 26, no. 4, Summer, pp. 60–69.
2. Uri Ram (1989) 'Post-Nationalist Pasts: The Case of Israel', in *Social Science History*, vol. 22, no. 4, Summer, pp. 513–45.
3. David Ohana (1997) *The Last Israelis*, Tel Aviv, Am Oved [Hebrew].
4. Ilan Pappé (1999) 'Were They Expelled? The History, Historiography and Relevance of the Refugee Problem', in Ghada Karmi and Eugene Cotran (eds), *The Palestinian Exodus, 1948–1988*, London, Ithaca, pp. 37–62.
5. Examples are Aharon Meged (1994) 'Israel Suicidal Urge', in *Ha'aretz*, 10 June [Hebrew]; Anita Shapira (1997) *New Jews, Old Jews* Tel Aviv, Am Oved; Shlomo Ahoronson (1997) 'Zionism and Post-Zionism: The Historical–Ideological Context', in Yechiam Weitz (ed.), *From Vision to Revision: A Hundred Years of Historiography of Zionism*, Jerusalem, Shazar Center, pp. 291–310.
6. Tom Segev (1989) *The Seventh Million*, New York; Idit Zertal, *From Catastrophe to Power* (the Hebrew title would be literally translated as *The Jews' Gold*), Tel Aviv; Haim Guri (1997) 'On Books and What is Within Them', in *Alpaim*, no. 14, pp. 9–30 [Hebrew].
7. Immanuel Sivan (1997) 'The Orientalist Debate', in *Alpaim*, no. 14, pp. 31–48 [Hebrew].
8. Efraim Karsh (1997) *Fabricating Israeli History*, London, Frank Cass.
9. Seffi Rachlevsky (1998) *Messiah's Donkey*, Tel Aviv, Yediot Aharonot.
10. Ministry of Education (1998) *Israel's Jubilee*, Jerusalem. The book was reported in Associated Press bulletins when it came out, and a review may be found at the Hebron Institute for Political and Religious Studies' website.
11. *Ha'aretz* (1998) 29 March [Hebrew].

4 ◎ Zionism, Anti-Zionism, Post-Zionism

Avishai Ehrlich

Post-Zionism is an ideological trend in Israel born out of the Israeli–Palestinian conflict at the end of the Cold War. During the Cold War local ethnic and national conflicts were exploited by the two superpowers in their contest for global hegemony. Many believed that in the 'new world order' these conflicts would become obsolete; some rushed to the conclusion that they would be defused. The Israeli–Arab conflict was seen by the post-Zionists as a case in point.

Integration into the world markets demanded economic liberalisation, and the post-Zionists believed that this would also encourage liberal democracy. They extrapolated from this that the imminent end to the conflict and the consequent integration of Israel (and the Middle East) into the globalisation process had created social forces in Israel that would struggle for peace and for the removal of the discriminatory nature of the Zionist state (ethnocracy, republicanism, ethnic democracy – the terminology varies.) If the process were to succeed, they held, it would change Israel into a secular democratic state. However, they were also aware of the alternative, neo-orthodox, nationalist tendencies that opposed this outcome.

This chapter takes issue with post-Zionism, and locates it within the wider context of the historical evolution of Zionism; it also contextualises post-Zionism, and the movements that opposed it, within the development of the Israeli–Arab conflict. I will present a different view of current world affairs and of the Israeli–Arab conflict, and will demonstrate the inherent contradictions among the post-Zionists.

In the first part, I will argue that Zionism gave rise not to one but to three main offshoots: statist (socialist), liberal and religious. Beside the common goal of establishing a Jewish state, each branch defined the Jewish situation and problems in modernity differently; each formed a different agenda and strove towards different goals, and each in turn had its heyday in the history of Israeli society.

Among Jews outside Israel, alternative conceptions of Jewish modernity developed which rejected Zionism's claim to be the sole representative of world Jewry in the twentieth century. These were a-Zionist or anti-Zionist in the sense that they did not regard a state for the Jews as a solution, or as the only solution, to Jewish survival in modern times. It will be argued that to each major Zionist ideological tendency there was a corresponding non- or anti-Zionist parallel: religious anti-Zionism, liberal anti-Zionism and socialist anti-Zionism.

Within Israel, however, only two forms of anti-Zionism emerged: religious and socialist. Liberal anti-Zionism did not develop as a political force during the mandate in Palestine, or in Israel. I will argue that post-Zionism in Israel has at present the makings of that missing liberal anti-Zionist element. Its development should be seen not so much as due to the late internal emergence of a wide social class whose interests are expressed by liberalism, but against the background of the demise of the socialist bloc and the decline of a social democratic agenda in the western states. Post-Zionism is the local Israeli ideological offshoot of capitalist globalisation in the Middle East. As such, it is the antithesis to Messianic religious Zionism (neo-Zionism as some post-Zionists call it) but is also in opposition to socialist anti-Zionism.

Zionism is evolutionary and contingent

Zionism did not begin as a fully comprehensive idea with all implications for the future clear cut. Political Zionism started as a simple utopian nationalist idea in the heads of several Jewish public figures in Europe in the last quarter of the nineteenth century, and from there it evolved. As Zionism became a political movement it inevitably engaged with political reality.

First, in trying to recruit members on the basis of its ideas, it faced competing movements among European Jewry. It had to elaborate and explicate its positions and define itself in contradistinction to other prevailing visions and movements related to contemporary Jewish life. The process of articulation and specification led to a distancing of the Zionists from other Jewish movements, as well as to splits in the Zionist movement and to the creation of different parties within it.

Second, as an international political movement, Zionism was too weak to achieve its goals by itself; it depended entirely upon international support. Zionism had, therefore, to adapt to the major power shifts, ideologies and changing regimes which occurred during the twentieth century. This need to adapt was directed not only by external necessity, but also from within by the major ideologies of the twentieth century – socialism, communism, liberalism, fascism, etc. – which strongly influenced the Jews of Europe. The world-views that prevailed among them influenced their attraction to Zionism and shaped the vision of the aspiring new Jewish society over which they struggled in the Zionist movement, thus giving rise to different parties and blocs.

Third, as a national movement Zionism was unusual. It aimed at creating an independent state, not in the space already inhabited by its national constituents, but rather by shifting those it claimed as its 'nationals' from Europe (and later on also from other parts of the world) and settling them far away in the Middle East, which was already inhabited by Arabs. This oddity among nationalist movements is at the core of the debate about whether Zionism is a 'return' of the Jews or a 'Jewish colonisation'. The reality of the process of nationalist (exclusivist) settlement (colonisation) against a growing Arab national movement opposed to and struggling against it was the major formative factor in the Zionist project in Palestine. This dimension, the protracted Israeli–Arab conflict and its ramifications, became a major constitutive factor of Israeli society, and of its economics, politics and culture.

As a result of all these developments, Zionism had, and still has, to articulate and re-articulate itself, to constitute and reconstitute itself as it faces opponents and historical junctions when crucial decisions have to be taken.

I would like to avoid defining Zionism at the outset and, following Nietzsche, argue that you can define things only *ex post-facto*, at their end, when the transformations have come to a halt. I think that Zionism is as yet an unfinished project which is continually changing. We can trace its trajectory to date; we can divide the Zionist process into stages; but I am reluctant to offer a definitive definition as yet. Some have argued that Zionism focused upon the creation of a Jewish state and that it was finished when the state was created over fifty years ago. During the last decade, some have been claiming that Zionism is finished and that we live in 'post-Zionist' times. These commentators have a fixed definition (explicit or implicit) of what Zionism is, or ought to be; and as it turns on a different trajectory they declare the phenomenon as 'post'.

I would like to demonstrate Zionism as still evolving, shaping and reshaping itself as a result of major decisions it has had to make. To this end, I will attempt to map the realm within which these debates take place.

Responses to modernity: Judaism–religion and/or nationalism?

Zionism was only one of several responses by European Jews to the Enlightenment. By separating church from state, the French Revolution launched a new principle of belonging. Identity, which was previously tied to membership in a universal, transnational, religious community was now transformed into a secular belonging to the national state. Through the invention of the nation, schisms between believers of different denominations and religions could be transcended or relegated to the private sphere. Unity through the church could be replaced with unity through the nation symbolised by the state.

The idea of membership in the national state (citizenship) forming the basis of solidarity and loyalty required, as in religion, that the individual had only one nationality. By the same logic that one cannot adhere to two religions simultaneously, one also cannot embrace two nationalities: nations were exclusive entities. Neither could this logic entertain the non-Christian idea that religion and nation are inseparable.[1]

Emancipation of the Jews and the granting of equal legal status in the state, first in France and later in other European nations, should be seen in the light of the same logic. Before granting them citizenship, Napoleon asked French Jewish deputies whether the Jews were a nation or a religion, for if they considered themselves a nation they could not, at the same time, be French. After long deliberation, the Jewish deputies answered that they considered Judaism a religion, whereupon the Jews of France were granted citizenship – 'French of the Mosaic religion'. The process of emancipation spread across Europe. Among themselves, however, the deputies noted that the question of either/or was essentially a Christian question.

This episode demonstrates that the first response of West European Jews to modern nationalism was to adopt the dichotomy of nation or religion and become nationals of their country of domicile; the religion of citizens in many Western nation states had become an individual, private and voluntary matter. The Enlightenment and emancipation enabled many Jews to enter professions hitherto closed to them, to settle outside the ghettos and to associate more freely with non-Jews.

Changes with regard to religion among Jews

These developments weakened the social control of the community and its religious leaders and created the secular Jew, someone of Jewish descent who decides for himself which religious Jewish laws (*halacha*) and customs he/she wants to keep. Religious Jews accept life as dictated by *halacha* because they accept the supreme authority of the Creator who determined its laws. Secular Jews see themselves as the authors of their lifestyles (free, in this sense). It is noteworthy that, according to *halacha,* a person is Jewish if s/he was born to a Jewish mother. Prior to modernity Jews adhered to a traditional way of life, as did other religious communities, and the only way to enter non-Jewish society was through conversion. A secular Jew – the 'non-Jewish Jew' in Isaac Deutscher's words – is someone born Jewish who did not convert but who also does not live by religious law and adopts an eclectic lifestyle. Secular Jews differ from traditional and religious Jews not only in the number of *mitzvot* they keep, but also in whether they perceive of their own observance as religion or as tradition and/or culture. The secular Jew is the direct product of the Enlightenment and emancipation.

Secularisation among Jews brought forth a reactive response from religious Jews. Secularisation without conversion creates the danger of 'pollution' – the blurring of demarcations between Jew and Gentile (assimilation). The reaction was a tightening of the community, stricter observance of *halacha* and stern adherence to external symbols and lifestyle. On an intellectual level it also led to greater emphasis on religious higher learning and the deepening of Jewish religious philosophy to counter the philosophy and morality of modernity. These ultra-orthodox are also known as *haredim* (fearful of the word of God) or *kanai'm* (zealots).

Another development, which started in the nineteenth century among German, French and Dutch Jews and spread to other parts of Western Europe and the USA, was Reform Judaism: the autonomous adaptation of Jewish religion to the modern bourgeois lifestyle (mostly influenced by Protestant culture). This was achieved by the abolition of the more obscure rituals, by changing the language of prayer from Hebrew to the vernacular, by incorporating instrumental and vocal music into prayer services, seating men and women together in the synagogue, and adopting modern clothing and education. Reform Judaism flourishes mainly in liberal regimes and among the highly educated middle classes who are well integrated in their societies. An intermediate trend between ultra-Orthodox and Reform in Germany was neo-Orthodoxy, which attempted a less radical synchronisation between Jewish orthodoxy and commitment to modernity.[2]

These four reactions to modernity characterised those Jews who lived through the Enlightenment in Western and Central Europe. In Eastern Europe the majority of Jews still lived a traditional (*masorti*) Jewish way of life until the end of the twentieth century. Traditional Judaism was less affected by modernity and by Jewish reactions to it. The indigent Jewish masses in Eastern Europe still lived mostly in the *stetl* (rural towns), as they were prevented by law from leaving the hinterlands for the developing urban centres.

Thus the radical secularists sought assimilation within the new nation-state or migration; the ultra-Orthodox preferred to maintain their separation and old ways of life within the nation-state of their domicile or to emigrate to America in search of tolerance. The Reform and neo-Orthodox took the intermediate attitude of making some changes whilst also trying to maintain a separate identity, relying too on the tolerance and pluralism of the modern liberal state. None of these groups saw themselves simply as Jewish nationalists, and they constituted the main articulation of modern identity among Western Jews.

Three Jewish responses to nationalism

Assimilation The first response to the granting of citizenship in the state was acceptance by the non-Jewish majority of Judaism as a 'religion only', and the adoption by Jews of the nationality of their country of domicile. Jews participated in national and cultural life, the army and national political parties. The fact of citizenship, the right to vote and democratisation mobilised them to take part in the struggle between competing ideologies in their nations. The ideological trends influential at the time also had their Jewish supporters.

Cultural nationalism A second reaction, mainly in Eastern Europe, where modernisation and democratisation were blocked by autocratic regimes, was the creation of the view that a nation is a community distinguished by its language and the culture created by that language. This trend was expressed in Eastern Europe chiefly by the Bund party which saw the Jews, as well as other national groups under the yoke of the Tsarist Russian Empire, as a nation by reason of their Yiddish language and culture. Like Christianity and Islam, Judaism was perceived as a transnational religion; believers in these religions were not of one nationality and, in the case of the Jews, there were several Jewish languages and thus potentially several Jewish nations.

The aim of the cultural nationalists was to preserve, cultivate and reproduce the nation through its culture. For this purpose the Bund stood against the policy of Russification promulgated by the Tsarist government, and fought alongside other liberal and socialist parties for the democratisation of the Empire and the right to self-determination of the nationalities within the Russian Empire. On the other hand, the Bund did not advocate centralisation of all Yiddish speakers in one territory to constitute a majority; nor did it seek a separate Jewish state. The Bund strove for cultural autonomy for the nationalities in a federal, democratic, large state; Yiddish speakers and other nationalities would be able to control their cultural reproduction through control of their own education system and other cultural institutions. Cultural nationalism was intended to combat acculturation and assimilation of smaller ethnic and national groups within the ruling state culture. In that respect it was a precursor of the current debate on multiculturalism. The Bund had wide support among the Jewish workers and lumpenproletariat in Eastern Europe between the late nineteenth century and the Second World War. Its followers were still steeped in tradition (in the *stetl*) but did not see themselves as religious; many were even atheists or agnostics. They were nostalgic about the culture they were preserving, as it was changing before their very eyes in the reality of industrialisation and mass emigration of Jews to America. The Bund as a mass movement was a major rival to Zionism.[3]

Zionism   Zionism was a third form of nationalism among the Jews in modernity. Theodor Herzl called the first World Zionist Congress in Basel, Switzerland, in 1897. This event is regarded as the birth of 'Political Zionism' and Herzl is officially recognized as its founder. Herzl believed that anti-Semitism is inherent and cannot be abolished by internal social, political change, and that it will prevail as long as Jews live as a minority in various countries. Hence his solution to anti-Semitism was for Jews to leave their countries of domicile and gather in one (any possible) place where they could form a majority and set up their own state. This idea of a 'state of the Jews' (not to be confused with a 'Jewish state') was open-ended. Herzl envisaged the state as a liberal democracy with equal rights for non-Jews and a separation of state and religion. Economically he stood for 'capitalism with a human face'.[4]

There are two important axiomatic features of Herzlian 'political

Zionism'. Firstly, that its 'imagined community' comprised *all* the Jews of the world (in contrast with the Bund view) and that Jewish unity was based not on religion but on the common suffering (anti-Semitism) of Jews as a minority in the places where they resided. The second feature of Herzlian Zionism was its secular nationalism: in the imagined 'state of the Jews', not only could state and religion be separated, but there would also be equal citizenship for people of different religions.

Herzl died in 1904, and by the time of his death the main features of Zionism were still embryonic, and had not yet been articulated. As they became specified, rifts and schisms occurred, with certain elements leaving the movement while others formed various parties within it, each of which struggled for leadership.

Main ideological decisions which shaped Zionism

Zion and religion

The first constitutive decision that shaped the future of Zionism was taken at the so-called 'Uganda Congress' in 1903, determining that the territory in which the Jews should strive to become a majority and establish a state should be the Jewish biblical Holy Land, Zion, Eretz-Israel (the land of Israel) or Palestine.[5] By fixing this territory as target, it was inevitable that Jewish religious hopes, messianic yearnings and mystical eschatological expectations would merge with the secular national idea. While it certainly gave the Zionist idea a tremendous boost among the poverty-stricken traditional Jews of Eastern Europe and helped it to become a mass movement, it was also the turning point from when the 'state of the Jews' became the 'Jewish state'. The myth of the return of the Jews to their promised land, the end of dispersion (*galut*), and the ingathering of exiles are all central themes of Jewish Messianic redemption myths. For the secularists the 'land of Israel' provided an identification with the biblical Jewish conquest of the land of Canaan and the period of statehood and kings (the 'first commonwealth'). For the religious it raised the need to return to holiness, the full return being not just a physical return to a place but a spiritual return to a full religious way of life, as many religious rules depended on place. For the religious it was unimaginable that state be separated from religion, as such a conception is inconceivable in *halacha;* a state of Jews must be also a Jewish state. The decision in 1903 was thus a pragmatic compromise between different aspirants to the goal of Zionism. It certainly helped to bring many traditional Eastern Europeans closer to

Zionism. Vital[6] claimed that Zionism was a revolution against the religious and traditional way of life, but this was not so. Shortly after its establishment, political Zionism started to temper its secularist ideology and accepted religious nationalism into its baggage.

Which way to build Zion? Liberalism vs. Collectivism

The second division which developed within Zionism had to do with alternative models of the society and economy of the envisioned state of the Jews. The two alternatives, following the developments of the twentieth century, were socialism and capitalism. The period from the turn of the nineteenth century saw a tremendous upsurge in socialist movements of different denominations in Europe. Socialists believed that the cure for all the illnesses of modernity lay in changing society from within. Rationalism, universalism, positivism and science, equality – legal and economic – would banish religion, superstition and prejudice; solidarity among working people would overcome nationalism, reaction and racism. Many Jews were attracted to socialism, especially in less developed states in Central and Eastern Europe.

In the early years of Zionist settlement in Palestine it became clear that Palestine was not an attractive destination for immigration. While millions of Jews moved to America, a mere trickle came to Palestine. Moreover, Palestine did not have natural resources to attract major private investors, and Jewish philanthropy would not suffice to maintain the few who came. Even worse, Palestine was not in the 'wilderness'; it would have to be colonised by force, and the Zionists did not have an allied state to back their venture. How then to colonise Palestine? Under these difficult circumstances even the liberal leaders of Zionism – and Herzl was a liberal in a nineteenth century sense – accepted economic practices which ran contrary to laissez-faire (an open economy which allows market forces to determine the flow of goods, labour and capital). With a native Arab population and economy, the Jewish settlers had to use exclusion and protectionism to enable the mostly poor immigrants to find work. In addition, nation-building required the appropriation of lands which, since they could not be seized by force, had to be purchased. The purchased land had to be nationalised in order to prevent its resale to native Arabs. The settlers had to be protected against competition from local native produce.

All these factors required a strong ideological collectivist solidarity and commitment rather than a utilitarian individualist ethos. Settlement projects had to be planned and scarce capital resources allocated according not to profitability but to priority in the strategic national plan. This demanded the command of politics and a planned economy, not laissez-faire capitalism.

A greater Israel, or smaller but more Jewish?

The third cardinal decision which defined Zionism related to the territorial borders of the Jewish state, and the ensuing Jewish–Palestinian conflict. The initial aspirations of Zionism included what is today south Lebanon, the Golan and most of Trans-Jordan. However, the decision did not lie in the hands of the Zionists but was concluded in the League of Nations; the borders were drawn by Britain and France. Zionist aspirations were thus curtailed to the area of the British Mandate in Palestine. In 1937, following the Arab Revolt, the Peel Commission first proposed the idea of partition. This was the first time the Zionist leadership was forced to take a stand on an issue which, until today, has been at the centre of the political divide in Zionism, both inside Israel and beyond. Ben-Gurion, leader of the largest party in the Jewish Yishuv and of the World Zionist Organisation, accepted the idea then, and again in 1947 when it was raised by the Anglo-American Committee and UNESCOP prior to the UN resolution of November that year.[7] The partition of Mandatory Palestine became fact as a result of the 1948 war, and lasted until 1967.

The issue of the borders of the Jewish state rose again in the wake of the June 1967 war. Israel gained control of all of the area of the former Mandate, but took heed of UN resolution 242 and did not annex it. Beyond the UN resolution was a more difficult dilemma: to annex would have meant absorbing a large Palestinian population and thus raising the ratio of Arabs to Jews, without granting the former citizenship. The stand adopted by that and all successive Israeli governments was to confiscate Palestinian land, settle it with Jews and displace the Palestinians. Although this was a much slower way to expand, we can see that the territorial borders were secondary to the principle of keeping the ratio of Palestinians down.

Religious anti-Zionism in Palestine and abroad

Ultra-Orthodoxy split from the Zionist movement and, in 1912, formed a worldwide rival, anti-Zionist organisation – Agudat Israel. The ultra-Orthodox (*haredim*) viewed Zionism from the early period (i) as an aggressive form of secularisation and cultural assimilation; (ii) as a rebellion against God, trying to force the redemption of the Jews by 'this-worldly' activism rather than patiently awaiting the Messiah's coming as promised by

God. For these Zionist transgressions, God brought the holocaust upon the Jews – so claimed the ultra-Orthodox anti-Zionists! (iii) The colonising activity of the Zionists brought the hostility of the Arabs, thus creating anti-Semitism and endangering the lives of Jews.

Religious Zionism

A large number of religious Jews remained in the Zionist movement, regarding it as their duty to battle against secular tendencies from within.[8] They formed the national religious wing – Mizrahi – within the World Zionist Organisation. Religious Zionism in Palestine did not reject the importance of building a Jewish society, and thus joined with the secular Zionists to encourage immigration, settlement on the land and institution building. While the ultra-religious separated themselves from secular Jewish society in Palestine, religious Zionists maintained a separate education system but otherwise participated alongside the secular in other societal institutions. They did, however, interpret the goals of Zionism from a religious point of view: state formation was not a goal in itself, only a means to the liberation of the land and to the spiritual return of all Jews to the religious fold. Within religious Zionism there was a strong Messianic element, influenced by Palestine's Chief Rabbi Cook, which viewed the return of Jews to the ancestral homeland as the beginning of redemption and as a sign of the coming of the Jewish Messiah. Religious Zionists recognised the Israeli state when it was formed, and accorded it religious significance in a special prayer. They participate in the army, in the government, in higher education and are economically active in the professions.

Socialism vs. Zionism

Socialists looked upon Zionism as a particularist movement which distracted sections of the population from the main purpose – the struggle to bring about radical change in their own societies by calling upon its members to leave their countries of domicile. Zionism was pessimistic about the likelihood of equality for Jews wherever they were in the minority; it did not advocate class solidarity as an answer to the national problems of the Jews, and called instead for national solidarity among Jews of different classes. From the inception of the movement, Zionist leaders connived with reactionary regimes to get support for Jewish immigration and settlement. For these reasons and others, most though not all socialists saw Zionism as a rival articulation of identity, and a bourgeois ideology. The majority of Jews who were members of socialist movements tended to reject Zionism; many were anti-Zionists.

Socialist Zionism

Despite these rejections, from the beginning of the Zionist movement there developed socialist brands of Zionism. Zionist socialists agreed with the Zionist axiom that there could be no solution to anti-Semitism for Jews in their home countries, but held that Jewish society in Palestine should be based on socialist principles. This view was attractive to many recruits to Zionism as it obviated the need to choose between Zionism or socialism, and permitted them to combine both in the new homeland. Moreover, a brand of socialist religious Zionism developed within the Mizrahi movement, which drew its socialist principles not from secular (Marxist) sources, but from Jewish scriptures, Jewish religious movements (the Essenes), and Jewish communitarian practices of charity and self-help.

After the First World War, the debate in the Zionist movement grew more heated. On one side were those who believed that Jewish society would be built by middle-class Jews immigrating with their property and know-how. On the other was the growing labour movement in Palestine, which claimed that the only way to develop Jewish Palestine under the prevailing harsh conditions and growing Arab opposition was by adopting the collectivist pioneering model. This model entailed mobilisation of funds and people from the worldwide Zionist movement, the nationalisation and centralisation of land purchases, strategic planned colonisation, and the creation of an autarkic, closed economy based on Jewish labour and separatist national institutions. All this required the development under a centralised leadership of a comprehensive welfare society, which would be able to absorb the poor immigrants and direct them towards national, rather than individual, goals. From the 1930s, Labour Zionism gained sway among Jews in Palestine, and a few years later in the world Zionist movement – though not among all the Jews in the world.

Socialist anti-Zionism in Palestine and Israel

Socialist anti-Zionism developed in Palestine as a reaction to the anti-Arab colonising policies of labour Zionism, and Jewish anti-Zionists formed the Palestine Communist Party in 1919.[9] Another wave of disappointment emerged among socialist Zionists in the early 1920s: their attempt to form an independent socialist organisation was crushed by the labour organisation.[10] Betrayed and banned, many returned to the Soviet Union while others joined the Communist Party, which became a small Jewish–Arab organisation with a Stalinist orientation struggling against Zionism and the British for national liberation of the Middle East. Socialist anti-Zionism was a direct result of the growing Jewish-Arab conflict, and stemmed from a universalist internationalist worldview rather than from a particularist nationalist one. Until shortly before the creation of the state of Israel (1948) it did not recognise the Jews in Palestine as a national group.

Matzpen was founded in the mid-1960s as a socialist anti-Zionist group; it had split from the Communist Party in disagreement with prevailing Soviet socialism and the lack of democracy in the communist regimes. Its members regarded Zionism as a form of colonialism and advocated the de-Zionisation of Israel and the formation of a unitary secular democratic state for Israelis and Palestinians within a socialist Middle East.[11]

Liberalism and Zionism

We have shown that within Zionism, and from its inception, parties emerged which attempted a synthesis between Zionism and other ideologies. After Herzl's death, the liberals, who were opposed to a synthesis of Zionism with religion, socialism or anything else, called themselves 'general Zionists'. During the1920s and until the mid-1930s, the leadership of the World Zionist Organisation was in the hands of the general Zionists. Its president, Chaim Weizmann, supported the labour movement in creating welfare collectivism, separatist institutions and a closed Jewish economy based on Jewish labour and protectionist policies; in this he incurred the opposition of liberal Jewish American leaders headed by Brandeis.[12]

There was another type of so-called liberal opposition to labour Zionism, which grew fast from the mid-1920s and was headed by Jabotinsky. However, his critique was directed mainly against the monopoly of power created by the labour movement and its organisation, and Weizmann's support of labour, not against the nationalist closure policies.

Laissez-faire liberalism, as it is understood today, was marginal in the Zionist movement. Though there was a Jewish bourgeoisie in the pre-state period,[13] it was politically weak and collaborated with labour under its leadership. Israeli economic policies were, until the late 1960s, not market-oriented but statist; the economy was in the service of building the Jewish national state and society. In the 1960s and 1970s, a corporatist model of economy developed; only from the mid-1980s has Israel opened itself up to liberalisation.

Liberal anti-Zionism abroad and in Palestine

Liberal anti-Zionism abroad[14] objects to the Jewish state because it sees Judaism as a universalist and anti-nationalist religion. Zionism sees Jews in national terms first, premised on the pessimistic disbelief in the possibility of Jewish emancipation and integration among non-Jews. In this respect, and in the policy of concentrating Jews in Palestine, Zionism concurs with extreme right-wing racist ideologies, which would separate Jews from Gentiles. Zionism is also anti-democratic, as it cannot conceive of a real equal status for non-Jews in a Jewish state.

Another type of liberal anti-Zionism emerged among some young intellectuals around Jabotinsky just before the First World War – right-wing nationalist secular liberalism. Its prophets were A. Horon and Y. Ratosh.[15] They raised the radical idea of severing the link between nationalism and the Jewish religion, and creating a new form of nativism: 'the Hebrew nation', linked to the land of Canaan. Judaism, they claimed, was created in the diaspora and is diasporic in essence, a religious cultural phenomenon.

The Jewish diaspora is not unique; other diasporas – the Hellenic and Persian – survived many centuries in antiquity, as did ethnic German in contemporary Europe. Judaism as a cultural religious entity does not need a state. Nationalism is first and foremost territorial and political. Like immigrants to the US who wish to shed their past and belong to the new nation, Hebrews make their own choice to define themselves as such. To Horon and Ratosh, being an Israeli or being a Hebrew is not the same; the state of Israel is not the realisation of their idea, which is linked to the diaspora and to Judaism. Another, milder, version of this Hebrew idea was advocated by Hillel Cook, also a close associate of Jabotinsky in the US. In 1947 Cook was against the division of Palestine and laid claim to the territories which are now Jordan. After 1967, Horon advocated the annexation of all the occupied territories; and in 1974 Cook advocated the establishment of a Palestinian state and separation of state and religion in Israel. He spoke about the Israeli nation founded by Zionism, which achieved its goal with its foundation. Israel must represent only those who live in it and not all the Jews. Cook and Jabotinsky's son, Ari, were elected to the first Israeli parliament on a strong anti-religious platform, which demanded the separation of state and religion.

Although the Canaanite idea was born on the right, it also found its way to the non-Zionist left, which aspires to remake Israel as a state for all its citizens – Jewish and Arab equally – rather than a state for Jews around the world.

Most Israelis identify with Zionism

It has been demonstrated that alongside each branch of Zionism, a branch of anti-Zionism also developed, namely religious, socialist and liberal anti-Zionism. Within Israel, liberal anti-Zionism was almost non-existent until the last decade.

We have tried to show that anti-Zionism does not relate primarily to the question of the territorial boundaries of the state, but rather to the Jewish nature of Israel. The original Canaanites stood for Greater Israel; Canaanism was territorial and political, and emphasised the state. Most socialist anti-Zionists advocate a unitary, secular, democratic state of Palestinians and Hebrews (as distinct from the Zionist belief that all Jews have an automatic right to citizenship); socialists emphasise the social aspect rather than the state-political. Socialist anti-Zionists are not concerned with where Jews or Arabs settle, provided that the same social and economic rules apply equally to all. Religious anti-Zionism relates to the religious–cultural aspect; for religious reasons it is anti-statist.[16] Religious anti-Zionism objects to Zionism because it created a Jewish society not based on Jewish religious law (*halacha*) and is thus anathema. Religious anti-Zionists envisage themselves living in the Holy Land even if it comes under Arab rule.

The bitter debates which, since Madrid and Oslo, divide left and right in Israel over the peace process are not directly related to Zionism versus anti-Zionism. The vast majority of Israelis are firmly for a Jewish state and identify with one form of Zionism or another. To argue that those who criticise various aspects of Zionist history or current policies are beyond Zionism is an unfounded exaggeration.

Post-Zionism

From the above discussion we move to post-Zionism: what it is? Where should it be placed and how should it be interpreted?

Post-Zionism is a vague term, more of a catchphrase. Gotwin[17] argues that post-Zionism fits with no definition of a coherent school of thought. Laurence Silberstein, whose important book introduces the post-Zionist debates to the non-Israeli English-speaking world, agrees that '[a]ll efforts to establish a fixed definition of an 'ism' such as postzionism are futile. As a dynamic process, postzionism's meaning undergoes constant change depending upon who is using it, where, and to what end'.[18] Nonetheless, he attempts to give an approximation:

> In a general sense, postzionism is a term applied to a current set of critical positions that problematise zionist discourse, and the historical narratives and social and cultural representations that it produced. Like the term zionism, postzionism encompasses a veriety of positions. The growing use of the term postzionism is indicative of an increasing sense among many Israelis that the maps of meaning provided by zionism are simply no longer adequate. To critics and detractors, postzionism presents a challenge to the basic principles and values of zionism. To its advocates, the postzionist critique is a necessary prerequisite to Israel's emergence as a fully democratic society.[19]

I would say that this description is too general; post-Zionism is full of contradictions. Silberstein's purpose was to map the forerunners of the post-Zionist debates and give a panoramic description of the scope of the arguments. My goals are more limited.

First, in contrast to the post-Zionists, my argument is that the Israeli-Arab conflict is not about to end. I wish to locate the post-Zionist trend in the fourth stage of the conflict, that of American global hegemony.

Second, I take issue with an underlying assumption in some post-Zionist writings that the growth of a 'willingness for peace' in Israel is determined from within, from the economic interests of those who benefit from the opening-up of Israel to the world. I would argue instead that the peace process was forced on Israel from outside. Indeed, Israel's burgeoning export industries needed access to world markets (not to Arab markets) and thus Israel had to break the isolation imposed on it by the Soviet and Arab secondary boycott. This aim was achieved primarily by the break-up of the Soviet bloc and the beginning of American global hegemony.

Third, following their determinist view about the conclusion of the Israel–Arab conflict, the post-Zionists paint the wrong picture of the issues which face Israeli society in the foreseeable future. In particular, I shall argue that, following several formal peace treaties, Israel will not become more secular and democratic, but will instead strengthen the ethos of 'ethnic democracy',[20] which relies more on Jewish tradition, 'soft Judaism' and Jewish religious symbols.

Fourth, the optimism of many post-Zionists about the inevitability of the conclusion of the conflict stems from a determinist, starry-eyed view of globalisation. The diminishing role of the state, the decline of nationalism, a world of peace through commerce – all this creates a contradiction between socialist post-Zionists and liberal post-Zionists. For socialist post-Zionists an egalitarian society is the goal. Pax Americana does not improve equality.

Locating post-Zionist discourse in the present stage of the Israeli-Arab conflict

The post-Zionist trend in Israel arose out of the atmosphere created in the late 1980s and 1990s. Like any cultural trend, it draws on the ideological capital available to it from previous periods. Each trend can be shown to have a 'history of ideas', but it is rooted in the events and the mood of its time. This is particularly true if the trend achieves some public resonance. It is my conviction that the post-Zionist trend must be understood against the background of the peace process. To understand this, I will sketch briefly the stages through which the Israeli–Arab conflict evolved.

The intra-state, inter-communal stage (1920–48)

The Israeli–Arab conflict has evolved in several stages or centrifugal circles.[21] In the first stage the conflict emerged between Jewish settlers and their newly founded, nascent society and the native Arabs in Palestine under the British Mandate. The conflict was expressed mainly through the Jews' creation of a separate, exclusive political community. The conflict was confined by the rule of the British government, which maintained law and order and prevented a decisive war occurring. The limits of power, which stemmed from a lack of sovereignty on either side, meant that Jews had to purchase land rather than take it by force, and that Arabs could not wage war against the Jews nor legislate against their immigration and settlement. British policy incurred the antagonism first of the Arabs in Palestine, as it favoured the Jews, and then of the Jews when, before the Second World War, the British tried to balance their policy and restrict Jewish state-building – a policy determined by changing international circumstances and growing Arab nationalism. This stage ended when the British decided to return their mandate to the UN and leave Palestine. Following the UN decision to partition Palestine, growing hostilities between irregular forces of Jews and Arabs resulted in the defeat of the Palestinians and the declaration of a Jewish state. The resolution was not accepted by the Arab states, which declared war on Israel – the first Israeli–Arab war, which ended with Israel holding 80 per cent of Palestine and most of the Palestinians becoming refugees, either remaining in Israel or fleeing from it.[22] The Palestinian state never came into being; its territory was annexed by Israel and Jordan.

Inter-state stage (1948–69)

During this period the conflict was mainly between Israel and surrounding Arab states, and assumed new forms. As well as full-scale wars in 1948, 1956 and 1967, there were border skirmishes and infiltration by state armies and irregulars, and attendant growing expenditure on militarisation. Economic war came about through direct boycott by Arab countries; a secondary economic boycott was imposed by appeal or pressure on non-Arab countries to ban all ties with Israel.[23] The conflict also took the form of ideological war – a concerted effort to isolate, debunk and ostracise one's opponent in international organisations and the world media.

During most of this period, the Palestinians played a secondary role, and their cause was claimed by different Arab states, who used the Palestinian issue in inter-Arab politics. In Israel, Palestinian citizens were held under military government, much of their land and property were appropriated and their status was as second-class citizens. Arab states confiscated much Jewish property and most Jews in the Arab countries, feeling insecure, emigrated.

In the first part of this period the Middle East was still influenced by the declining colonial powers, Britain and France. After 1956, the pro-colonial regimes were replaced by revolutionary nationalist governments in several Arab countries, and the superpowers – the Soviet Union and the USA – began the process of penetration and competition in the region.

Superpower stage (1969–88)

The beginning of the superpower stage is marked by the war of attrition between Israel and the Arab states following the June 1967 war. The superpowers supplied their clients with arms and new technologies, thus subsuming this conflict – as happened elsewhere – into the Cold War and their own global contest. Consequently, the Israeli–Arab conflict became a war by proxy between the superpowers, who fought indirectly via their clients (for example, in 1973). The military build-up at this stage reached proportions far beyond the economic and scientific capabilities of the warring sides. As a result, the opponents become economically and militarily dependent on their patrons and received from them a spiralling level of foreign military and economic aid. After 1967, diplomatic and economic ties between Israel and the Soviet bloc were severed; this increased Israel's isolation and denied it access to significant world markets.

The Israeli–Arab conflict also became central in the ideological war between the superpowers. Zionism was equated with racism in a UN resolution backed by the Soviet bloc and Arab and Islamic states. On the other hand, the US demanded the right of Soviet Jews to emigrate, and made it a condition for economic transactions with the USSR.[24] The Palestinians were brought to the forefront of the conflict when, with Soviet and Egyptian support, they formed the PLO in 1969.

At this point, the economic aspect of the conflict affected the global economy. The use of oil and petrodollar power by OPEC countries in solidarity with the Arabs following the 1973 war caused turmoil and a slow-down in Western economies. The US stepped in to fight the secondary boycott against Israel and break OPEC's power. This stage drew to its end when Anwar Sadat decided to break Egypt's alliance with the Soviet Union – a development brought about through disappointment with the Soviets' inability to force an Israeli withdrawal from Egyptian soil and supply Egypt with superior military technology. The new affiliation between Egypt and the US heralded a new era in the Middle East: Pax Americana. The peace treaty between Egypt and Israel was triangular: between the US and Egypt, and between Egypt and Israel. Egypt received annual economic and military aid and, in return, it had to recognise Israel and sign a formal peace treaty. Israel had to return all occupied Egyptian territory, as stipulated by UN resolution 242 and, in return, Israel received a large aid package as compensation for redeployment. Since then until the present day, both sides also receive annual economic and military aid. This pattern of triangular peace agreements became the model for future US-brokered accords with Israel.

American global hegemony (1988–)

Towards the end of the 1980s, it became clear that the ailing Soviet bloc was no longer able to aid and arm its Middle Eastern clients. The beginning of this stage is best marked by the Stockholm conference in 1988, where Arafat announced his willingness to recognise Israel, cease the armed struggle and enter negotiations. This was a precondition set by the US and the Europeans to end Arafat's isolation in Tunis and afford him recognition as the leader of the restive Palestinians in the impending Middle East peace talks.

The evolution of the Israeli–Arab conflict can be represented graphically by three concentric circles, each symbolising one of the stages described above. The inter-communal stage between Palestinians and Jews is the inner circle, the core of the conflict; the inter-state stage is the intermediate circle, and the superpower stage forms the outer circle. With the demise of the Soviet Union, the outer circle ceased to exist and the Cold War – cold only in Europe and America – finally ended. Many national conflicts which had been subsumed into this rivalry served no purpose in the new world architecture; the continuation of some became dangerously disruptive to the 'new world order' and had to be defused; others which presented less of a threat to the outside world were left to linger on. The Israeli–Arab conflict fell into the first category, as it is played out in an area which fulfils a major role in the world economy and sits close to the soft belly of Europe.

The defusion of Middle East conflicts was not easy: more rogue states had been identified by the US in this region than anywhere else (Iraq, Iran, Libya, Sudan, Syria), and the 'dual containment' policy against Iraq and Iran was not particularly successful. The Islamic belt stretching from Pakistan via Afghanistan and the Muslim ex-Soviet republics to the former Yugoslavia threatened globalisation with a 'clash of civilizations'. It was in this arena that the US chose to demonstrate its new role as 'Globocop', in the 1990 Desert Storm against its former ally Saddam Hussein.[25] The invasion of Kuwait and the Arab coalition against Iraq also contributed to the break-up of Arab solidarity and, following the war, Arab nationalism was at its nadir. It is against this background that the Madrid and Oslo initiatives should be seen.

An interlude: the myth of the end of the conflict – or conflict management?

It is beyond the scope of this chapter to deal in any depth with the general question of how conflicts end.[26] Suffice it to say that protracted conflicts (Ireland, Cyprus, Yugoslavia) can lie dormant for generations after what looks like a resolution, and then flare up when conditions change. The Israeli–Arab conflict, in my view, follows this pattern.

It is my contention that the post-Zionists conflate what are two separate situations: formal peace and end of conflict. In their eagerness to see the conflict end they become believers of the crude ideological generalisation that capitalist globalisation heralds the end of zero-sum thinking and the universal end of conflicts. For example, Shafir and Peled write:

> The Israel–Arab conflict had remained at an impasse so long as it was viewed solely in security terms, as an ethnic or national confrontation. The conflict

became 'solvable' when it was reconceptualised as the main obstacle to the full participation of Israeli business in the international economy, at a time when the economic stakes in the global race between 'winning' and 'losing' countries became enormously high. In the new global economy, favorite countries have become not the big ones, but rather the faster 'integrators'. Under this new thinking, territorial, economic, and power redistribution were subjected to the primacy of economic growth. Thus the potential was created for replacing a zero-sum game, in which one side's gain is the other side's loss, with an open-ended approach, in which opposing sides might both come out ahead by compromising.[27]

Without underrating the value of peace from above, to end national conflicts entails much more than ending war. Conflict includes the whole gamut of violent activities, from high- to low-intensity operations; it entails economic activities, from economic sanctions and boycott (primary and secondary), to political use of economic resources for the creation of strategic dependency, and lack of international economic co-operation and prevention of private initiatives. Conflicts have an ideological dimension, expressed by the discourse created to portray the opponent internally and externally. Conflict means the inculcation and reproduction of hostile, conflictual attitudes (hatred, retribution, fear, distrust, prejudice) towards the opponent in curricula, religion and culture, through the politics of memory. Conflict also entails institutional segregation and closure against the opponent in terms of differential legal treatment and/or social discrimination, and avoidance of social contact and relations. In a protracted conflict, where it is a constitutive aspect of the identity of the opponents, ending it requires the ability to bring about reconciliation and create another, non-contradictory identity over time.

My argument is that currently neither Israel nor the Palestinians or Arab states are able or willing to terminate their conflict. There is, however, international – and internal – pressure on them to avoid major conflagrations and open up market opportunities to the world. I claim that this view is more realistic; it differs from the unreserved optimism of the post-Zionists.[28]

The peace agreement with Egypt belongs to the period of the third stage of the conflict, though its logic is located in the fourth stage, after the demise of the Soviet Union. The logic of the US-brokered peace between Egypt and Israel lies in the fact that conflict between two allies of the same super-power weakens that power, which must therefore act to reduce tension and increase solidarity within its camp. The peace agreement was the first measure that removed the threat of a major war which could endanger the very existence of the Jewish state. The peace agreement entailed the fixing of borders. Establishing mutually and internationally recognised borders between two sovereignties is a necessary, but not sufficient, condition of peace; it is not in itself a guarantee of peace or of an end to conflict between states.

The agreement with Egypt punctured the first hole in the second (inter-state) circle of the conflict, and was a breakthrough in the long-term principled refusal of the Arabs to recognise Israel in any form. Israel's military might and Egypt's commitment to stay out of a military coalition against Israel also considerably reduced the chances of any other Arab country going to war with Israel. As a result, Israel could reduce its security budget and divert funds to other uses. The first peace was, therefore, most valuable, and the price paid for it was deemed worthy by the Israeli leadership. However, it was not followed by more agreements until the demise of the Warsaw Pact. The agreement did not prevent another war by Israel against Lebanon in 1982, the first war where an Arab capital city was captured by Israel; until 2000 large tracts of south Lebanon remained under Israeli control. Following on the heels of the return of Sinai, the Lebanon war severely tested the peace treaty with Egypt. Relations between Israel and Egypt have remained cold and formal ever since. Hostility to Israel is popular and is maintained in the media and in education curricula in schools; social and economic relations are limited to official channels. Egypt is also hostile to Israel in international forums.

Peace with Jordan was the first result of American global hegemony, and was made possible by the weakening of Arab solidarity following the Gulf War of 1990–91. It was worthwhile for Jordan to atone for its previous (profitable) sin of being the way-station for Saddam's Iraq. In the wake of the Gulf War, Jordan's policy was reversed to appease the US. The borders and other issues outstanding between Israel and Jordan were not difficult to resolve, as there had long been understanding and co-operation between them. As a result of the Gulf War and this second peace agreement, the gaps in the second circle multiplied: other Arab states – mainly in the Gulf and the Maghreb – relaxed their attitudes and established open contacts with Israel; other Islamic states, such as Indonesia, or those with a large Muslim population, such as India, followed suit. The overall effect of this process was the breakdown of the international economic isolation of Israel and the opening of new markets for its exports. All these, however, although important, were secondary to what I claim as the main factor in the rapid economic growth of Israel in the 1990s, namely the collapse of the Soviet Union.

Israel was one of the chief beneficiaries of the fall of the Soviet bloc. Because of Soviet support for the Arabs during the conflict, Eastern bloc countries severed diplomatic and economic relations with Israel. Soviet influence was also responsible for many neutral states refusing to establish relations with Israel. The collapse of the Soviet Union brought Israel's isolation to an end. Diplomatic relations were renewed or established for the first time and, in their wake, major new markets in Central and Eastern Europe and in Asia were opened to Israel.

A second advantage gained by Israel from the collapse of the Soviet Union, and the attendant growing economic and political instability across its territories, was the major wave of immigration from the former USSR. To date the total number of immigrants has been more than a million. Beside the impact on the demography of Israel, and the reversal of the declining natality, the immigration brought Israel a huge amount of human capital. The immigrants included a much larger proportion of highly educated people than had the pre-immigration Israeli population, with a particularly high percentage of scientists. The timing of the immigration was opportune as it coincided with the burgeoning revolution in communications, computing and biological, genetic and medical research. Owing to its military–industrial complex, Israel had already developed these areas; with the influx of the immigrants Israel was ideally positioned to benefit from this revolution.

Another factor which helped Israel to capitalise on the fall of communism was the aid promised by the US for absorbing the Soviet immigrants. The aid, in the form of guarantees of US$10 billion, gave Israel access to funds at cheap rates of interest. American economic aid was part of the deal to bring Israel, under the premiership of Shamir the 'peace opponent', to the negotiating table in Madrid.

The coalescence of all these factors – opening markets, immigration of an expert labour force, fortunate timing and cheap capital – brought to Israel the economic boom which it enjoyed during the first five years following the peace process. In contrast to some of the post-Zionists, I argue that the explanation underlying the high rate of economic growth in Israel in the first years after Madrid and Oslo is not peace with the Arabs, but the collapse of the Soviet Union, the end of competition between socialism and capitalism and the opening up of the international economy under US hegemony. The optical illusion is simply because several major events happened at the same time. The collapse of the Soviet Union ended the isolation of Israel and normalised its relations with most countries save a few Arab and militant or Islamic fundamentalist countries. The trading partners responsible for the major expansion of exports by Israel were not Arab countries but new markets in Europe, Asia and America. The normalisation and renewal of diplomatic and economic relations with those countries also enabled Israel to improve its terms of trade, to replace expensive home-produced goods with much cheaper imports, thus increasing the purchasing power of Israeli consumers.

Arguments with post-Zionism

The post-Zionists argue that economic changes, liberalisation and privatisation created in Israel a growing stratum, or class, whose interests lie in ending the Israeli–Arab conflict, integrating economically in a new Middle East and (non sequitur) secularising and democratising Israel. I disagree. The base-superstructure Marxist metaphor is too simplistic to analyse the changes taking place in Israel. Its transparent purpose is to create the political myth that post-Zionism has a wide social base. From this point of view, the proponents of post-Zionism can posit themselves as the political alternative to neo-Zionism (religious Zionism).[29] I would like to suggest some counter propositions:

- The peace process is imposed on Israel from outside. It stems from the new architecture of the international system following the end of communism and the demise of the Soviet Union. The debate among Israel's power elite is about timing, whether the process plays against Israel or for it, and about the inevitability of the need to cede most of the occupied territories and finalise the borders of the state. One position, represented by Rabin, Peres and Barak, accepts the inevitable, grasps the nettle, concurs with the US's and Europe's wish to contain and stabilise the conflict, and tries to maximise the benefits for the concessions made. The other approach, represented by Shamir, Netanyahu and Sharon, was to delay and prevaricate in order to gain time, even at a certain price, in the hope that some external conditions may change. The changing attitudes in public opinion polls and in voting represent not so much a change in economic interests, but rather the slow realisation of the inevitable, which had been hidden from Israelis by an internally centred, jingoistic public discourse. This discourse is slowly breaking up under the pressure of global events and global media.

To substantiate the proposition that the will for peace stems from growing economic interests, it must be shown that a wide enough global class already existed in Israel in the period preceding the 1990s.

- There is confusion as to the economic benefits for Israel from making peace with the Arab countries. Most of the economic benefits of the 1990s came to Israel from the fall of the Soviet Union and not from direct economic relations with the Arab countries. Shimon Peres's ideas of a new Middle East with Israel as its hub immediately encountered negative responses from the Arab countries as a conspiracy for neo-colonialism. This attitude of suspicious hostility is not going to disappear for quite a long time. If peace is understood in the formal, minimal sense, and not as the end of the conflict in the foreseeable future, then the benefits for Israel lie not in the surrounding Arab world but rather with its normalisation in the family of nations, and the end of its outcast status. From the beginning, Zionism created a total separation between the Jewish economy and the surrounding Arab economies. Owing to the Arab boycott after 1948, Israel's areas of specialisation suited its trading partners, mostly far away in the West. The secondary boycott managed to isolate Israel in other countries, some of which are now burgeoning economies demanding products from Israeli military industries, tele-communications, agribusiness, pharmaceuticals and electronics. It is these markets that Israel covets. The poor developing countries in the Middle East have neither the money nor the need for what Israel sells. They can only be exploited for their cheap labour. It follows from this that the interests of Israeli industrialists are not necessarily best served by ending the conflict; they are served by the lifting of the ban on Israeli goods elsewhere. This has been expressed in Barak's concept of separating Israel from the Palestinian state and his slogan 'we are here and they are there!'

- It does not necessarily follow that the growing will for peace in Israel also indicates a growing willingness to forgo the Jewish character of the state and society. In fact, some of the strongest arguments for giving up terri-tories are in order to improve the demographic ratio of Jews to Arabs. It also does not follow that a willingness to return much of the territories occupied in 1967 also indicates a willingness to redress the situation created in 1948, to accept and compensate refugees, to grant full national equality to Arab citizens, to forgo the Law of Return which grants all Jews the right of citizenship, and to make Israel a secular, democratic state.

- Peace, in the formal limited sense imposed on Israel by the international community, means, however, that the spatial expansionist stage of Zionism must end. Israel will have proper borders with its neighbouring Arab states, including the Palestinians; these borders will be internationally recognised and guarded. To the extent that expansion and Judaisation of the land were the basic tenets of Labour, Likud and the National Religious Party, these movements are at the end of their ideology. However, this is not the end of Zionism but rather another turning point in its evolution.

Healing the rift between maximalist and minimalist zionists (hawks and doves) after a traumatic withdrawal from occupied territories and the evacuation of settlements may possibly, though not inevitably, become the major task of Israel's power elite in the near future. The internal healing and conciliation can, in my view, draw only on the common denominator of the majority – their Judaism, whatever this term means to different Jews. Israel is not going to become more orthodox or less modern in the technological sense,[30] but it will adopt through wide consensus a more Jewish public discourse in terms of symbols, norms and customs and within the national education system; indeed this process has already begun. This is not going to be the 'hard Judaism' of the ultra-Orthodox or the messianic settlers, which has become anathema to many, but rather streams of 'soft Judaism' more palatable to various strata of Israeli Jews.

What can be said about the suitability of various streams of Israeli Judaism for this transformation? Religious messianism is already on the decline, and will sink further as it loses its main *raison d'être* after withdrawal from the occupied territories. Ultra-Orthodoxy cannot provide a model of life for the majority as it is a sect, an elitist religion. The types of religion that may provide the necessary Jewish ideology will be as listed below.

Meimad (the name comes from the Hebrew initials for *Jewish state, democratic state*) This dovish Zionist religious group broke away from militant settler nationalism and the growing religious zealotry of the National Religious Party. The movement is now an affiliated faction within the Labour Party bloc. Meimad belongs to the orthodox stream of Judaism but retains a strong commitment to modernity. It denies that there is an inherent contradiction between Jewish religion and democracy. It welcomes innovation and change of tradition within the limits of *halacha*. It is also for democracy and against 'political religion', that is, the use of political power in order to enforce a religious way of life by legislation. It can act as a bridge to religion for many labour voters. Meimad is, however, an elite movement of people from a mainly occidental, educated, upper middle-class background, and has limited appeal beyond those parameters.

The Reform movement   The main trend in American Judaism established an offshoot in Israel (Progressive Judaism), first among American immigrants. It is gaining followers among the Israeli-born and some Russian immigrants who have a secular lifestyle but seek to combine tradition and modernity and maintain gender equality in their services. Reform Judaism is involved in battles against Orthodoxy's monopoly of religion in Israel: Orthodoxy refuses to recognise Reform or to validate its Rabbis' authority to convert, marry and divorce. As there is only religious marriage in Israel, and as conversion confers rights of citizenship, the denial has severe repercussions: it shifts the battle between Reform and Orthodox in the USA to Israel and as such has contradictory dynamics. This conflict threatens to alienate American Jewish solidarity with Israel. In order to avoid this and to gain sympathy in Israel, the movement in the USA became more committed to Zionism and makes more efforts to gain supporters among Israelis. Reform (Progressive) Judaism gained support in Israel among secularists who, in the absence of the separation of state and religion, favour religious pluralism and see Reform as an alternative to the despised Orthodox religion. Reform Judaism attracts people from some Labour socialist circles (Mapam). Its appeal, like Meimad's, is confined mostly to educated, middle-class, occidental Jews and does not reach the lower strata of Israeli society. Meimad, which is orthodox in style, nonetheless adopts a more conciliatory approach towards Reform. While the two groups do not pray together, Meimad would integrate the Reform movement in Israel into its political organisation.

Shas   This religious oriental party is the most important development in Israeli Judaism and on Israel's political map.[31] It has enjoyed a meteoric rise since it was founded in 1984 – in protest against Ashkenazi Orthodox discrimination against the Sephardi religious – to become the third biggest party after Labour and Likud. Shas is positioned to attract wide strata among the Israeli population. Unlike Ashkenazi Orthodoxy, Shas is not an exclusive sect but a wide open church[32] willing to incorporate not just orientals but any Jew. Shas followers are involved in all aspects of Israeli society and combine modernity with tradition.

From the nineteenth century, traditional Ashkenazi rabbinic authority and its interpretation and implementation of *halacha* were increasingly curtailed by European states and their legal institutions. Middle Eastern rabbinic tradition, on the other hand, was more autonomous in the Ottoman *millet* system and came closer to providing solutions to daily problems arising from modernisation. Judging from the rulings of Rabbi Yossef, the spiritual leader of Shas, the movement adapts very well to modernity. Shas also has the appeal of a populist protest movement fighting for justice for the poor and disadvantaged. It bears a resemblance to Erbekan's Welfare Party in Turkey. Shas is quickly becoming a threat to both Labour and Likud, and positions itself as counter-establishment. It thrives on its leaders' confrontations with the law, and it is building an alternative establishment of its own.

As Likud and Labour implemented their policies of privatisation, they tried to abolish universal welfare. Instead they channelled funds to religious institutions, among them those of Shas. In turn, Shas distributed the funds to the poor oriental sectors of the population it sought to attract, thus building loyalty and political dependency on the party. However, Shas remained dependent on whoever controlled the Treasury and had to serve in coalition governments; but it brought with it the support of the poor oriental masses.

Shas represents religion as tradition, much as it still exists in traditional Muslim society – a collective way of life passed on from bygone times. This way of life binds the individual into a collective ethnic identity and represents unity between past and present. Although the hard core of Shas's leaders studied in ultra-Orthodox institutions, Shas aims to create not a virtuoso religion but rather a way of life in which all can participate.

As long as war divided Israelis from the rest of the Middle East, their Jewish identity was relatively secure. Israeli Jews may be killed, but they did not assimilate – at least not at the rate prevalent among Jews in the former Soviet Union, the USA and Europe. The opening of Israel to neighbouring countries threatens Israelis with the problem of assimilation, especially if the peace process develops. This will be particularly true among secular, educated, affluent and mobile Israelis and among the very poor, uneducated, mainly oriental groups, where the stigma of assimilation matters less.

Contrary to the assumption that peace will polarise relations between religious and secular, the reverse is more likely. Israeli Jewish identity was created through the wars. If there are open borders, Israeli Jewish identity will have to be maintained in other ways, from within. This would necessitate strengthening Judaism as a tradition, as a separate way of life, as it existed between the different ethnic groups in the Ottoman Empire.

The status of the army as the secular national symbol will subside. With the resolution of the border issue, army service will cease to be a symbol of Israeliness. The bitter issue of avoidance of military service by the ultra-Orthodox will decline as the army moves from conscription to voluntary professional recruitment.

Following the end of the expansionary stage of Israel, one can also foresee a reduction in the role and status of the High Court, at present another symbol of secularism. Since the foundation of the state, the court served as legitimator of much of the colonising practices of the state as well as adjudicator on breaches of human rights and illegal activities of the security forces stemming from the occupation. The High Court helped the state to maintain a measure of rule of law; it served as the 'wise arm of the state'. The courts were held in high esteem. Consequently, the High Court presidents were able to increase the purview of their jurisdiction. Stalemate in parliament and lack of legislation on matters between religious and secular gave the High Court wide scope for intervention. The liberal attitudes of the courts led to growing confrontation with the Orthodox. However, there are now indications, in the reform of the court system, that the High Court wishes to limit confrontations with other judicial institutions (parliament and the rabbinic courts), and make access by the public more difficult.

There is, however, another reason for my belief that Zionism is about to shift and turn inwards. Israel is undergoing a process of massive privatisation. The break-up of the welfare state and the opening of Israel to global competition is causing a major restructuring of the economy. As a result, much of the 'low-tech' sector is being closed through replacement by cheaper imports or foreign labour. The claim that everybody benefits from globalisation is false; disparity between rich and poor has grown so rapidly that Israel has become one of the most inegalitarian societies among industrialised nations. Moreover, it has made this transition within a very short time. Growing relative deprivation, rather than absolute poverty, is what creates resentment in the poor classes. The 'new economy' benefits narrow sections of the population, but causes wide and permanent structural unemployment among the older, less educated, mainly oriental (and Arab) people living far from the main business centres. These people have not enjoyed the peace dividend; indeed the Jews among them form the bulk, not the leadership, of the anti-peace camp.

Both Likud and Labour are committed to privatisation and are against the resurrection of the welfare state. However, they need the votes of the popular poor, but instead of improving their material situation they entice them through appeal to tradition and the notion of Jewish unity.[33] I have elaborated on this issue in order to counter the post-Zionists' presentation of the alternatives facing Israel as an apocalyptic dichotomy between post-Zionism and zealotocracy.[34] I have shown that the likelihood of 'soft Judaism' is more plausible.

Post-Zionism as a local version of ideological globalisation

The battle cries of the diminishing role of nationalism and of the territorial nation state, together with claims that capitalism has overcome its major contradictions, are as yet unfounded;[35] the state will not disappear under the rule of the market; the 'Third Way' – that middle road between social democracy and liberalism – is stumbling from crisis to crisis in Europe; and 'the end [of the Israeli–Arab conflict] is nigh' sounds more like a religious slogan calling sinners to repent than a reflection of the current situation in the Middle East.

A significant number of academics associated with post-Zionism originated among the Zionist left, which may explain some of their vehemence at the hegemonic history and sociology created by labour Zionism. Gotwin attacks the post-Zionists because, in effect, they collude with right-wing Zionism in their efforts to destroy Israeli collective memory and promote what he calls 'privatisation of memory'. Gotwin sees the emergence of post-Zionism against the background of the struggle for and against privatisation: 'This connection can explain why the new historiography with its various contradictions ... gained a central place as a cultural phenomenon in the social and political context of privatisation – and gains its legitimation from this struggle as well as legitimising it'.[36] Gotwin, who is opposed to privatisation of memory, argues that collective memory is the only remaining obstacle on privatisation's road to becoming the hegemonic ethos in Israeli society.

I suggest another explanation for the appeal of 'liberal globalisation' to the post-Zionists. Post-Zionism appears at the same time as the demise of socialism (Soviet and social-democratic); it is no wonder that its proponents are in search of a substitute ideology. If the vision of socialism receded, at least the vision of peace remained and would be a goal in itself. In fact, some of the more coherent post-Zionists retain a hidden Marxist pattern in their 'problemstellung'.

- They explain the 'new willingness for peace' in Israel by directly attributing it to the economic interests of social classes (reductionism).

But they replace the 'progressive class'; instead of it being the working class it is capitalists and civil servants.

- They have a crude determinist belief in the linear connection between the progress of globalisation and the end of national conflict. Economy determines everything.

- They pose themselves as a vanguard and view the unfolding of the future in apocalyptic manner: 'post-Zionism or zealotocracy!' (which sounds like 'socialism or barbarism').

Quo vadis post-Zionism? The split between left- and right-wing post-Zionism

Recently, however, some of the post-Zionists have become aware of the contradictions of capitalist globalisation and are not willing completely to shed their social conscience and accept globalisation lock, stock and barrel. They are caught between their Marxism and their liberalism. This leads Uri Ram to distinguish in post-Zionism two trends: Liberal post-Zionism and Radical post-Zionism. It is interesting that the word 'socialist' is not to be used, in the same way that anti-Zionism is not mentioned.

Ram ends his article in *Israeli Sociology* with the sad observation: 'Poverty, inequality and the sense of deprivation turn the lower strata easy prey to populist chauvinist and clerical politics of the neo-Zionist right and leave the democratic-dovish-secular post-Zionist "left" as an isolated group of an elitist minority ... and so the liberal post-Zionist trend is in essential contradiction which threatens to dismantle it'.[37]

Conclusion

Zionism has been transformed; in this respect the post-Zionists were correct, but not in the way they had hoped. At the root of present events there was a major shift in the ideological make-up of Israel. Present events indicate a major political earthquake: labour Zionism as a secular, left-leaning ideology is dead, and so is the Labour Party. The secular liberal Zionism of Herzl, Jabotinsky and the early Likud is also dead. Both have been replaced by religion as the source of political legitimation for the state of Israel and for its continued control and colonisation of the whole of

Palestine. The majority of Israelis have not become more observant; far from it, although even this may follow. Rather, political religion is the use of religion to explain the cohesion and uniqueness of the ethnos, its history and ethos; it is the use of religion as an argument for the claim to territory and justification of political measures to defend the national project.

Is there a way out of the present situation? The struggle between Palestinians and Israelis could easily deteriorate into a regional war. There are many internal and regional actors who seek to escalate the conflict. Messianic and nationalist extremists in Israel hope for a regional war and the breakdown of peace between Israel, Jordan and Egypt. Only under conditions of general war can the ethnic cleansing of Palestinian Israeli citizens and Palestinians from the occupied territories take place. On the Arab/Islamic side, there are pan-Arabists and fundamentalists who dream of doing away with the pro-American Arab regimes and the creation of Arab/Islamic unity which will destroy the Zionist entity and liberate the Middle East from American domination. These dangers are further exacerbated by the presence on both sides of weapons of mass destruction.

While terrorism (including state terrorism) is a complicating factor used by both sides in the conflict, the real issue is colonialist occupation by Israel. In any event, Bush must decide whether it suits American interests to include the Israeli–Palestinian conflict within the US definition of the 'war on terrorism'. Until now the pro-American Arab regimes have withstood popular protest and are resisting the more extreme forces in their midst. The recent Beirut summit conference adopted a moderate Saudi plan for regional peace and normalisation of relations between Israel and the Arab states. The proposal is based on UN resolution 242. Although this is not acceptable to Israelis because it includes the demand for a just solution of the Palestinian refugee problem, it is an opening for negotiations. Since 1948 the Israeli–Palestinian conflict has been subsumed within the wider Arab–Israeli conflict. The Arabs took over leadership of the struggle and subordinated Palestinian interests to their own. During most of this time, the Arabs resolved to reject any compromise solution with Israel (for example, at the Khartoum summit of 1967). However, since the signing of peace agreements between Israel and Egypt, and between Israel and Jordan, pro-American Arab states have distanced themselves from the Israeli–Palestinian struggle and have allowed the Palestinian leadership to speak and act autonomously. The Beirut summit may indicate a turning point for renewed involvement by the Arab states in the Palestinian issue due to the impasse reached by the Palestinians themselves. This renewed involvement may develop in two ways: either towards an overall Pax Americana agreement, or towards a new, more brutal phase of Israeli–Arab conflict.

Nor is Israel independent. Its capacity to act in the conflict is dependent on the ability to align its interests with those of the US. An example can be found in the configuration of Israel's arguments against the Palestinian Authority to fit within the framework of the US 'war on terrorism'. In this respect Sharon was much quicker to grasp and utilise the repercussions of 11 September than Arafat. The suicide attacks on civilians inside Israel ill-serve the Palestinian cause. Sharon's government has managed to wrap the war for a 'Greater Israel ' in the guise of a 'war against terrorism'.

NOTES

1. Y. Dan (1997) *On the Sacred*, Magnes, The Hebrew University [Hebrew].
2. M. Meir (1988) *Response to Modernity: A History of the Reform Movement in Judaism*, Oxford, Oxford University Press.
3. Y. Peled (1997) *Cultural Autonomy and Class Struggle: The Development of the National Program of the BUND 1893–1903*, Hakibbutz Hameuchad, Bnai-Brak [Hebrew]; Y. Peled (1991) 'Cultural National Autonomy', in *Theory and Criticism*, no. 11, pp. 163–75 [Hebrew]; E. Nimni (1991), *Marxism and Nationalism*, London, Pluto Press.
4. N. Gross (1999) 'Herzl's Economic Thought', in *Not on the Spirit Alone*, Magnes, The Hebrew University, pp. 89–105 [Hebrew]; Amos Eilon (1976) *Hertzl*, Tel Aviv, Am Oved Afakim.
5. Eliahu Beniamini (1990) *States for the Jews: Uganda, Birobidzhan and 34 Other Projects*, Tel Aviv, Hakibbutz Hameuchad [Hebrew].
6. D. Vital (1982) *The Zionist Revolution*, Oxford, Oxford University Press.
7. S. Dotan (1980) *The Partition Dispute in the Mandate Period*, Jerusalem, Y. Ben Tzvi [Hebrew].
8. A. Shapira (ed.) (1983) *The Religious Trend in Zionism*, Tel Aviv, Am-Oved [Hebrew]; S. Almog, J. Reinharz, A. Shapira (eds) (1994) *Zionism and Religion*, Jerusalem, The Zalman Shazar Center for Jewish History [Hebrew].
9. S. Dotan (1991) *Reds*, Kfar Saba, Shevna Hasofer; G.Z. Israeli (1953) *MPS, PKP, ICP: History of the Communist Party in Israel*, Tel Aviv, Am Oved.
10. Z. Sternhell (1995) *Nation-building or Reform of Society*, Tel Aviv, Am Oved, Afakim [Hebrew].
11. N. Yuval Davis (1977) 'Matzpen – The Socialist Organisation in Israel', Researches in Sociology, The Kaplan School of Economics and Social Sciences, The Hebrew University [Hebrew].
12. D. Sheari (1990) *From Just Zionism to General Zionism*, Jerusalem, Reuven Mass; S. Zalman Avramov (1995) *On a Party Which Disappeared and on Liberalism*, Tel Aviv, Dvir [Hebrew].
13. A. Ben Porat (1999) *Where Are Those Bourgeois? History of The Israeli Bourgeoisie*, Jerusalem, Magnes, The Hebrew University [Hebrew].
14. Y. Gorny (1990) *The Quest for Collective Identity*, Tel Aviv, Am Oved [Hebrew]; Elmer Berger (1942) *Why I am a Non-Zionist*, New York; E. be H. Arendt (1945) 'Zionism Reconsidered', in *The Menorah Journal*, Autumn; R. Tekiner, S. Abed Rabbo and N. Mezvinsky (eds) (1988) *Anti-Zionism: Analytical Reflections*, Brattleboro, Vermont, Amana.

15. J. Diamond (1986) *Homeland or Holyland: The 'Canaanite' Critique of Israel*, Bloomington, Indiana University Press; Y. Shavit (1984) *From Hebrew to Canaanite*, Tel Aviv, Domino [Hebrew]; B. Evron (1988) *A National Reckoning*, Tel Aviv, Dvir.

16. A. Ravitzki (1988) *Religion and State in Jewish Thought*, Jerusalem, The Institute For Democracy [Hebrew]; G. Veiler (1976) *Jewish Theocracy*, Tel Aviv, Am Oved, Afakim [Hebrew].

17. See D. Gotwin in Y. Weitz (ed.) (1997) *Between Vision and Revision: A Hundred Years of Zionist Historiography*, Jerusalem, Shazar Institute, p. 325 [Hebrew].

18. Laurence J. Silberstein, (1999) *The Postzionism Debates*, New York and London, Routledge.

19. Ibid., p. 2.

20. S. Smooha (1997) 'Ethnic Democracy: Israel as an Archtype', in *Israel Studies*, vol. 2, no. 2, Ben-Gurion University, pp. 198–241; R. Gavison (1999) 'Jewish and Democratic, a Rejoinder to the Ethnic Democracy Debate', in *Israel Studies*, vol. 4, Spring, Ben-Gurion University, pp. 44–72; A. Dawty (1999) 'Is Israel Democratic? Substance and Semantics in the Ethnic Democracy Debate', in *Israel Studies*, vol. 4, no. 2, Ben-Gurion University, pp. 1–15.

21. A. Ehrlich (1993) 'A society in war: the national conflict and the social structure', in U. Ram (ed.) *Israeli Society – Critical Perspectives*, Breirot Publishers, pp. 253–74 [Hebrew].

22. Hillel Cohen (2000) *The Present Absentees: The Palestinian Refugees in Israel since 1948*, Jerusalem, The Institute for Israeli–Arab Studies [Hebrew].

23. Y. Elitzur (1997) *Economic Warfare: 100 years of economic confrontation between Jews and Arabs*, Ramat Gan, Keneret.

24. N. Chomsky (1999) *Fateful Triangle: The United States, Israel and the Palestinians*, updated edition, London, Pluto; Avi Shlaim (2000) *The Iron Wall: Israel and the Arab World*, New York and London, W.W. Norton.

25. A. Ehrlich (1992) 'The Gulf War and the New World Order', in R. Miliband and L. Panitch (eds), *Socialist Register*, London, Merlin, pp. 227–38.

26. J. McMurty (1988) *Understanding War – A Philosophical Inquiry*, Canadian Papers in Peace Studies, no. 2, Toronto, Science for Peace; J. Stoessinger (1985) *Why Nations Go to War*, Fourth edition, New York, St Martin's Press; R.I. Rotberg and T.K. Rabb (eds) (1988) *The Origins and Prevention of Major Wars*, Cambridge, Cambridge University Press; J.S. Nye (1997) *Understanding International Conflicts*, New York, Longman; C.W. Kegley Jr. and G.A. Raymond (1999) *How Nations Make Peace*, New York, St Martin's Press.

27. G. Shafir and Y. Peled (eds) *The New Israel: Peacemaking and Liberalization*, Boulder, Colo., Westview, especially Introduction, p. 2, and chapter 10, 'Peace and profits: the globalization of Israeli business and the peace process', pp. 262–3, which makes this paragraph sound like a manifesto. For another view see J. Nitzan and S. Bichler (1996) 'From War Profits to Peace Dividends – The New Political Economy of Israel', in *Capital and Class*, no. 60, pp. 61–94.

28. See A. Tal (2000) 'The fiction of the end of the conflict', in *Ha'aretz*, 27 July.

29. I. Pappé (2000) 'Israel at a Crossroads Between Civic Democracy and Jewish Zealotocracy', in *Journal of Palestine Studies*, vol. xxix, no. 3, Spring, pp. 34–44.

30. Y. Sheleg (2000) *The New Religious in Israel: Recent Developments Among Observant Jews in Israel*, Jerusalem, Keter [Hebrew].

31. Y. Peled (1998) 'Towards a Redefinition of Jewish Nationalism in Israel – The Enigma of Shas', in *Ethnic & Racial Studies*, vol. 21, no. 4, July.

32. S. Fisher (1999) 'Shas Movement', in '*50 to 48' Theory and Criticism*, special issue, Van-Leer Institute, Hakibbutz-Hameuchad, pp. 175–85 [Hebrew].

33. D. Gotwin (2000) in *Mikarov*, no. 3, Winter.
34. U.Ram (1999) 'Between Weapons and the Economy: Israel in the Glocal Era', in *Israeli Sociology*, vol. 2, no. 1, Tel Aviv University, pp. 99–146 [Hebrew]; Pappé (2000) 'Israel at a Crossroads'.
35. P. Hirst and G. Thompson (2000) *Globalisation in Question*, second edition, Cambridge, Polity; L. Panitch (ed.) (1994) 'Between Globalism and Nationalism', *Socialist Register*, London, Merlin; L. Panitch (ed.) (1999) 'Global Capitalism Versus Democracy', *Socialist Register*, London, Merlin; L. Panitch (2000) 'The New Imperial State', in *New Left Review*, March–April.
36. See D. Gotwin in Weitz, *Between Vision and Revision*, p. 343.
37. Ram (1999) 'Between Weapons and the Economy', p. 136.

5 ◎ Zionism, Post-Zionism and Anti-Zionism in Israel

Jews and Arabs in Conflict Over the Nature of the State

As'ad Ghanem

In recent years the post-Zionist debate in Israel has occupied the headlines and enjoyed broad media coverage. The interest in the new context of analysis presented by practitioners of the social sciences and by historiographers of the Palestinian–Israeli conflict is, without a doubt, one of the most positive innovations in the history of scholarship in Israel. The new 'discoveries'[1] made by a group of young scholars, led by Professor Benny Morris of Ben-Gurion University of the Negev and Dr Ilan Pappé of the University of Haifa, along with a number of other 'new' historians, were a sort of renewed disclosure of the recent history of a cruel and bloody conflict. Subsequent to the revelations made by Morris, Pappé and others, sociologists such as Dr Uri Ram of Ben-Gurion University, Dr Yoav Peled of Tel Aviv University and others focused on understanding the history of the last two decades and the present, and even made so bold as to predict the future.

There is no doubt that the social scientists' writing about recent developments in Israeli society would not have been possible, or at least could not have blazed a new trail, without the writings of their predecessors who challenged cherished Zionist narratives of the conflict, especially concerning the violent and cruel mass expulsion of the Palestinians from their country and their consignment to refugee camps in neighbouring countries. These historians had to deal with a variety of extremely serious challenges on the way to publishing the conclusions of their research. In addition to publishing new findings about a topic that had been studied for years and seemed to offer nothing new, these historians performed focused archival research and showed that the historical narrative of Israel, as disseminated in Israel and to the world, is full of distortions and warped to favour one side in the political debate and propaganda war between Israel and the Arab world. These scholars also had to deal with the successful and well-marketed narrative in which Israeli historians claimed, contrary to all logic, that it was the Jews who were threatened and that only they suffered from the results of the conflict and from the establishment of the state of Israel.

Israeli public opinion, most of which is *engagé* (despite some assertions of the contemporary post-Zionist debate), viewed the new scholars and their findings with hostility, and, frequently with the encouragement of the Israeli academic and political establishment, hurled charges of collaboration with the enemy, self-hatred, and many other similar negative expressions at these historians. Their findings, however, struck many Palestinians and Arabs as nothing new, but merely a repetition of historical truths already documented and published by many Palestinian and Arab historians, and even learned from Palestinian parents who witnessed what happened in 1948 and told their children at every available opportunity.

The post-Zionist argument promulgated by these social scientists and others was largely built on the findings of the 'new historians'. It was able to penetrate the debate about the past and propose a scientific, empirical alternative for analysing and understanding the contemporary situation in Israeli society. This argument, along with an evaluation of its significance for the Palestinians in Israel, is the subject of the present chapter.

In my opinion, the acid test of the development of post-Zionist currents in Israel is the situation of the Palestinian minority *vis-à-vis* the state and in the light of expected changes in the positions and attitude of the Jewish majority and in the nature of the policy adopted by the state *vis-à-vis* the Palestinian minority. I will have little or nothing to say about current official policy toward the Palestinian minority in Israel, or about the situation of the Palestinian minority as a reflection of that policy, since I have dealt with this elsewhere.[2]

In this chapter I will deal at length with two key aspects relevant to my topic: the attitude of the Jewish majority towards the Palestinian minority and its position in the state; and the attitude of the Palestinian minority towards Zionism and towards the character of the State of Israel. My hypothesis is that the positions held by the two components of the Israeli population, Jews and Palestinians, are substantially different from those presupposed in a post-Zionist context. The Jews sustain traditional Zionist values and the Arabs hold strongly anti-Zionist positions, even though the two groups agree formally that they are citizens of a shared state. This formal 'agreement' holds no possibility of the development of a shared 'Israeli' identity such as exists in any other democratic country.

The public commitment of Jews in Israel to the Jewish–Zionist and ethnic character of the state

Zionism as a national movement that aspires to establish a Jewish state appeared at the end of the nineteenth century. An elitist group of intellectuals of the Jewish faith decided to take action in the spirit of nationalism that had begun to rise in Europe and in light of the discriminatory and racist policy of European regimes against members of the Jewish faith. Initially Zionism drew on national and ethnic movements that had developed in Central and Eastern Europe based on an ostensible blood relationship among all members of the ethnic group along with the aspirations of their originators and theorists to find other connecting threads (real or imaginary) of shared history, culture, religion, and origins, including the geographical location that they conceived of as the group's original home.

Europeans, including members of the Jewish faith, reacted with suspicion toward the new movement, but by slow stages it was able to attract various groups of Jews in Poland, Germany, the Austro-Hungarian Empire, Russia and elsewhere, and to persuade them of the need to emigrate to Palestine (which they called 'Eretz Israel' or 'Jerusalem'). The first emigration from eastern Europe, in 1880–1882, accounted for only a few tens of people, certainly less than a hundred. This was followed by additional waves of Jewish immigration to the country, which accelerated following the establishment of Israel in 1948. Added to the tens of thousands of Jews who had always lived in the country, and natural increase, this produced what is today a Jewish majority in the country of some 82 per cent, or about five million of the six million citizens of Israel.

Before they arrived in the country these Jewish migrants were exposed to various processes of persuasion about the Jewish national project. The Zionist movement and its representatives, such as the Zionist Organization, used education and propaganda as means of persuasion, exploiting the particular history of each region to persuade its Jewish residents of the need to emigrate to Palestine and participate in the building of a Jewish state in the ancestral homeland. There is no doubt that the efforts of the Zionist movement bore abundant fruit, manifested in the emigration of tens of thousands of Jews from their original countries to Palestine.

The vast majority of the Jews who immigrated into Palestine did not know Hebrew before they arrived. Their knowledge of Jewish history, Jewish culture, and even Jewish religion and its rituals was minimal and superficial. Similarly, it is plausible that their commitment to an ethnic

Jewish state was weak and poorly developed. In Israel, thanks to the efforts of the state and its elites, the Jewish immigrants experienced accelerated processes of recruitment to a national ethnic Jewish project. These processes produced a dramatic increase in the level of commitment evinced by Jews toward the Jewish state and its Zionist objectives. This commitment helps the state and its leaders to take action towards realizing Zionist objectives and to strengthen the Zionist state, steps that clearly harm the native Palestinians in Israel, the West Bank and Gaza.

The literature about the Jewish majority's attitude to the Arab minority in the country and related issues—such as the Israeli–Palestinian conflict and its solution, recognition of the Palestinians as a people and not only as part of the larger Arab nation, relations with individual Arabs, and the individual and collective equality of the Arab citizens of Israel—grapples with two key questions. First is the change in the attitude of the Jewish majority toward Arab citizens of Israel and the Palestinian people in general, of whom the Israeli Arabs are a part. Has there been any such change? If so, in what direction has it been—towards rapprochement or a further hardening of the majority's attitude against the Arab citizens of the country? Second, are there different streams among Jews concerning the Arabs and related issues? That is, with regard to their attitude toward Arabs, do the Jews in Israel constitute a monolithic group?

To the first question the literature offers two contradictory answers. The 'entrenchment' model is based on the prevalent perception in the Arab world, among the Palestinians and segments of the Arab community in Israel,[3] that the Jews are hardening their attitude toward the Arab citizens of Israel and manifesting rigid positions that become more inflexible over the years. This model was given expression in the literature in the work of the Palestinian scholar Khalil Nakhleh[4] (1978, 1982), who maintained that over the years the Jews manifested unyielding attitudes towards the Arab citizens of Israel and adopted obstinate and uncompromising positions on questions that relate to the Arabs, their heritage, their property and their rights.

In contrast to Nakhleh, Sammy Smooha (1992) developed an 'accessibility' model,[5] according to which the Jews have displayed increasingly conciliatory attitudes toward the Arabs over the years. On questions that have to do with co-existence with Israeli Arabs, such as personal relations with Arabs, a resolution of the Palestinian problem and equality for Arabs, he maintains that the Jews' position is marked by an increasing willingness to move towards the Arabs and their needs, demands, and positions.

As for the second question, concerning the existence of different Jewish currents concerning the Arabs, there are three models. The first, presented by Nakhleh in his treatment of the attitude of the Israeli Left toward the first Land Day in 1976, holds that all Israeli Jews, except for negligible groups of non-Zionists, manifest the same attitude towards the Arab citizens of Israel. According to him, even the Zionist left in Israel conforms to positions that resemble those of the other political currents within the Jewish majority, which come down to rejection of Arabs, support for the seizure of their property for 'Jewish' goals, and the absence of a willingness to move towards them on the question of equality with the Jewish majority and their acceptance as equal citizens.[6]

According to the second model, presented by Ian Lustick in his book on Israeli policy toward the Arabs,[7] the Jews can be divided into two main groups – supporters of the right wing and supporters of the leftwing on the Israeli political map. With regard to their attitude to the Arab citizens of Israel, these groups are distinguished by the fact that supporters of the left hold more conciliatory positions than do supporters of the right. This difference exists but is irrelevant when it is a question of a willingness to move in the direction of shared management of the country. The differences exist exclusively with regard to practical questions of a moderate or rigid attitude, in the context of a general consensus that Israel is a Jewish state and the state of the Jews and must guarantee Jewish supremacy.

The third model, offered by Sammy Smooha,[8] holds that the Jewish majority falls into four distinct groups in its attitude toward the Arabs. The 'conciliationist' stream, which is the most liberal, supports full citizenship for the Arabs and their equality and integration into Israeli society. It sees no contradiction between Zionism and democracy but would opt for democracy should it come into contradiction with the Jewish–Zionist character of the state. Second, the 'pragmatist' stream desires equality for the Arabs but insists on guarding the security interests of the state and its Jewish-Zionist character. This stream supports greater equality for the Arabs, rejects a military regime over them, supports efforts to reduce the socio-economic disparities between Jews and Arabs, and acknowledges that the state does not do enough on behalf of the Arabs. The 'hardliner' stream gives primacy to the security needs of the state and its Jewish and Zionist character, prefers the Jewish–Zionist character of the state to its democratic nature, and supports rigid control of the Arabs. Its members believe that it is impossible to rely on the Arabs, suspect that they pose a potential threat to the security of the state, and do not believe that closing the economic gap between Jews and Arabs should be a central goal of the state. Finally, the 'exclusionist' stream believes that the Arabs should accept Jewish hegemony without protest or leave the country, and views this as a goal towards which the state should aspire. Its members are unwilling to accept an Arab in a position of authority over them at work and believe that the state does too much for the Arabs.

A fourth model, represented by Hanna Herzog,[9] divides the Jews into five groups with regard to their attitude to the Arabs. The first, unbending nationalism, supports the identification of Israel with exclusive Jewish dominance and insists on its unique security problems that justify an unbending attitude toward the Arabs. The basic assumption of this stream is that the Arabs in Israel are affiliated to the enemy and will remain so; accordingly they must always be treated with suspicion and kept under control and supervision. This stream is represented chiefly by supporters of right-wing parties. The liberal nationalist stream holds that the Jews' treatment of the Arabs must be pragmatic in order to neutralize them as a security threat and induce them to display maximum loyalty to the state. Its members believe that there are 'good and loyal' Arabs who should be treated well, and 'bad and hostile' Arabs who should be treated with an iron fist. The basic attitude of the supporters of this stream is built on the assessment that the Arabs can be manipulated into maximum loyalty to the Jewish state. This stream is represented by supporters of the Likud and some supporters of Labour. The third stream, that of 'Jewish democracy', considers the question of how to give the Arabs maximum equality without impinging upon the Jewish–Zionist character of the state. This current is supported chiefly by broad sectors of the Labour party. Fourth, the 'equality for all' stream favours full equality for Arabs on the basis of their shared citizenship with Jews. Emphasizing the democratic and egalitarian nature of the state, they believe that this should be preferred in the event of a contradiction between its Jewish and democratic characters. This stream is represented chiefly by supporters of the Zionist left. The fifth stream, 'no problem', holds that there should be absolute equality between Jews and Arabs and that in every case democracy should be preferred to Zionism. According to this stream, the Arabs are equal citizens in every respect. In practice it is represented by the tiny group of non-Zionists or anti-Zionists among the Jews.

The discussion in the literature and the various classifications of Jewish attitudes toward Arabs constitute the essential background for understanding the analysis that follows. My first hypothesis is that Jewish immigrants undergo a process of recruitment that causes them to increase their commitment to the Jewish–Zionist state and its objectives. This recruitment was carried out through a number of means by institutions of the state-in-the-making before independence and continued thereafter by the state and its organs to the present day.[10] My second hypothesis is that the Jewish majority displays a high level of commitment to the Jewish state and its Zionist objectives, manifested in a variety of expressions, and that this commitment has not declined over the years. My third hypothesis is that there are differences among the four political and ideological currents concerning the level of their commitment to the ethnic Jewish–Zionist state, but not concerning the existence of such commitment. In the discussion that follows I shall relate to the first two hypotheses. The third has been discussed by others, such as Smooha and Herzog; for want of space I will not repeat a view similar to theirs, but merely refer to their works on the subject.[11]

The Jewish commitment to the ethnic Zionist character of the state and attitudes toward the Palestinians in Israel

The Jews in Israel hold extremely stable ethnic values that are accepted by almost all. In the final analysis the Jews are not interested in a neutral state but in a state committed to their concerns and prepared to serve them even at the expense of its other citizens.[12] According to a survey conducted in 1995, a majority of Jews in Israel support the ethnic state and its policy toward the Palestinian-Arab minority. The Jews see Israel as a Jewish state and even as the state of the Jewish people; almost all of them (96.4 per cent) want to preserve the Jewish majority in the country. They want to preserve this situation and the general idea that stands behind it and to strengthen it on various levels. The change over the years is not unequivocal; there have been ups and downs in the extent of the Jewish majority's commitment to the various manifestations of the Jewish character of the state (see Table 5.1). It is true that in a historical perspective there is a slight decline in the percentage of those who define Israel as the homeland of the Jews, but this is so small that it is difficult to speak about any serious change whatsoever. Today, as in the past, the vast majority of the Jews (73.4 per cent in the 1980 survey; 72.1 per cent in the 1995 survey) believe that Israel is exclusively the homeland of the Jews. In the more recent survey the same percentage of the Jews in Israel (72 per cent) agree to a definition of the state in law as the state of the Jewish people, without including its Arab citizens in this definition; only 27.9 per cent are willing to support the formulation that Israel is the shared homeland of Jews and Arabs.

TABLE 5.1: HOW JEWS DEFINE ISRAEL (JEWISH SAMPLE ONLY)

Israel today is:	1980	1985	1988	1995
The homeland of the Jews	73.4	77.0	76.6	72.1
The shared homeland of the Jews and the Arabs	26.2	22.5	22.4	27.9
The homeland of the Arabs	0.3	0.5	1.0	0

The attitude toward the Jewish–Zionist character of the state again points to an entrenchment in the positions of most Jews in the country. It is true that the percentage of those who favour increasing the Jewish-Zionist character of the state has declined over the years (from 76 per cent in 1980 to 59.1 per cent in 1995); but they are not moving to the other side, which would like to moderate this character. Rather, they have switched to support for the idea that the situation should remain as it is (19.4 per cent in 1980 and 35.6 per cent in 1995). There are two possible explanations for this movement. One is that some Jews have become slightly more moderate and think that there is no need to intensify the Jewish–Zionist character of the state. The other is that some Jews believe that the Jewish–Zionist character is strong enough and needs no reinforcement. The change does not indicate any moderation of principles that would embody a breakthrough in the Jews' willingness to compromise concerning the Jewish–Zionist nature of the state. The percentage of those who support the idea that the Jewish–Zionist character of the state should be reduced actually declined between 1985 and 1995. The law that gives the Jews their numerical superiority and permits them, in addition to other things, to preserve the Jewish–Zionist nature of the state is the Law of Return, which grants every Jew in the world the right to immigrate to Israel and immediately acquire citizenship on a par with that

TABLE 5.2: THE JEWISH MAJORITY'S ATTITUDE TOWARD THE JEWISH-ZIONIST CHARACTER OF ISRAEL (JEWISH SAMPLE ONLY)

Today Israel within the Green Line is a Jewish–Zionist state with an Arab minority. What is your opinion of the Jewish–Zionist character of the state?

	1980	1985	1995
It should be strengthened	76.0	62.7	59.1
It should be left as is	19.4	31.3	35.6
It should be moderated	4.6	6.0	5.4

of long-settled Jews, but does not permit this to other citizens, including Arabs. This law is supported, even today, by a majority of the Jews (68.1 per cent), who believe that the Law of Return should be kept; only 3 per cent of the Jews favour its repeal.

TABLE 5.3 (JEWISH SAMPLE ONLY)
What would you prefer in the event that the democratic–egalitarian character of the state comes into contradiction with its Jewish–Zionist character and you are forced to choose between them?

	1980	1985	1988	1995
I would certainly prefer its democratic–egalitarian character	41.7	23.0	18.7	21.9
I think that I would prefer its democratic–egalitarian character but cannot be certain		18.6	27.2	23.8
I think that I would prefer its Jewish-Zionist character but cannot be certain	58.3	27.9	36.9	24.6
I would certainly prefer its Jewish–Zionist character		30.5	17.2	29.7

TABLE 5.4 (JEWISH SAMPLE ONLY)
Should the state give preferential treatment to Jews or Arabs?

	1980	1985	1988	1995
Significant preference for Jews	66.6	59.1	47.9	45.8
Some preference for Jews	19.2	21.7	25.9	28.3
No preference for either Jews or Arabs	15.7	18.8	25.5	25.6
Some preference for Arabs	0.3	0.4	0.7	0.2
Significant preference for Arabs	0.1	0.0	0.0	0.1

With regard to the nature of the state as both Jewish and democratic, most Jews, when asked to choose between these two components, prefer the Jewish to the democratic. This preference has held stable over the years. More than half of the Jews would rather live in a state that is Jewish but not democratic than in a democratic but non-Jewish state. This preference is compatible with the Jews' similar position concerning the role of the state in conflicts between its citizens, taking into account their particular national and ethnic affiliation. They believe that the state should give preference to Jews over its Arab citizens. Most of the Jews (about three-quarters) support the fact that the state is an agent that intervenes on the side of the Jews. This majority believes that the state should prefer the Jews to a great extent or to some extent over the Palestinian Arabs.

With regard to symbols and the Jewish hegemony over them, most Jews are unwilling to make any change in order to include the Arabs and give them representation on the symbolic level. A vast majority (91.1 per cent in the 1980 survey and 85.6 per cent in the 1995 survey) is opposed to any change in the symbols of the state, such as the flag and anthem, to enable the Arabs to identify with and be included in them. These are Jewish symbols and derive from the Jewish heritage; the Jews in Israel consider them to be their own and are not willing to allow the Arabs a hand in shaping them.

A large percentage of Jews do not favour institutional integration of the Arabs and support the continuation of exclusive Jewish control. In the 1995 survey, a significant proportion of the Jews (40.5 per cent) were opposed to the inclusion of Arab political parties in a parliamentary coalition with equal status and full responsibility for public policy; another large group (38.6 per cent) would accept the inclusion of the Arab parties in a coalition, but only under certain conditions. Almost a third of the Jews (32.2 per cent in 1995) believe that only Jews should be employed in government ministries; 27 per cent believe that Jews and Arabs should be hired, but with preference for Jews. Only 21.8 per cent believe that Jews and Arabs should be hired on an equal footing; 19 per cent support employing Jews and Arabs in the civil service in proportion to their share in the general population.

According to the 1995 survey, many Jews support outlawing some Arab political parties and movements and forbidding others to be elected to the Knesset. Almost half the Jews (45.6 per cent) support outlawing the Communist Party; only a quarter (25.3 per cent) opposes this (the others have reservations on the subject). This is despite the fact that the Communist Party is a combined Jewish and Arab party known for its moderate positions, although most of its electorate is Arab. A majority of the Jews (72.2 per cent) do not agree or tend not to agree that the Islamic Movement in Israel, which represents a significant sector of the Arabs in the country, be allowed to contest Knesset elections. In addition, a significant number of Jews (30.9 per cent) believe that Arabs should not even be allowed to vote in Knesset elections. All in all it can be argued that a majority of the Jews are not happy with the fact that 'Arab' parties that represent Arab interests participate in

Knesset elections. Broad sectors of the Jewish population seem to believe that the Knesset is an institution that should include only Jewish parties that represent Jewish interests.

Social segregation of Jews and Arabs as part of the structural separation that distances Jews from Arabs and makes it possible to direct benefits to the Jewish citizens is part of the ethnic policy. This policy is supported by a broad segment of the Jewish population. On the social-structural level a significant percentage of the Jews are not willing to work under an Arab superior. If we add to this those Jews who prefer to have a Jewish supervisor we find that there is a Jewish majority that at least prefers to work under a Jew and not an Arab. This same attitude and preference applies also to living in separate neighbourhoods or a mixed neighbourhood.

TABLE 5.5 (JEWISH SAMPLE ONLY)
Are you willing to work under an Arab boss?

	1980	1985	1988	1995
Absolutely	9.2	8.9	7.5	11.0
Yes	24.1	22.9	17.8	19.6
Yes, but I prefer a Jew	23.3	20.8	19.6	25.6
No	43.4	47.4	55.1	43.8

TABLE 5.6 (JEWISH SAMPLE ONLY)
Are you willing to live in a mixed neighbourhood of Jews and Arabs?

	1980	1985	1995
Absolutely	7.1	7.2	7.1
Yes	16.0	17.4	13.2
Yes, but I prefer Jews	22.3	21.6	23.4
No	54.6	53.7	56.4

From a cultural perspective, a large percentage of the Jews wish to preserve the supremacy of Hebrew culture and language and are not willing to include Arab culture and language in the moulding of Israeli culture or to participate in a cultural amalgam with the Arabs. A significant percentage (30.1 per cent in the 1995 survey) believe that Arab culture should not be treated as an important part of the national culture in Israel; 39.7 per cent have reservations about treating Arab culture as an important part of the national culture. A solid majority (59.9 per cent) are opposed to the playing of Arab songs on Hebrew radio broadcasts; 70.7 per cent believe that there should be no legal requirement for the names of streets and localities to appear in Arabic as well as in Hebrew, even though Arabic is by law an official language of the country. Some 48.6 per cent are opposed to or tend to oppose the possibility that Jews and Arabs in Israel create shared values and customs.

Recently a number of Jewish politicians have rejected the equal participation of Arabs in Israel in democratic decisions such as a referendum about an Israeli withdrawal from the Golan Heights, the West Bank and Gaza District, and even East Jerusalem. These views are accepted as legitimate among the Jews. According to the 1995 survey, a majority of the Jews (59.9 per cent) agree that a Jewish majority should be required in decisions about the future of the Golan and the West Bank and Gaza District; that is, in such decisions the views of the Palestinian–Arab citizens, who are considered to be automatically willing to hand over these territories to Syria and the Palestinians, should not be counted.

The ethnic character of the state is supported by a high proportion of the Jews. They want to preserve the situation in which the Arabs are excluded from all consideration. A majority of the Jews do not include the Arabs in their definition of 'Israeli'; according to the 1995 survey, 51.7 per cent of the Jews believe that the adjective 'Israeli' applies only to Jews and not to Arabs. A significant percentage of them are not pleased with the very presence of the Arabs and expressed a position in favour of the state's looking for and using every opportunity to encourage Palestinian citizens to emigrate in order to reduce their number in the population. According to the 1995 survey, a majority of the Jews (53.1 per cent) agree to increased supervision of the Arabs in Israel; 39.4 per cent were in favour of the expropriation of Arab land within the Green Line for the needs of Jewish development.

TABLE 5.7 (JEWISH SAMPLE ONLY)

Do you think that the state should search for and exploit every opportunity to encourage Israeli Arabs to emigrate in order to reduce their number in the population?

	1980	1985	1988	1995
Yes	49.5	42.4	39.9	36.7
I have reservations	31.4	33.7	36.9	35.0
No	19.1	23.9	23.2	28.3

The Jews reject the possibility of the establishment of a democratic, egalitarian state in Israel. According to the 1995 survey, an overwhelming majority (91.1 per cent) do not agree that Israel should cease to be a Jewish Zionist state and be turned into a consociational democracy, in which the Jews and the Arabs would be recognized as equal national groups, be represented in proportion to their weight in the population and be equal partners in running the country. An even larger majority (95.5 per cent) is not willing for Israel to become a liberal democracy, to stop being a Jewish– Zionist state, to repeal its recognition of Jews and Arabs as separate groups, to permit them to compete freely, and to give those among them who so wish the right to live as neighbours and intermarry.

The Jews are satisfied with the ethnic state; they wish to perpetuate and even to reinforce it. According to the data presented here, the Jewish population supports an ethnic state and its policy toward the Palestinian–Arab citizens, who are in crisis as a result.[13] The findings surveyed above show that the post-Zionist era has yet to touch the Jewish population in everything connected with the status of the Palestinian minority in the state. It may well be that there is a willingness among the Jews to move toward the Palestinians in Israel on questions related to individual equality and localized improvements in various areas of life; on the other hand, the Jews are resolutely opposed to and adamant on matters associated with collective equality for the Palestinians in Israel and the nature and vocation of the state as a Jewish– Zionist state.

The Palestinians in Israel as an anti-Zionist group

In the context of the standard social-science analysis in Israel, scholars assume that the Palestinian minority in Israel has experienced an accelerated process of change, like other minority groups in democracies. The argument is that in the aftermath of the war in 1948 and the initial traumatic experience of the collapse of the Palestinians' social and political system, the Palestinian minority began to travel a normal path in all areas of its development. Hence I call the chief model in research about the development of the Palestinian citizens of Israel the 'normal development model'.

When it comes to relations with Israel as a state, the key assumption of the normal development model is that the Palestinians in Israel have come to accept their status as a national minority and seek to continue to live in Israel without demanding self-determination within the state and without cutting themselves off from it. What is more, many scholars assert that the Arabs recognize and accept the existing situation in which they are a minority in a Jewish state and are interested in improving their status as part of the existing Israeli context, even if this improvement cannot lead to full equality. The best expression of their acceptance of their status as a minority in the Jewish state, according to this model, may be the process of 'Israelization'. Smooha, for example, argues that they have developed a strong and stable Israeli identity in addition to their Palestinian identity. With regard to the process of Israelization, some scholars argue that the influence of Israeli society and the increasing interaction with Jewish society have caused the Palestinian minority to experience an accelerated process of modernization. This process leads to the gradual adoption of modern values and norms that are different from those prevalent in this community in the past, as well as from the accepted values in Arab society elsewhere in the Arab world. In a later article Smooha argues that the Palestinian Arab citizens of Israel are experiencing a process of Israelization that leads them to acquiesce in their status as a minority in the state of Israel and are also coming to terms with Zionism and with the Jewish–Zionist character of the state. In essence, Smooha argues that the Palestinians in Israel accept their inferior status in the Jewish–Zionist state, adapt to what the Jews are willing to give, and compromise on the question of fundamental rights that might come to expression in the achievement of full and genuine equality for the Palestinians in Israel.[14]

The data that I collected through a general survey about the political aspirations of the Palestinians in Israel contradicts these assumptions. According to this data, the Palestinians in Israel express a strong desire for equality with the Jewish majority, and a great support for anti-Zionist views and rejection of the state's Zionist character.[15]

The overwhelming majority of the Palestinians in Israel want full equality between the Jews and the Arab citizens of the country; while a small number choose 'almost full equality', only a negligible fraction would be happy with 'partial equality' or believe that 'equality is not necessary'. What is the substance of the equality that the Palestinians in Israel want to achieve? I shall attempt to answer this question below.

The Palestinians in Israel, as stated, want to achieve equality with the Jewish majority. For most of the respondents this must be full equality. In response to the question, 'how important is the achievement of full equality in the state for improving the collective situation of the Palestinians in Israel?', 93.8 per cent replied that it was 'very important' or 'important'. This equality was emphasized when we presented the panel with a variety of areas where there are disparities between Jews and Arabs in the country: public services, the allocation of resources, employment in the civil service, participation in government, and equality in determining the nature and objectives of the state (see Table 5.8).

TABLE 5.8 (ARAB SAMPLE ONLY)

What degree of equality do you think there should be between Jews and Arabs in Israel, in the following domains? (per cent)

	full equality	almost full equality	partial equality	equality is not necessary
Public services	85.5	10.8	2.8	0.9
Allocation of resources	80.3	14.7	3.9	1.1
Political representation	69.8	18.9	9.5	1.7
Civil service positions	76.1	16.2	6.2	1.5
Participation in government	66.5	20.4	11.9	1.2
Defining the nature of the state	60.8	24.3	12.2	2.6
Defining the objectives of the state	61.4	21.6	13.7	3.3

The Palestinians in Israel are not happy with their living conditions, and want the state to serve them on an equal footing with the Jews, allocate equal resources, provide equal public services, distribute civil service positions on a fair basis, permit them to participate fully in government and parliamentary coalitions, and give them an equal voice in defining the nature of the state and its objectives. In their eyes the state must serve all citizens equally. In essence they demand that the state be 'the state of its citizens' and not a state that favours one group of citizens (the Jews) at the expense of others. All of this is expressed in their demand to modify the character of the state.

Questions that relate directly to the state indicate that the Palestinians in Israel reject its Jewish–Zionist character, manifested in the clear preference given to Jews in all areas related to the state, its future, society, and citizens in general. The respondents are conscious of the fact that Israel serves primarily the Jews and not all its citizens; a majority (66.3 per cent) believe that 'the state of Israel, by its overt objectives and policy, manifests itself as only for the Jews'; only 33.7 per cent think that the overt objectives and policy of the state indicate that it is 'a state shared by its Jewish citizens and the Palestinians in Israel'.

In what way do the Palestinians want to revise the nature of the state? They believe that they should achieve equality, something they deem to be problematic and even impossible in an Israel that is a 'Jewish–Zionist state.' About half (48.2 per cent) think that 'Israel has no right to exist as a Jewish-Zionist state.' In response to another question, the vast majority (86.4 per cent) support the abolition of this character. In the eyes of most of them (58.6 per cent), the state has no right to intervene in order 'to preserve a Jewish majority'. This has a double implication. First, they do not believe that the state should intervene to preserve a Jewish majority in the state; that is, it should not encourage Jewish immigration. Among other things, this entails repeal of the Law of Return, which applies only to Jews, and an end to state activity in Israel and abroad that encourages Jewish immigration. Second, nothing should be done to impede or prevent a process whereby the Palestinian citizens of Israel, or any other group, could achieve a majority in the state; that is, the state should not be ethnic or an agency that intervenes in favour of one particular ethnic group among its citizens. In practice, this means the abolition of the ethnic–national character of the state and its conversion into a civil state with a liberal attitude toward citizenship and citizens. According to the survey data, a majority of the Palestinians in Israel (89.9 per cent) believe that it is important to alter the current nature of the state and adopt a different one. Their preferred definition is 'the state of its Arab and Jewish citizens' (66.5 per cent).

TABLE 5.9 (ARAB SAMPLE ONLY)
Israel should be: (per cent)

1.	Only the state of the Jewish people	2.6
2.	The state of the Jewish people and its Arab citizens in Israel	17.2
3.	The state of its Arab and Jewish citizens	66.5
4.	The state of its Arab citizens in Israel and of the Jews and the Palestinian people wherever they are	11.9
5.	Other	1.8

Conclusions: the post-Zionist debate and its significance for the Palestinians in Israel

The post-Zionist debate and the significance of its conclusions for Israeli society are extremely critical for all components of the Israeli entity and its place in the region. The assumption that Israeli Jewish society is gradually developing a post-Zionist identity and norms has major significance for the feasibility of Israel's integration into the Middle East and the Arab world as well as for future possibilities of a resolution of the Israeli–Palestinian conflict. Latent assumptions of the post-Zionist debate also have decisive

importance for internal Israeli issues of economics, politics, state–society relations, and so on. In particular, the debate is associated with the power relations
among the groups that make up the Jewish population as well as the relations
between this group, taken as a multi-part whole, and the Palestinians in
Israel.

One might expect the Israeli post-Zionist age to be accompanied by far-
reaching changes in the attitude of the Jewish majority and the state to the
Palestinian minority in Israel, leading them to be more tolerant and to
promote egalitarian policies *vis-à-vis* the Palestinian citizens. In this event, the
status and position of the Palestinians in Israeli society would change substantially; the state would be concerned with mechanisms of equality and
even affirmative action *vis-à-vis* the Palestinian minority; it would recognize,
in its own name and that of the Jewish majority, the historical injustice done
to the Palestinians and to those who remained within the boundaries of the
state after the 1948 war. The land that was unjustly expropriated would be
returned to its Palestinian residents; the situation of discrimination would be
wiped out and replaced by a policy of equality. A unifying Israeli identity
would be created. A liberal democratic or consociational regime would
replace the current ethnocracy.[16]

On the other side, one may assume that the Palestinians in Israel would
feel freer as citizens of the state of Israel. They would integrate into its
economic, social, and cultural processes in a normal fashion and not, as today,
in a crisis fashion.[17] The development of a shared Israeli identity would lead
to far-reaching changes in the components of identity among Palestinians in
Israel and in the meaning of these components.

The findings presented and analysed in this paper show clearly that the
Jews hold ethnocentric Zionist attitudes and reject any possibility of compromise concerning the nature of the state. There is no doubt that the mod-
ifications that ought to take place in their attitudes to the Palestinians in Israel
are not taking place. There are no signs in the field to indicate that the Jews
will be willing to modify these attitudes at any time in the near future. On
the other hand, the Palestinians in Israel maintain anti-Zionist positions that
reject the nature and objectives of Israel as expressed today by the official
policy, despite their acceptance of their Israeli citizenship.

Contrary to the expectations that might be derived from the post-Zionist
debate, these attitudes herald not acceptance and development of a shared
identity, but rather the emergence of severe and even violent confrontations
between the Jewish majority and the Palestinian minority, which will no
longer accept being discriminated against and which aspires to equality in the

state while developing methods for combating its Jewish–Zionist character and its expression toward them – discrimination.

NOTES

1. Arab and Palestinian scholars and biographers had documented and presented most of the findings of the 'new historians' long before the publication of the results of their researches.
2. As'ad Ghanem (1998) 'State and Minority in Israel: The Case of Ethnic State and the Predicament of Its Minority', in *Ethnic and Racial Studies*, vol. 21, no. 3, pp. 428–48; Nadim Rouhana and A. Ghanem (1998) 'The Crisis of Minorities in Ethnic State: The Case of the Palestinian Citizens in Israel', in *IJMES*, vol. 30, pp. 321–46.
3. Among the Arab citizens of Israel this approach is represented chiefly by the Sons of the Village Movement, a Marxist group that calls for the establishment of a secular democratic Palestinian state in the entire territory of mandatory Palestine. For many years this movement refused to cooperate with Zionist Jews, on the grounds that all Zionists are the same, engaged in the theft of Arab land, discriminating against Arabs, and despoiling them of their property in order to promote the Jews and the Jewish–Zionist character of the state.
4. Khalil Nakhleh (1978) 'Israel's Zionist Left and "The Day of the Land",' in *Journal of Palestine Studies*, vol. 7, no. 2, pp. 88–100; Khalil Nakhleh (1982) *The Two Galilees*, Arab World Issues Occasional Papers, no. 7, September.
5. Sammy Smooha (1992) *Arabs and Jews in Israel Vol.* 2, Boulder, Colo., and London, Westview.
6. Nakhleh (1978) 'Israel's Zionist Left'.
7. Ian Lustick (1980) *Arabs in the Jewish State: Israel's Control of a National Minority,* Austin, University of Texas Press.
8. Sammy Smooha (1989) 'A Typology of Jewish Orientations toward the Arab Minority in Israel', in *Asian and African Studies*, vol. 13, nos. 2–3, November, pp. 155–82.
9. Hanna Herzog (1990) 'The Right to be Included: Israeli Jewish–Arab Relations', Discussion Paper no. 3, Tel Aviv University, p. 90.
10. Many devices and means are used to recruit Jews to strengthen stable Zionist values, operating in many channels and planes, including propaganda before they reach the country, education in the formal and informal educational systems, the media and the regular daily preaching of Zionist values, preference for the Jews, the army as an agent of intentional socialization, separation of Jews and 'natives' in workplaces and residential areas, and the like.
11. Smooha (1989) 'A Typology'; (1992) *Arabs and Jews*; Herzog (1990) 'The Right to be Included'.
12. The data are drawn from public opinion surveys of representative samples of the Jewish and Arab-Palestinian populations of Israel, aged 18 and over. The interviews were conducted face to face using a closed questionnaire prepared for the study.

Year	Jewish sample	Arab sample
1980	1267	1140
1985	1205	1203
1988	1209	1200
1995	1200	1202

The surveys in 1980, 1985, and 1988 were conducted by Professor Sammy Smooha of the Department of Sociology and Anthropology at the University of Haifa. The 1995 survey was conducted by Professor Smooha and Dr As'ad Ghanem of the Department of Political Science of the University of Haifa. I would like to thank Professor Smooha for permitting me to make use of the data he collected.

13. See Rouhana and Ghanem (1998) 'The Crisis of Minorities'.

14. For more details on these issues see ibid., and Nadim Rouhana (1997) *Identities in Conflict: Arab Citizens in an Ethnic Jewish State*, New Haven, Yale University Press.

15. The statistical figures presented in the next paragraph were collected through a survey that I conducted as part of my doctoral dissertation at the University of Haifa, on 'Political Participation by the Arabs in Israel,' under the direction of Professor Gabriel Ben-Dor of the Department of Political Science, and Professor Majd al-Haj of the Department of Sociology. The representative countrywide sample encompassed 768 respondents selected randomly using the Kish method. The sampling error was 3–4 per cent.

16. On future possibilities for development of the regime in Israel, see Sara Ozacky-Lazar, As'ad Ghanem and Ilan Pappé (1999) 'Theoretical Options for the Future of the Arabs in Israel', Givaat Haviva, The Institute for Peace Research; As'ad Ghanem, Nadim Rouhana and Oren Yiftachel (1998) 'Questioning "Ethnic Democracy",' in *Israel Studies*, vol. 3, no. 2; Rouhana (1997) *Identities in Conflict*.

17. See Rouhana and Ghanem (1998) 'The Crisis of Minorities'.

6 ◎ From *Galut* to *T'futsoth*

Post-Zionism and the Dis><location of Jewish Diasporas*

Ephraim Nimni

No te gustan mucho mis ideas, esas ideas 'raras' que les meten a los muchachos en la cabeza en Humanidades, esas ideas que ni vos ni la parentela pueden concebir del todo, que te alejan del viejo y rancio sentido tribal, que te integran con los demás de una manera u otra, con los demás que según vos (y los tíos y las tías) deben permanecer aparte, mientras muchos, muchísimos de ellos (de los demás) piensan que somos nosotros los que debemos permanecer aparte. Esas ideas que te hacen comprender que si Israel arrasa una escuela en Egipto o una aldea entera en el Líbano es un pueblo agresor, pero que no podes manifestar a la hora de comer porque nunca falta una tía que te diga dignamente, despectivamente y ominosamente: *Di Vist an idischer anti semit.*[1]

Eduardo Guidiño Kieffer, *Carta Abierta a Buenos Aires Violento*, Emecé Editores, Buenos Aires, 1970, p. 132

For the last 35 years, Jewish diasporas lived under the firm hegemony of the narrative of Zionism. This narrative continuously reaffirms the centrality of the State of Israel for Jewish diasporic life and politically subordinates the interests and security of Jewish communities to those of the State of Israel. Given the wide acceptance of this narrative, it comes as no surprise that the post-Zionist debate in Israel is generating a very apprehensive reaction in large sections of organised Jewish communities outside Israel. For if the post-Zionist project proposes the upgrading of the status of non-Jewish citizens in Israel and the downgrading of the status of non-Israeli Jews,[2] then mainstream 'organised' Jews[3] outside Israel invariably see in the post-Zionist project a serious danger to the hegemonic narrative through which their collective identity is expressed. For at least two generations, mainstream diaspora Jews have generally accepted Israel-centred versions of the Zionist discourse, which invariably sees the state of Israel as a key player of Jewish life and, furthermore, sees diaspora Jews as instruments or assistants in the achievement of Zionist goals and Israel's strategic interests. Those Jewish communities and individuals that have accepted the logic of this hegemonic discourse are bound to feel disappointed or have their Jewish identities dislocated by demands to make the state of Israel a state of its citizens. This disappointment notwithstanding, I shall try to argue here that this diasporic dislocation will have a beneficial effect on the ethos, identity, and lifestyle of Jewish communities in the diaspora. Instead of devoting precious energies and resources to supporting the Israeli government of the day in its conflict with the Palestinian people – a faraway conflict, not connected to their immediate circumstances, Jewish communities could instead concentrate their efforts on building vibrant diaspora Jewish institutions and make a decisive contribution to the institutionalisation of multiculturalism, a condition *sine qua non* for Jewish diasporic survival and continuity. It will be a mistake to believe that this shift in priorities is unprecedented. As a noted contemporary critic of post-Zionism reluctantly admits, it is hardly remembered today that the idea of a Jewish nation-state was, in the not too distant past, opposed by the majority of Jewish intellectuals and civic leaders in the diaspora precisely because such an idea threatened, in their view, the continuity and well-being of Jewish diasporic life.[4]

The decline of what was, up to now, the hegemonic Zionist narrative will have a dislocating effect on contemporary secular Jewish identities in the diaspora.[5] If the Israeli State was to dilute or remove the Law of Return from the centre of its political imaginary and downplay the position of diaspora Jews in the symbols of the state, it would come as a shock to many secular diaspora Jews, as they believe that they play a key role in the survival of the State of Israel.[6] Under these circumstances, diaspora Jewish communities will have to rethink and reassess the status of the State of Israel in their dislocated identities. However, this dislocation, far from destroying the fabric of diasporic Jewish culture, will, on the contrary, cement and strengthen it. Continuous over-identification with and, in many cases, subservience to the State of Israel's realpolitik has considerably weakened the vitality and autonomy of Jewish diasporic life. Even if political Zionism made repeated and far reaching pragmatic concessions to Jewish diasporic demands,[7] mainly as a result of pressure from organised Jews in the USA, the aim of political Zionism was and is to supersede and make obsolete Jewish life in the diaspora by 'ingathering the exiles' (Hebrew *kibbutz galuiot*). To understand the dynamics of this complex and contradictory relation, it is necessary briefly to evaluate the impact of political Zionism on the identity of Jews in Western liberal democracies.

Zionism and diaspora Jews

The term 'Zionism' has several different and sometimes confusing meanings, and some of these should be briefly surveyed. Zionism refers to several initially disparate political and cultural projects of Jewish national emancipation, and it is important to note that there are cultural–national projects for Jewish emancipation that are explicitly anti-Zionist.[8] These diverse Zionist projects are not only different, but appear to be opposed to each other. For example, Martin Buber, the pre-eminent twentieth-century Jewish philosopher, claimed to be a Zionist while he argued that:

> We describe our programme as that of a bi-national state – that is, we aim at a social structure of two peoples living together. The foundations of this structure cannot be the traditional ones of majority and minority, but must be different. We do not mean just any bi-national state, but this particular one, with its particular conditions, i.e., a bi-national state which embodies in its basic principles a *Magna Carta Reservationum*, the indispensable postulate to rescue the Jewish people. This is what we need and not a 'Jewish State'; for any national state in vast, hostile surroundings would mean pre-meditated national suicide.[9]

Likewise, the Jewish humanist philosopher and founder of the Hebrew University of Jerusalem, Judah Magnes, defended his version of Zionism when he argued in 1946 that:

> We oppose partition not only for the reasons that are usually given, but because partition is going to mean the intensification of chauvinism on both sides. When you draw these borders, when you draw these frontiers and have the Jewish schools on the one side of the line and the Arab schools on the other side, have you any idea what is going to be taught in them? Well, I have. There is going to be hatred by the Jews of the Arabs and hatred of the Jews by the Arabs.[10]

While the above may sound today extraordinary, visionary and bold, something that if genuinely implemented at the time would have saved thousands of lives, much Jewish and Palestinian pain, agony and destruction (not to mention that which is still to come), these statements were made before the creation of the Israeli state, when the Jewish population in Mandatory Palestine was a minority. The exponents of these ideas were a small group of isolated liberal intellectuals, important for their vision and academic achievements, but not for their contribution to Zionist thought. Contrary to Hazony's conspiratorial interpretation,[11] these liberal intellectuals had a negligible influence on the future development of the Zionist movement. A better-known and perhaps more influential argument is that of Asher Ginzberg, who, writing under the pen name of Ahad Ha'am, opposed the demand for mass emigration of Jews to Palestine and argued from what he believed was a Zionist perspective for the creation of a 'spiritual' Jewish centre in Palestine. Utilising rhetorical devices directly borrowed from the prevailing European anti-Semitic discourse of the period, he rebuked the Zionist leadership for their settlement policies in Palestine and for believing that the land was empty.[12]

While these and other less-known dissenting views within the Zionist movement questioned whether the aim of Zionism should be the creation of a Jewish nation-state in Palestine (and, in some cases, elsewhere), these views were ultimately defeated and consigned to oblivion by the triumph of the rhetoric and project of political Zionism, the idea that the aim of Zionism was to constitute a Jewish nation-state in Palestine to ingather the Jewish diaspora. Some historians of the Zionist movement (as well as some contemporary post-Zionist writers) attribute this success to the leadership of Chaim Weizmann and David Ben-Gurion. However, it is necessary to go beyond the circumstantial activities of leading personalities, and to understand that this success resulted from two interrelated factors. First, the model of the nation-state uniquely captured the imagination of most nationalist movements of the period, and Zionism was not an exception. In a world order that is so manifestly cruel to refugees and dispossessed cultural minorities, the goal of a separate nation-state is a seductive and devilish political inducement to those oppressed minorities who wish to protect their national or ethnic heritage, or have their voices heard in the international arena. Zionism, like other minority movements for emancipation through the creation of an ethnic state, fell into this trap, which usually ends up in a curious and indecent metamorphosis: casualties of ethnic persecution who seek emancipation are transformed into cruel oppressors.[13]

Second, as is the case in many other nationalist movements, the term 'Zionism' was an empty signifier,[14] having a plurality of meanings that inevitably resulted in internal struggles for hegemony, the aim of which was to capture and fix the meaning of Zionism. 'Political Zionism', the idea that the ultimate aim of the Zionist movement was to construct a nation-state in Palestine to ingather the Jewish diaspora, became the undisputed hegemonic force within the movement. Following the pattern of every successful hegemonic movement, political Zionism itself[15] became the movement, and the distinction between 'Zionism' and 'Political Zionism' ceased to have any meaning. Surplus meaning was expunged, and what was not, strictly speaking, political Zionism became an appendix of the Zionist discourse, or an historical curiosity devoid of contemporary political value. Consequently, for the period in which the Zionist movement made its most strident appeals to the Jewish diaspora, it was already consolidated as a movement that aimed to build and support a Jewish nation-state in Palestine and to empty the diaspora by mass Jewish migration to Palestine.

The success of political Zionism was due not only to its hegemonic appeal, but also to the circumstances of its birth. Zionism first emerged in Central Europe in the last quarter of the nineteenth century, when the idea of the nation-state was at its zenith and the rhetoric of enlightened rationalism was challenged by ideas of blood and belonging. It reflected the burgeoning disappointment with the ideals of enlightened liberalism, and appealed chiefly to assimilating Jewish intellectuals who felt betrayed by what seemed to them to be Europe's abandonment of ideas of equality regardless of ethnicity and religion. However, if the ideals of equality and fraternity were being questioned in this period, one important ingredient of the philosophy of the Enlightenment − its universalising certainties − was not. The young Zionist movement was seduced by the period's universalising rhetoric, and fell prey to universalising assertions based on painful conjunctural experiences. European modernity prepared the ground for a distinctive and unprecedented subjugation of minorities. The modern persecution of European Jews (and other territorially scattered minorities) resulted from the nationalisation of the state and the territorialisation of the nation, and was urged by the pivotal demand for congruent cultural and political boundaries.[16] Nation and state were made synonymous, and all citizens of the state were required to pledge loyalty to the official nation. Cultural diversity within the borders of the nation-state was viewed at best with suspicion and at worst as a form of subversion of the existing order. During the early days of the French Revolution, this idea was expressed by Count Clermont-Tonnerre to the French National Assembly: 'To the Jew as a man − everything; to Jews as a nation − nothing'. A century later, the compelling opinion of the period is clearly expressed in the famous dictum of John Stuart Mill: 'Free institutions are next to impossible in a country made up of different nationalities'.[17] European Jews, Roma (Gypsies) and Armenians were among the most territorially dispersed ethnic communities, and for this reason were deemed unsuited to constitute nation-states. It is then no coincidence that territorially scattered ethnic minorities were among the most persecuted in the Europe of nation-states. Adelbert von Chamisso wrote an influential Kafkaesque novel about a man

who lost his shadow.[18] This was taken to mean that a man without a nation
defies recognised categories and provokes revulsion.[19] Leon Pinsker, one of
the precursors of modern Zionist thought, took the argument one step
further by elevating this condition to the status of a perennial existential
malaise: 'Judeophobia', he says, is a perennial existential illness for which
there is no cure.[20] In this way, the modern persecution of European Jews,
one that resulted from the nationalisation of the European state and its
concomitant distrust of difference, was elevated by the foundational
ideologues of Zionism to the status of a transcendental, ahistorical existential condition.

Zionism and Jewish diasporic identity

The term 'Zionism' was first coined in the 1880s by Nathan Birnbaum in
Germany. The term 'anti-Semitism', perhaps not coincidentally, was coined
in the same country only a few years earlier.[21] At the threshold of the
twenty-first century, it is now clear that the plight and immense suffering of
European Jews in the period 1885–1945 were not, as Pinsker asserted, the
result of the incurable, intrinsic Judeophobia of European societies, but the
result of wider trends, the cause of which had little to do with Jews and
Judaism as such. In particular, the European nation-state model was, at best,
not well disposed to the recognition of ethnic diversity, and Jews, as the
quintessential European stateless minority, suffered the brunt of this
problem. In fact, the experience of the period 1946–2000 shows a very
different picture, for even if racism and xenophobia continue to ravage
European and North American liberal democracies, Jews are no longer their
prime targets. In fact, the favourable situation of North American and West
European Jewry has led to unprecedented levels of Jewish assimilation,
something that has moved some contemporary Zionists to assert that if the
trend continues, the continuity of Jewish existence is not at all assured.
Paraphrasing the founding father of political Zionism, Theodore Herzl,
some go as far as to say that 'lack of anti-Semitism' is more pernicious to
Jewish continuity than anti-Semitism itself.

When anti-Semitism is no longer a threat, assimilation becomes for
Zionists the main danger. In situations where there is no visible anti-
Semitism, Zionists search for it with a magnifying glass, for without anti-
Semitism, political Zionism loses its *raison d'être*. This must not be taken to
mean that the loss of Jewish identity is not a difficult and painful problem for
most Jews in liberal democracies. Assimilation and loss of Jewish identity is a

source of considerable anxiety and fear for many diaspora Jews regardless of what attitude they take in relation to Zionism, and the issue should be understood and debated. The manifestation of this anxiety is dramatically expressed in the cold calculations of statisticians and demographers. Sergio Della Pergola, a respected Jerusalem-based demographer, argues that at the beginning of the twenty-first century roughly 38 per cent of all Jews reside in Israel, where the growth rate of the Jewish population is 2 per cent per year. In contrast, he argues, the absolute numbers of diaspora Jews is declining at a rate of 0.3 per cent a year, mainly due to assimilation. Della Pergola concludes that in less than 30 years, if current trends continue, Israel will have the majority of the world's Jews without receiving a significant influx of Jewish immigrants. Della Pergola contends that the absolute numbers of Jews will soon begin to decline owing to assimilation in Western liberal democracies, while the sources of Jewish immigration into Israel are, at the threshold of the twenty-first century, more or less exhausted.[22] Since the collapse of the Soviet Union and the significant emigration of Jews from it, the overwhelming majority of diaspora Jews live in a few 'first world' liberal democracies (US, France, UK, Canada, Germany, Argentina, and Australia). After the massive emigration to Israel and the West, Della Pergola argues, there are more Jews in France than in the former territories of the Soviet Union, and that the Ukraine has one of the highest contemporary rates of Jewish assimilation.[23]

It is not unreasonable for secular diaspora Jews to wish to protect their heritage for the benefit of future generations. For them, Jewish continuity cannot be expected to be a matter of indifference. However, the Jewish predicament in liberal democracies is complex. One the one hand, Jewish communities are happy with individual freedoms and liberties, something unimaginable in the not too distant past. On the other, these very freedoms and liberties are decimating these communities through voluntary assimilation to the dominant society and culture. The problem is compounded by the liberal attitude towards minorities. Contemporary liberal democracies do not help or encourage the cultural preservation of the collective identity of ethnic and national minorities. In the words of Charles Taylor, they are often 'inhospitable to difference'.[24] Often in liberal democracies, voluntary assimilation conceals the considerable unfair advantages of the dominant culture, and in these circumstances diaspora Jews and other minority cultures are entitled to protection in what are de facto multi-nation states.[25] This argument also has implications for the Palestinian citizens of Israel in the post-Zionist project, and will be discussed below. Until the onset of the debate about multiculturalism, individual members of minorities were encouraged to assimilate to the dominant culture (the 'melting pot' theory) to enjoy the benefits and responsibilities of full equality. This view is vigorously challenged by contemporary advocates of multiculturalism, but so far with few tangible results, particularly in the area of collective minority rights.[26]

In following the cruel and despotic logic of a world of nation-states, political Zionism offers a seductive solution to the Jewish diaspora problem of assimilation through the success of its colonial enterprise in Mandatory Palestine and, later, in Israel: *nationalise Judaism*. As Yossi Beilin argues in support of Herzl, anti-Semitism protects Judaism. From the moment Jews are accepted as equals and anti-Semitism is rejected, the world opens a broad door for the assimilation of those Jews who do not live in a Jewish sovereign (national) community.[27] Territorial concentration in Israel is the answer to Jewish survival; at least it makes the Israeli state and its concomitant real-politik the centre of Jewish life. However, the overwhelming majority of diaspora Jews in liberal democracies rejected the invitation to migrate to Israel. Those who wanted to migrate did so unhindered; the vast majority who stayed in the liberal democratic diaspora did so of their own free will. In the call for the ingathering of diasporas, Zionism has proved to be an abject failure. What made the Jewish state in Palestine viable was not the unencumbered action of a handful of dedicated Western political Zionists to nationalise Judaism and ensure Jewish cultural survival, it was the Arab regimes' vindictive displacement of Arab Jews, who were totally outside the European problematic discussed above. But first and foremost, there was the urgent existential threat to physical survival of the displaced Jewish masses in Central and Eastern Europe before and after the Second World War. As Yossi Beilin candidly argues, if the gates of the US and other Western countries had remained open for Jews fleeing persecution throughout the twentieth century, the Zionist settlement in Palestine would have been a small episode.[28] Moreover, and in a remarkably candid statement for a former senior Israeli minister and leading Zionist politician, Beilin argues that the (Jewish) holocaust prevented most states opposing the creation of a Jewish state in Palestine. Moreover, Beilin argues that without the (Jewish) holocaust, the end of the British Mandate over Palestine would have heralded the creation of an Arab state with a Jewish minority, and most Jews would have left it for Europe or the United States.[29] This situation also has a contemporary complicating impact on the Israeli–Palestinian conflict: if the twentieth century's cruel persecution of European Jews influences Western attitudes to Zionism, then the Palestinians' clamour for justice is heard with difficulty. Palestinians not only suffer inhumane and unjust treatment, but as the 'Jews' Jews', their clamour is treated with suspicion by a guilt-ridden West.

From the perspective of diaspora Jews, particularly those living in the West, the Zionist discourse offered, for the first two decades of the State of Israel, an ambivalent, contradictory model. On the one hand, organised Jewish communities resented the doctrinaire Zionist demand for Jewish migration to Israel. The US and other Western countries were their homes, the place where they saw their social, economic and political future, the place where they wanted their offspring to put down roots while protecting and nourishing their Jewish culture. Liberal democracies treated them overall as equal individuals. They benefited from their equal status, and integrated into these societies as full and often loyal participants. This contradicted the gloomy, fatalistic predictions of anti-Semitism and persecution made by Zionist ideologues, and, before 1967, Western diaspora Jews resented Zionism for this. For diaspora Jews, Israel was, at best, one of the philanthropic causes they supported, and a place for the less fortunate destitute Jews of the world who do not share in the good fortune of their politically and economically wealthier Western brethren. Give money? Yes. Send your children or migrate? An emphatic no! Israel's status was similar to that of an asylum for the elderly and the indigent, which it is charitable to help, to which to send hard-luck cases, but towards which we show our constitutive difference by such very acts of charity.[30]

On the other hand, organised Western diaspora Jews feared for Jewish continuity. Thanks to all the available opportunities for integration and participation in liberal democracies, Jews integrated well, with opportunities and possibilities unimaginable to previous generations. However, this remarkable success was pushing their offspring away from Judaism. They were satisfied with their integration, but liberal democracy did not offer them an assurance, and in some cases the possibility, of Jewish continuity. The assimilatory pressures and fears of loss of heritage generated anxieties that tainted their satisfaction with their sense of equal participation and citizenship. To be sure, the problem is not specifically Jewish; it is the result of a significant deficiency in the modality of the liberal democratic nation-state, one that advocates democracy and individual equality with assimilation as a compensation for the loss of identity. Liberalism in Western nation-states puts minorities in an impossible and often cruel predicament, for it seeks to suppress minority identity and culture without violating individual rights.[31] Multiculturalism was not yet an option and even today, with the resurgence of the politics of difference, liberal democracies are still reluctant to accommodate fully minority demands for the institutional recognition of cultural diversity. It will be argued below, however, that the politics of difference offers diaspora Jewish communities a way of lessening their dependence on Zionism for the renewal of Jewish identity. The post-Zionist debate in Israel is an important catalyst for this. If post-Zionism is to have a beneficial effect in lessening the Jewish monopoly over the identity of the Israeli state and thus facilitatinge the integration of Palestinian citizens, it will also have an unsuspected beneficial effect on Jewish diaspora communities by dislocating their Israel-centred identities to recover a more autonomous and diaspora-centred identity which is more in tune with their lifestyles and immediate circumstances. There is nothing unprecedented here. Contemporary Judaism developed its characteristics in a diasporic situation, and Jewish territorial sovereignty handicaps Judaism's multifaceted character, which is unmistakably associated with its minority status and the creative tensions associated with it. The unexpected and unintended result of the Zionist project of nationalising and territorialising Judaism resulted in the creation of a different nation: the Israelis.

After 1948, Zionist discourse offered some certainty about continuity, so diaspora Jews reluctantly accepted some Zionist cultural artefacts. Their children visited Israel for short periods, hoping to return with an acceptable suitor that would ensure Jewish continuity for another generation. They remained, however, very wary of the Zionist grand scheme of things, and protected the autonomy of their respective communities. Zionism defeated the last bastion of diaspora resistance with a skilful manipulation of the events that surrounded the 1967 war. For weeks, the images beamed to the Jewish world were the spectre of a new Jewish holocaust,[32] perpetrated this time by Arabs aiming for a *Judenreines Palestina*. The argument was designed to strike a sensitive chord in diaspora Jews, skilfully using painful memories to overcome the last diasporic line of resistance to the Zionist project. The weapon was the manipulation of a hidden but very painful scar of persecution and destruction. By evoking memories of the Jewish holocaust, skilfully re-presented as something waiting to happen to Israel in 1967, Zionist discourse successfully bridged the gap between Israel as the object of diaspora charity and the separate proud sense of a lucky diasporic self. The image of a Jewish diasporic separate identity was erased. When the Jewish holocaust looms large, we are all in the same boat.

A masterstroke of Zionist propaganda was the images beamed on the eve of the Six-Day War. I vividly remember pictures of the most advanced tanks of the period advancing in an offensive formation, visibly showing a stylised Star of David, insignia of the *chail shirion*, the deadly mechanised corps of the Israel Defence Forces (IDF), but moving alongside an old pious Jew with a long white beard, robed in his prayer shawl, wearing his ritual phylacteries, and rhythmically leaning forward while reading devotions from his prayer book.

It was the utter incongruity of this image, the juxtaposition of opposites, that gave it its most powerful impact. For 23 years after the holocaust, the only similar images that diaspora Jews had seen of mechanised divisions next to pious Jews with yellow Stars of David, were images of the *Wehrmacht* or the *Waffen SS*. Now the awesome power of a mechanised army corps, the most vivid symbol of military might and modern warfare, previously associated with the Jews' deadly enemy, was paradoxically the axis of the military might of an army of Jews. The image conveyed with unique clarity the political Zionist message: we are a 'normalised' nation-state. In a cruel world of Gentiles, we collectively became Gentiles by mastering the offensive weapons of the Gentiles, and for this reason we will survive. In the slogan of the extreme right-wing terrorist wing of the Zionist movement, 'In blood and fire fell Judea and in blood and fire Judea shall arise!'[33] The message was carefully calculated to touch the raw nerves of the sons and daughters of Holocaust survivors, and it did. The quintessential image of the defenceless learned and spiritual Jew, which in the Zionist view epitomises the fundamental shortcomings of diaspora life and was the object of Zionist derision and revulsion, appeared shielded by the armour of Gentile Jews mastering the most awesome weapons systems that military technology of the period could provide. The Star of David was no longer 'the yellow star of shame' of those who, Zionists believed, were taken 'like sheep to the slaughterhouses', but the glorious emblem of the deadly weaponry of an elite mechanised army corps. The brute force that was then seen as antithetical to Jewish values became the very symbol of a revived Zionist version of Judaism that was by its own definition contrary to the spiritual values of diaspora life. In an era when a nation-state could not guarantee the viability of its minorities, Jewish spirituality and intellectual power were seen as hopeless and useless. Instead, the seduction of the opposite – physical strength, glossy armour and paraphernalia, military glory and awesome weapons systems – dramatically transformed diaspora Jews' perceptions of Jewish continuity.

The absurd power of this incongruity is thus revealed. If, as a minority, the Jewish generation that followed the Jewish holocaust carried the painful scar of feeling defenceless in the face of the deadly and arbitrary might of the idea of the nation-state taken to its ultimate conclusion, it was *only* a militarily powerful Jewish nation-state that could defend them from this. The price was simply the transformation of post-emancipation Jewish diasporic humane and spiritual values into their opposite. This was entirely predicted in 1938 by the most powerful Jewish mind of the twentieth century:

> I would much rather see reasonable agreement with the Arabs on the basis of living together than the creation of a Jewish State. ... my awareness of the essential nature of Judaism resists the idea of a Jewish State with borders, an army and a measure of temporal power, no matter how modest. I am afraid of the inner damage Judaism will suffer – especially from the development of narrow nationalism within our ranks.[34]

While Einstein's words may sound prophetic today, it is implausible to argue that Judaism has an 'essential nature', even if this is qualified by the author's subjective understanding. Our argument is not that Zionist zealots have defaced some 'essential' or 'genuine' Jewish diasporic humane values; most ethnic, religious or cultural groups cannot claim to have fixed, essential values, and certainly not a complex multifaceted group such as the Jewish people. Much in the same way as no ethnic group can claim a monopoly over suffering, no ethnic group can claim that humane values are peculiarly theirs. The argument here is that following Jewish emancipation in Europe, and as a result of the absorption of the main tenets of the philosophy of the Enlightenment into the newly emancipated Jewish culture, and considering the precarious position of non-territorial minorities in a world of nation-states, a new type of 'hybrid' Jewish diasporic culture emerged, which relied on the authority of universal values of freedom and dignity to guarantee its own survival (see below). The disenchantment with these ideas marks the origins of political Zionism, and it is no coincidence that political Zionism aimed at transforming these diasporic values into their opposite. Likewise, and for the same reasons, it is wrong to argue that pre-modern, Orthodox Judaism, as it is officially sanctioned by the Israeli state, is 'genuine' Judaism. The late Israel Shahak correctly showed, in an important book, the anti-democratic and racist character of versions of Orthodox Judaism supported by the Israeli state.[35] Shahak, however, weakened his argument by unwillingly accepting the underlying premises of the arguments he justifiably critiques. This is particularly so in his essentialised understanding of Judaism and in his refusal to consider that the discursive premises of democracy and human rights subvert and undermine the positions he is criticising. These democratic subversions facilitate the emergence of alternative forms of Judaism that are antithetical to the ideas he so vehemently denounces. For example, the proponents of the Jewish Enlightenment (*Haskalah*) attacked the rabbinical establishment fiercely, and some condemned orthodoxy as superstition and ignorance.[36] They were not less 'authentic' Jews because of this. In refusing to consider this option, Shahak paradoxically plays into the hands of his enemies, for they too – and, unfortunately, Shahak – assert the unpalatable interpretation that Orthodox Judaism is the 'genuine' one.

Whatever interpretation of Judaism was adopted in the relative success and tolerance of Western liberal democracies, Jewish anxiety was not for physical survival but for continuity. To the generation that followed the Jewish holocaust, Western liberal democracies offered great opportunities wrapped in the danger of loss of identity. Sorrowful memories of the Jewish holocaust fuelled many repressed anxieties and proved to be the Achilles' heel in the defences of diaspora pride and identity. This was finally understood by Zionists, who very rapidly consigned to oblivion their widespread disparaging remarks about lack of (non-Zionist) resistance during the holocaust,[37] and concentrated instead on a commonality of victimhood, in which the achievements of the Israeli state were the best possible insurance against any hypothetical future Jewish genocide. The trial of the war criminal Adolf Eichmann marked the beginning of this campaign.[38] The heroic Jewish rebellion of the Warsaw Ghetto was cleansed of non-Zionist protagonists, and Marek Edelman, the anti-Zionist Bundist deputy commander of the Jewish Fighting Organisation who led the surviving combatants to safety through the Warsaw sewerage system, was airbrushed from history because he remained in Poland and supported the rights of the Palestinians. On the commemoration of the fiftieth anniversary of the rebellion of the Ghetto in Warsaw, the then prime minister of Israel, Yitzhak Rabin, requested of Lech Walesa, the Polish prime minister, not to be made to share a platform with Edelman.[39] 'Never again' was the slogan, for which the subtext is 'never again because Israel will not permit it'. This has not impeded right-wing Israeli governments from turning a blind eye to the persecution and killing of Jews when it suited their realpolitik. For example, Israel could have saved many Jews from torture and death at the hands of Videla's military dictatorship in Argentina (which included in leading government positions many self-declared anti-Semites). Instead, the Israeli government pursued a multimillion-dollar arms deal with the military dictatorship, with which, according to former minister Yossi Sarid, it had a 'very close relationship'.[40] However, after the 1967 war a new ideological venture was consolidated. Norman Finkelstein calls it the 'holocaust industry', which was used to deflect criticism of Israel's inhumanity towards Palestinians and to disarticulate the last bastions of Jewish diaspora resistance to Zionism. Through its deployment, Finkelstein argues, a formidable military power with an abysmal human rights record has cast itself as the 'victim' state and managed to mobilise in its support US diaspora Jews, one of the most successful ethnic groups in that country.[41]

After 1967, when Israel occupied what remained of Palestine, and the last bastions of diasporic resistance to Zionism were finally defeated, political Zionism became the almost uncontested political project of organised diaspora Jewry. Fear for Jewish continuity in Western liberal democracies and fear of a new Jewish holocaust as portrayed by the 'holocaust industry' were the two significant ingredients in the Zionist triumph. In particular, support for Israel mutated from being a philanthropic activity to a transaction akin to an insurance policy. For diaspora Jews in liberal democracies, the possibility of a mishap (new holocaust) is a low risk, yet the impact of the continuous activities of the 'holocaust industry' impairs a balanced assessment of the risk. With the help of an inconsequential fringe group of Jewish holocaust deniers and racially motivated others, the scars of the painful experiences in the first part of the twentieth century are continuously reopened by the 'holocaust industry', not allowing the wound to heal with the passing of time.[42] Irrational fears of an implausible destruction of their own communities pushes many diaspora Jews in liberal democracies to believe that nourishing a strong Israel is in their own immediate interest. Here the post-Zionist project of downgrading the status of diaspora Jews in the State of Israel's imaginary sounds to them like an insurance company no longer interested in their policies. A more balanced discussion of the strengths and achievements of diaspora Jewry and of contemporary anti-Semitism is urgently required.

Diaspora Jews, particularly in the US, were led to believe for decades that their contributions were crucial to the well-being of Israel, but from the utterances of a younger generation of leaders they discover that their contributions are in fact insignificant. The two metaphoric images indicated by the Hebrew title of Beilin's book help to illustrate the point. The first is the aunt from Long Island who sends packages of food and clothing to her Israeli relative every month. But when told, after the 1967 war, that this was no longer required (West Bank and Gaza Palestinians have entered the Israeli labour force, making the country wealthier), she refuses to accept this and requests the parcel to be kept for her. The second is Beilin's own grandfather, a Zionist leader who died before Beilin was born, but who, the young Beilin was told by his parents, went to the US. The discovery by a disappointed young Beilin of the death of the Zionist leader from 'America' becomes a metaphor for the Israeli Zionist disappointment about the eagerly awaited Jews from 'America' who never came.[43] Beilin, as an ardent Zionist leader, sees the impending parting of ways between diaspora Jews and Israelis as a great danger. Unable to understand the resilience of Jewish diasporic existence and blinded by a Zionist myopic lens, Beilin considers that diaspora Jewry will be doomed if it parts ways with Israel, and develops an implausible master plan to prevent this from happening.

This parting of ways could be beneficial for both diaspora Jews and Israelis. Diaspora Jews will recover the autonomy and institutional plurality that was the hallmark of Jewish communities after emancipation. More importantly, they will be free to concentrate on issues that matter to them most – Jewish continuity and the strengthening of diaspora institutions. Likewise, Israelis could construct a civil society free from bigotry and ethnocentrism, one that promises the possibility of Palestinian integration. However, most post-Zionist writers concentrate on the specific Israeli problematic without noticing that post-Zionism also has something important to offer to diaspora Jews.

From a diaspora Jewish perspective, a new, post-Zionist, vibrant Jewish diaspora identity will allow diaspora Jews to extricate themselves from the Israeli–Palestinian conflict, a conflict that, by its distinctive characteristics, is alien to their own diasporic existence: they cannot resolve it, they have not caused it, and they find themselves increasingly dragged into it. More importantly, diaspora Jews could renew an unequivocal commitment of the humanist principles of the *Haskalah*, the Jewish enlightenment, this time benefiting from the advances of contemporary multiculturalism. Under these circumstances, diaspora Jews could confidently work with other ethnic and national minorities for a long overdue reform of the nation-state, a reform that would institutionalise multiculturalism and generate collective rights for themselves and other ethnic and cultural minorities.

Jewish emancipation and the transformation of the diaspora

In the present conditions of the Jewish diaspora, a credible post-Zionist alternative must address the issues that cause anxiety to secular diaspora Jews in liberal democracies, issues of Jewish diaspora continuity and anti-Semitism for which political Zionism puts forward seductive but ultimately unsatisfactory answers. These themes have been present in the West since the emancipation of the Jews, following the triumph of the philosophy of the Enlightenment and the ideals of the French Revolution. It is worthwhile for the purposes of our discussion briefly to survey these developments.

The origins of Western secular Judaism lay in the *Haskalah* (Hebrew for 'enlightenment') whose practitioners called themselves *maskil/maskilim* (enlightened). This eighteenth- and nineteenth-century movement attempted to reconcile Jewish culture and religious values with the tenets of the European philosophy of the Enlightenment. It also spearheaded a significant transformation of the meaning of the term 'Jewish diaspora'. The movement was influential in the West until the 1880s, the period that witnessed the emergence of Zionism. Moses Mendelsohn pioneered the movement in Germany; its goal was to interpret Judaism with a modernist rational discourse and oppose the irrational, mystical and isolationist tendencies of orthodox Judaism.[44] Mendelsohn was, enigmatically, an orthodox Jew, but this did not prevent him from confronting the dogmas of Jewish orthodoxy. The aim was to create a hybrid combination of Jewish cultural themes with a modern European rationalist method of argumentation. The appeal was to a reasoned exegesis of the Torah and to the rejection of blind dogma as expressed in the Talmud. The *maskilim* used biblical Hebrew as the Jewish language in direct opposition to the orthodox prohibition on the use of the sacred language for secular purposes. They tried to differentiate themselves from what they considered the 'backward' condition of the Jewish masses in Eastern Europe, for whom the vernacular language was Yiddish. The ghetto, the cultural milieu of the *Ostjude,* was considered primitive, superstitious and ignorant, to be soon superseded by the more educated and cultured modernising ethos of the modern *Haskalah.* In following the logic of the philosophy of the Enlightenment, the *maskilim* believed that they were riding on a wave of Jewish progress, and constructed a hierarchical evolutionary model that located the *Haskalah* at its pinnacle. The *maskilim* eliminated from Jewish ritual and custom practices that are incompatible with the tenets of modernity. In the reformed ritual, women were treated as equals, and services were simplified or adapted to Enlightenment themes. Passover began to signify a celebration of universal freedom, and not covering males' heads in rituals became both an act of integration into modern society and a defiance of Jewish orthodoxy. From here the reform movement in Judaism emerged, a movement that is bitterly opposed by orthodoxy to this day. For example, the principal source of friction between diaspora Jewry, which is overwhelmingly non-orthodox, and the official (orthodox) religious authorities in Israel is the status of reform and conservative rituals. The *Haskalah* movement also led to an important Jewish cultural renaissance, for it gave great impetus to a new form of Jewish secular philosophy, to various forms of Jewish artistic expression and to a prolific literature generally associated with the themes of modernity. The movement laid the foundation for the identity of the secular Western Jew, by democratising Jewish existence and asserting the newly created hybrid Jewish culture as a lasting component of the heritage of the Enlightenment.

One of the most important changes introduced by the ethos of the *Haskalah* was a significant transformation in the meaning of the concept of Jewish diaspora. The term 'diaspora'[45] (διασποραο) is of Greek origin, meaning a dispersion of minorities of the same ethnicity across several political boundaries.[46] The traditional Hebrew meaning, however, is different. In Jewish religious scripts and their exegesis, the term used is *Galut* or *Golah* (plural *Galuiot*) – exile.[47] This term has an intricate religious meaning and has been subjected to considerable commentary and exegesis. It expresses the condition of being uprooted from the homeland and subject to alien rule. It strongly suggests alienation, both in the etymological sense of being resident aliens, and in the sociological sense of estrangement from the surrounding society. Jewish prophecy has it that the diaspora (in the sense of *Galut*) is a punishment for the sins of the Jewish people, for which they will be apocalyptically redeemed at the end of the days (*achrit hayamim*). The Zionist movement, while secular in its origins, adopted this term to indicate the lack of authenticity of Jewish life in the diaspora and the validity of its ultimate goal of ingathering the diasporas/exiles (*Kibbutz Galuiot*). The *Haskalah*, however, took a different view. By advocating the emancipation and integration of Jews into the societies they lived in, they radically departed from the traditional meaning of *Golah*. First, there was a demystification of the holy land as an object of redemption.[48] Emancipated Jews were advised to regard the lands where they lived as their political homes, overcoming in this way any sense of alienation. Second, the nation-states where they lived and to which they proclaimed their loyalty with differing degrees of success, no longer entailed *Golah* (exile), but *T'futsoth* (dispersion), which is very close to the original meaning of the term 'diaspora'.[49] In Israeli Hebrew, Zionist references to the diaspora generally use the term *Golah*, and only recently has the term *T'futsoth* gained currency.[50] It is in the shift from *Golah* to *T'futsoth* that it was possible for emancipated Jews to find ways to integrate with the nation-states of residence and at the same time demand recognition for their specificity and way of life.

In the development of this hybrid enlightened Jewish identity, and in the rejection of the alienation of the pre-modern understanding of 'diaspora', the *Haskalah* paved the way for the integration of Jews into modern societies simultaneously as individuals and as collectivities. Individual integration met with varying degrees of success, depending on the country and period. The collective integration of Jews as a distinctive group faced severe obstacles in the Europe of nation-states.

Post-*Haskalah* diaspora Jewry and a post-Zionist Israel

One of the key slogans of the *Haskalah* movement was 'to be Jewish at home and a man outside'. The slogan shows the constitutive weakness of the argument. The two elements of the equation are separable only through a dogmatic application of cosmopolitan universalism, which, in the conditions of the nineteenth- and twentieth-century modern nation-state, was impossible. The concrete expression of 'the rights of man' was inevitably inserted into the premises of the dominant (national) culture of the state, and 'man' was not a universal abstraction but a concrete cultural creature within the parameters of the official ethnicity of the state. Joseph De Maistre, the conservative thinker and sharp critic of the philosophy of the Enlightenment, captures the argument nicely: 'During my life, I have seen Frenchmen, Italians, Russians, and so on; thanks to Montesquieu, I even know that one can be Persian; but I must say, as for man, I have never come across him anywhere; if he exists, he is completely unknown to me'.[51] In concrete terms, the philosophy of the Enlightenment posited abstract notions of cosmopolitan equality which, in the conditions of the recently democratised Western European nation-states, inevitably meant equality on the terms of the dominant or majority culture. In the demand for a monocultural nation-space as a condition for equality, the demand for sameness and equality were constructed as synonymous. While in pre-modern European societies the ethnic and national identity of the subjects was of little importance to the rulers, under the conditions of the recently universalised parochial equality of the European nation-state, there was relentless pressure on minorities to abandon minority cultures as the price for emancipation and civil rights. The period's enlightened alternative to De Maistre's unequal and privilege-ridden pluralism was the totalising and oppressive equality of Clermont-

Tonnerre. There was of course the road of secession and the constitution of a new nation-state. Many followed this route, which left territorially scattered minorities in an impossible situation. In a Europe of nation-states hurtfully insensitive to its own diversity, Zionism offered to Jews a seductive, but ultimately untenable, escape from the dilemma.

Mendelssohn's position was firmly anchored in the liberal tradition. He argued that the state as an instrument had no purchase on beliefs and opinions and, consequently, had no right to ask for changes in Judaism as the price for emancipation and civil rights.[52] This put Mendelssohn and the *maskilim* in an impossible dilemma. In a Europe dominated by the images and ideas expressed by Chamisso, Clermont-Tonnerre, Stuart Mill and Pinsker, the alternatives were assimilation or marginalisation, and neither was guaranteed, owing to recurrent bursts of anti-Semitism. The latter was the expedient conduit for every cause that attempted to undermine the liberal status quo, and the Dreyfus affair, so influential in Herzl's thought, was its exemplary occurrence. Therefore, as the Zionists predicted, many *maskilim* assimilated and abandoned Judaism, and others (a small minority) became Zionists. On this point, political Zionism correctly understood the logic of the monocultural European nation-state.

However, political Zionism had from the start an ambivalent attitude towards the *Haskalah*. It admired the secularisation and revival of the Hebrew language, which it considered an important ingredient in the nationalisation of Judaism, but scorned the *maskilim* for what it considered their naive, universalist and self-defeating position. The political Zionist critique was that the *Haskalah* set itself a contradictory and thus impossible task. On the one hand it sought the emancipation of Jews, meaning the recognition of individual Jews with rights and obligations universally endowed to each individual by the principles of the philosophy of the Enlightenment. On the other hand it recognised the impossibility of such emancipation without abandoning the collective attributes of the Jewish condition, the sense of a distinctive community with a minority culture that required recognition and protection. According to the Zionist diagnosis, the *maskil* would end up by assimilating to the majority culture, a move that, for many, would prove impossible because of the resurgence of anti-Semitism that this assimilation would provoke. In the Zionist perception, the *Haskalah* was aiming inexorably towards assimilation; this would be checked only by the revival of endemic European anti-Semitism. The seductive alternative that political Zionism offered – territorial concentration for collective emancipation (becoming a 'normal' people) – was in their view possible only with a Jewish nation-state in which Jews were the ethnic majority. It is here, however, in the proposed Zionist solution, that the contemporary fallacy of the argument is manifested.

During the period when the *Haskalah* was most active, in the eighteenth and nineteenth centuries, the European nation-state was, to put it mildly, not well disposed to the recognition of cultural diversity. The cruel dilemmas denounced by political Zionism were the immediate reality not only for Jews, but for other non-territorial minorities. In spite of these tangible limitations, however, many Jewish communities flourished in Western Europe and in Germany up to the holocaust. After the Second World War, the largest Jewish community in the world – in the US – as well as the British and French communities and other smaller communities in the Americas and Australia, did not experience the cyclical anti-Semitism ominously predicted by Zionists. Assimilation rates are high, but in most of those countries Jews are among the most successful ethnic minorities. Here Jews see the diaspora as their home and the Zionist equation of *Galut* with diaspora is firmly rejected by most organised Jewish communities in liberal democracies.[53]

Second, much in the same way as it fossilises anti-Semitism, the Zionist critique of the *Haskalah* fossilises the nineteen-century nation-state model, a characteristic that is also evident in Zionism's inability to stop seeing Israel as an ethnic state. The argument is easily disarmed by the transformations experienced by the Western European nation-state in the second part of the twentieth century. The European Union is a de facto multicultural and multilingual political framework in which the idea of ethnically based states has no place. If the idea of a state based on one ethnicity is perceived to be regressive and anachronistic, the argument has direct and immediate implications for the Jewish state; this gives considerable justification to the post-Zionist position that Israel should be a state of its citizens. Recent advances in multiculturalism as a critique of the monocultural nation-state provide an alternative, more viable model to the pessimistic Zionist prediction of Jewish alienation and perennial anti-Semitism.

Third, the Zionist ethnic nation-state argument is self defeating, for as the long history of the Israeli–Palestinian conflict shows, it is impossible surgically to isolate communities in ethnically cleansed territories; when this is attempted, the international community justifiably considers this a punishable war crime. The Pandora's box recently opened with the war crimes tribunal for the former Yugoslavia will eventually have major implications for Israel.

Fourth, the Zionist demands for territorial concentration were neither feasible nor desired by European Jews in nineteenth- and twentieth-century Europe. When European Jews were forced to migrate, except for a small minority of dedicated idealists, they preferred, if they had the choice, the United States or other Western liberal democracies to the uncertainties of mandatory Palestine, and even to the privileges of the State of Israel. The same applies to South African Jews abandoning South Africa. In the case of Soviet Jews during the cold war, 'Let my people go' was the slogan of the period, endorsed by Zionists and non-Zionists alike. The subtext for Zionists, however, was 'let my people go to Israel only'. In the unusual Soviet nationalities law, Jews, even if they suffered anti-Semitism and other disabilities, were a constituent nationality of the Union, a privilege not afforded in liberal democracies. Some Jews and Germans (the numbers varied according to international circumstances) were allowed to emigrate in what the Soviets called a 'family reunion scheme' to their 'homelands' (Israel and Germany respectively). After considerable humiliation and degrading treatment, the Jews who were allowed to leave were stripped of assets and Soviet citizenship and given exit visas to Israel. As there were no direct links between the Soviet Union and Israel, the stateless Jews were taken to Vienna, en route to Israel. In Vienna, the overwhelming majority expressed the desire to go the United States instead, taking advantage of the laws in force during the Reagan era, which automatically accepted as refugees escapees from 'behind the Iron Curtain'. (Similar laws exist today in relation to Cuba). World Zionist Organisation officials and envoys from Israel were astonished by this reaction, and the Israeli press took a very dim and derogatory view of these Jewish refugees, calling them *noshrim* (dropouts).[54] Israel made strong representations to have these Jews flown directly to Israel, where Israeli citizenship was to be bestowed upon them on arrival. In these circumstances, they were no longer stateless refugees, and therefore no longer qualified for asylum in the USA. There was also considerable official Zionist animosity towards the American Jewish Joint Distribution Committee (the 'Joint') for helping these stateless Jews to go from Vienna to the US. With the collapse of communism, preferential treatment by the US was abandoned, and post-Soviet Jews had their emigration choices restricted. From this time, they began to go to Israel.

Recent developments in multicultural theory and practice provide an alternative model to political Zionism, one that allows for a more feasible realisation of Jewish individual and collective emancipation as proposed by the *Haskalah*. Even before the idea of multiculturalism, some partial and tenuous recognition of minorities was afforded by the liberal democratic nation-state. The issue has however come to the fore with the current interest in the politics of recognition and with the demands for collective rights for national and ethnic minorities. In a multinational state that offers institutional safeguards for ethnic and national minorities, the position of the *maskil* is now plausible and coherent. Their individual and collective attributes are recognised and protected by the state without the need to build a nation-state in which they will be a majority. If the *Haskalah* model was severely undermined by the rigidities of the European nation-state model, a post-*Haskalah* project is eminently feasible in the era of multi-culturalism and multinational states, and consistent with the lifestyle and wishes of secular Jews in contemporary liberal democracies. We shall briefly examine how a post-*Haskalah* model will meet the two main Jewish diasporic existential anxieties: Jewish continuity and anti-Semitism.

The question of anti-Semitism has been extensively discussed above. The conclusion is that Jewish life in the second part of the twentieth century showed little empirical support for the political Zionist and 'holocaust industry' assertions about the ahistoricity of anti-Semitism. The contem-porary persistence of racism and bigotry, this time directed towards other groups, shows that the phenomenon is not exclusively directed to Jews, but is the result of more generalised trends that have little to do with Judaism. A recognition of the collective rights of minorities, conferring upon those minorities a legal corporate personality, and anti-vilification laws akin to existing individual defamation legislation, would help to create the secure environment that might alleviate persecution anxieties. In this, diaspora Jews have a common project with other ethnic and national minorities, and post-*Haskalah* Jewish communities will find a sense of mission and an imprint of their collective personality. This sense of mission is appealing and mobilising, for it relates to an immediate Jewish interest as well as having a wider application in favour of other minorities. Its implementation would involve considerable rethinking of the nation-state and the recognition of a minority institutional space in a multinational state, all of which is entirely congruent with the goals and aims of a post-*Haskalah* Jewry.[55]

The question of assimilation is more complex. Secular Jews have every right to worry about the continuation of Jewish society and culture in future generations. In multicultural societies, Jews and other ethnic minorities must have the right and opportunity to maintain and transmit their culture and way of life to future generations.[56] In liberal democracies, however, the rate of assimilation to the majority culture is high; this occurs chiefly through intermarriage. Voluntary assimilation cannot be prevented and should be respected: the individual right to exit an ethnic community cannot be compromised in any democracy, liberal or otherwise. However, except in societies where numbers are small, there is in nation-states a marked imbalance of opportunity arising from the imbalance of power between minorities and majorities. The majority culture, by the sheer weight of numbers, resources, enshrined state institutions and powerful mechanisms of social acceptance, has a distinct advantage over minority cultures in assimilating members. Moreover, the institutional and legal framework in most nation-states is not neutral but oriented to the goals and values of majority cultures. Jews and people from other ethnic minorities are compelled from early childhood to comprehend and manage their difference, something that is irrelevant to their majority-culture peers. Public holidays are biased towards the culture of the majority, and the exercise and participation in a minority culture requires some continuous individual effort and often inconvenience, while participation for members of the majority culture is effortless, unreflected upon, and a natural aspect of state life. This is why individual members of minorities who wish to have an easy life are well advised to assimilate to the majority culture. In these circumstances, to argue that assimilation is a purely individual affair is to unfairly promote, willingly or unwillingly, the ethos and values of majority cultures to the detriment of minority cultures.

If assimilation cannot be understood to be only a private individual affair, in multicultural, multi-nation states fairness to minority cultures must entail collective and distinct cultural rights, as well as the possibility of minority institutional organisation and representation in the apparatus of the state in ways that are not available to others.[57] Jewish communities must be able to enjoy collective representation and participation in state institutions and to accommodate members who marry outside the community without loss of status or community standing. Some reform Jewish communities do this and, in the spirit of the *Haskalah*, secular Jewish marriages will greatly facilitate this task. A higher public visibility of Jewish representative institutions, as well as securing a public space for minority cultures, is the goal of the politics of recognition, and this will ensure that assimilation is not a one-way affair. Majority cultures in liberal democracies can easily accommodate minority members who wish to assimilate to the majority; in much the same way, minority cultures, including Jews, must be able to accommodate members of the majority who wish to assimilate to the minority. They will have the institutional framework and the public profile to do so. This argument is not new in Jewish history. Similar arguments were advanced by the Jewish Socialist Party – the Bund – the historian Simon Dubnow, and the Jewish socialist thinker Chaim Zhitlowsky.[58] All three were, in different ways, products of the *Haskalah*. The general conceptual ideas were derived from the model for national-cultural autonomy developed by Bauer and Renner.[59] What is new is that, with the crisis of the nation-state and the liberal democratic retreat from the model of ethnically based states, the argument is now feasible in the light of recent developments in the politics of recognition and multicultural theory.

While the *Haskalah* project ran into difficulties in the quest for collective rights for Jews in the young ethnocentric nation-state liberal democracies, a post-*Haskalah* model that incorporates the ideas of the *Haskalah* adapted to the contemporary circumstances of multinational states, multiculturalism and the politics of recognition has not only a much better chance of succeeding, but is more realistically connected to the circumstances and lifestyle of diaspora Jews. After all, the model is much better suited to Jewish diasporic circumstances than is the protection of the Jewish diaspora by a remote Jewish state. As the post-Zionist debate in Israel acts as a catalyst for dislocating Jewish diaspora identities from the Israeli state, there is a considerable complementarity between Israeli post-Zionism and a diasporic post-*Haskalah* project. The parting of ways will be a significant advance for both diaspora secular Judaism and a less ethnocentric Israel.

One final argument remains for elucidation in the parting of the ways between Israelis and diaspora Jews. Is the identity of secular Israelis Jewish or Israeli?

Israel's diaspora, Jewish or Israeli?

A peculiar Israeli dimension undermines the postulates of political Zionism. For a movement that is riddled with paradoxes, one of the most glaring ones is that its ideology was soundly defeated by its resounding practical success. The unexpected, and perhaps unintended, result of the Zionist settlement and the creation of a Jewish state, was a remarkable process of ethnogenesis, a kind of ethnic engineering that has few parallels in contemporary nation-building. Israeli secular society, instead of becoming Jewish, became increasingly Israeli, with specific cultural and linguistic characteristics, mores and customs that are not shared with diaspora Jews. This is not to say that Israeli society is homogenous. Close to 20 per cent of Israeli citizens are Arabs, the original Palestinian inhabitants of the country, who remain alienated and institutionally discriminated against by the Jewish state. The remaining 80 per cent, Israeli Jews, constitute a diverse, multi-ethnic society culturally dominated by the Israeli core.[60] The vociferous minority of orthodox Jews should be excluded from this equation (surveys in Israel have consistently shown an inverse relation between religion and an Israeli identity). Likewise, a sizeable proportion of the more religious Jews from Sephardic and Arab backgrounds remain alienated from the mainstream after more than three generations. There is also the largest community of new arrivals, the Russian Jews, who show little signs of cultural integration. Yet the Ashkenazi substratum of earlier settlers, now several generations old, with the incorporation of a significant number of more secular Sephardic and Arab Jews, has, through the medium of Israeli Hebrew, constituted a new community of culture and destiny and, it is fair to say, a new ethnicity. This is not to say that Israeli society is homogeneous, nor that it should be homogeneous, but simply that the constitution of this Israeli ethnicity within its limited boundaries transcends the space of Zionist political engineering. The exhaustion of the elite that participated in its construction does not herald its demise as a cultural community.

Israeli Hebrew, through the influence of North American English, immigrant languages (mainly North African Berber and Arabic), but above all through the influence of colloquial Palestinian Arabic, has changed the original biblical Hebrew's grammar and syntax. This diglossic discrepancy between the written and colloquially spoken language is a good indicator of the process of ethnogenesis, the consolidation of a new ethnic group. A note of caution must be sounded, however, in relation to the in-between situation of what the Israeli establishment calls 'oriental communities' (*edot hamizrach*).[61]

The position of Jews from Arab and Sephardic backgrounds is complex and cannot be discussed here in detail. Statistically, this ethnically diverse group constitutes a slight overall majority of the total Jewish population. Most of them came in the early years of the state, from countries that were marginal to the European Zionist endeavour. Their presence, however, was vital to ensuring the demographic viability of the Jewish state. Their displacement from their home countries was the outcome of the process of decolonization and, to some degree, of vindictiveness towards local Jews for the Palestinian defeat of 1948. But they were not welcomed with open arms. The so called 'oriental' Jews (*mizrahim*) were not the immigrants preferred by the Ashkenazi Zionist elite, which was waiting in vain for the bulk of Western Jews to come. Their integration into Israeli society was dominated by patronising attitudes (such as sending them to peripheral areas and housing them in sub-standard accommodation), and ethnocentric and racist notions of enforced acculturation, demanding that they abandon their 'backward Levantine' and 'Arab' cultural markers. All of this has been amply document by Israeli social sciences.[62] This led to a legacy of alienation, bitterness and marginalisation, which lasts until today, three generations down the line. Even if some isolated individuals have been successful and upwardly mobile, this group continues to occupy relatively marginal positions in Israeli society. There is also among these communities a sense of loss of identity through their enforced acculturation. While a large group remains religious and insulated from existential doubt concerning identity, among the most secular, there is a perception that their identity is reluctantly and unfortunately Israeli. They resent the harm imposed upon them by growing up in a society that ridiculed their parents' culture, they resent the shame and humiliation inflicted on their parents and grandparents, but admit they lost the nexus to their parents' and grandparents' culture, and that there is no easy way back to it.[63]

Another demographic characteristic makes this community (religious and non-religious alike) more Israel-centred. While the majority of world Jews are Ashkenazi, a significant majority of Sephardic and Arab Jews reside in Israel, where they constitute a slight majority of all Jews living there. This leads us to another paradox of Zionism: the main target of the process of ingathering diasporas were Western Jews, among whom Sephardic Jews are a small minority. As Sephardic and Arab Jews have fewer ties with the diaspora, they are by necessity more Israel-oriented and depend upon institutional support from the Israeli government.

With the proviso that the relationship between the Ashkenazi Israeli elite and the Sephardic and Arab Jewish communities is complex and multi-faceted, it is still possible to identify a significant secular group that has, as a result of the process of aggressive acculturation, become an integral part of the new Israeli ethnicity. This group did not enter Israeli culture empty handed, however. In recent decades, it has made a decisive and original contribution to the Israeli cultural and artistic milieu, though the medium of Israeli Hebrew, in plays, popular music, comedy, poetry, and so on. To the horror of Ashkenazi supremacists and 'modernist' sociologists, this group stamped an unmistakable 'Levantine' imprint on contemporary Israeli culture, introducing a further element of differentiation from Western diaspora Jewish culture.

The idea of a *sui generis* Israeli ethnicity is not new and has accompanied the Zionist movement since its early settlement in Palestine (mainly through the notion of *shlilat hagolah* – negation of the diaspora). It was also the brainchild of a group of intellectuals and writers in the early years of the state and before. These intellectuals initially flirted with the proto-fascist ideas of the extreme right wing of the Zionist movement, including the *Brit Habyrionim*, and finally broke with Zionism by taking the idea of Hebrew singularity to a bizarre conclusion: Israelis are not Jews, but a new Hebrew nation destined to redeem all Semitic peoples in the Middle East. These people were derisorily called 'Canaanite'[64] by their opponents, a term that stuck curiously; it is how this movement was known thereafter. Some of its leaders were accomplished poets, sculptors, writers and academics, but it never made any serious inroads into Israeli politics, though its influence on the Israeli artistic scene was significant. A 'moderate' Caananite faction argued that 'Hebrews' are the descendants of Zionist settlers only, and that the Zionist settlement in Palestine generated two new nations: the Israeli Hebrews and the Palestinian Arabs. It called upon Israelis to share the land between these two national movements.[65] These ideas had an unmistakable influence on the Israeli peace movement.

Another dimension of Israeliness that allows for an identification of Israeli culture and a simultaneous comparison with Western diaspora Jewish culture is the position of Israeli émigrés in cities where there is a large concentration of diaspora Jews. From the early days of the Israeli state, there has been a significant emigration of Israelis, mainly to developed Western liberal democracies. While in some cases these were recent immigrants who decided to return home, and reintegrated with relative ease into their countries of origin, there is also a very significant emigration of native Israelis. In traditional Zionist discourse, these emigrants are called *yordim* (those who descend, the antonym of the Hebrew *olim*, those who ascend), in order to shame them. There is a large number of Israelis living abroad; some put the figure at about 20 per cent of the population. From several studies of Israeli migrants to the US[66] and Canada, as well as from my own circumstantial observation in London and Sydney, the conclusion is that Israeli emigrants behave like most other migrant minorities. They socialise mainly among themselves, language being a decisive barrier for interaction with others, and define their diasporic identity in terms of their country of origin.

Rina Cohen in Toronto has carried out a comprehensive study of Israelis abroad.[67] After analysing a significant number of case studies, Cohen's conclusions are strongly oriented towards the idea that Israeli migrants constitute a distinctive ethnic community. In Cohen's words, while 'remaining a marginal part of the general Jewish community, they have developed distinctive Israeli communal activities involving politics, recreation, culture, and entrepreneurship'.[68] The reason for this, she argues, is that there is a discrepancy between the ethnic identity of the veteran Jewish community and the ethnic identity of Israeli Canadians. They have even created an Israeli *shikun* (crowded tenement block), which leads to intensive interaction. Unable to fit into the established Jewish community, they have developed their own ethnic activities and institutions, from day-care centres to nightclubs, Cohen argues. While the local Jewish community defines itself (and is defined by others) in terms of religion, Israelis define themselves in terms of nationality and language.[69] One of Cohen's informants, an Israeli who lived in Toronto for more than twenty years, explains that she does not socialise much with Jews:

> It's another style of friendship. We don't have to phone two weeks in advance before we visit a friend. We just pop in or organise parties on the spur of the moment. … Most of the parties include Israelis. When Canadians are present we have to break teeth and speak English and when we slip into Hebrew, they'll remind us that we are too loud, or plain rude.[70]

Even if it would be fair to say that this experience is common to many Latin and Mediterranean people who live in an Anglo-Saxon society, when taken into consideration with the other elements discussed above, it clearly indicates a distinctive ethnic identity.

In conclusion, the existence of clear cultural and linguistic markers strongly suggests that secular Israelis constitute a separate national and ethnic community, which is in many ways significantly different from that of secular diaspora Jews. While religious Israelis may not fully share in this identity, and some recent arrivals may remain marginal to it, it is sufficiently inclusive to bring together the secular Ashkenazi elite with significant sections of the descendants of Sephardic and Arab Jews. The subject remains more or less taboo in Israel, because it undermines constitutive Zionist myths about the unity of the Jewish people. The post-Zionist debate is removing these barriers, uncovering the clear and unavoidable bifurcation between diaspora Jews and Israelis.

The argument also has considerable implications for the Palestinian minority of Israeli citizens. Even if a post-Zionist Israeli state were to remove all ethnic Jewish elements from its symbolic legal and political system, Israeli ethnicity will remain, as in liberal democratic nation-states, the official ethnicity of the state. While the disabilities suffered by Palestinian citizens will be of a different order, they will still be a national minority in an Israeli state. Here we return to the argument of Martin Buber in the 1940s quoted above, but this time in reverse! Without a *Magna Carta Reservationum* – that is, without providing full, collective differential rights for the Palestinian national minority – post-Zionism will not be able to bring about full equality of citizenship for them.

Conclusion: post-Zionism and post-*Haskalah* diaspora Jewry

The post-Zionist debate in Israel is a catalyst for two different but interrelated processes: the transformation of the old nation-state ethnic model to a more modern democratic state of citizens, and the dislocation of Jewish diasporas from being Israel-centred to being diaspora-centred. The Zionist project severely underestimates the resilience and vitality of the Jewish diaspora and fossilises a nineteenth-century model of the nation-state. The direction in the West is to remove the linkage between ethnic categories and the organisation of the state and, in some cases (the European Union), to weaken the idea of the nation-state altogether. Both tendencies discredit the idea of ethnic states and do not augur well for the Zionist model. The recent wars in former Yugoslavia show the heavy price paid when disaffected minorities wish to build ethnic states. The emergence of a distinct Israeli ethnicity further undermines the idea of a Jewish state and enlarges the gap between Israelis and diaspora Jews. The State of Israel as a state of its citizens will be in a much better position to resolve the perennial conflict with the Palestinians and will express more scrupulously its own ethnic composition.

The process will also be beneficial for diaspora Jews, for it will allow them the freedom to focus their identity and resources on the support and maintenance of their own diaspora culture and way of life. The dichotomy – either Zionism or Jewish assimilation – is disingenuous, as it ignores the vitality of Jewish diasporic life. Jewish diaspora continuity is assured not by a strong Israel, but by the development of strong multicultural institutions and by the transformation of liberal democracies into multinational states with collective rights for all ethnic minorities. A post-*Haskalah* emancipatory discourse, one that integrates into the ideas of the *Haskalah* recent advances in multiculturalism, will allow diaspora Jews to balance the protection and nourishment of their own ethnic identity and the necessary public and institutional recognition of Jewish specificity with their full integration as citizens in their states of residence. Strong Jewish institutions and a strong Jewish education supported by a multicultural state are the pillars of Jewish continuity. The recent momentous changes in the West promise to remove the obstacles faced by earlier versions of the *Haskalah*, and finally allow Jews to be both at once, concerned human beings and concerned Jews.

Zionism was the product of one of the most difficult, painful periods of Jewish history. It resulted from the unfortunate tragic circumstances of European Jewry in the nineteenth and the first half of the twentieth centuries. It dragged into its problematic Middle Eastern Jews who did not share those unfortunate circumstances. These circumstances, that were not of Jewish making, were dangerous, mean and inhospitable to Jews and other non-territorial minorities in Europe. They propelled many Jews towards a seductive nationalisation and territorialisation of Judaism. The success of the Zionist colonial enterprise in Mandatory Palestine did not result in the ingathering of the Western diaspora, but in the creation of a new ethnic division in Judaism, that of the Israeli Hebrews. While this was in many ways the unintended and unexpected result of the Zionist enterprise, it was in others its intended but unreflected consequence. The Zionist project of creating a new Jew through the medium of a language in which the vast majority of Jews are not fluent, and in Middle Eastern conditions very different from those of West, was bound to create in the long run a different ethnic group. Of course, the founding fathers of Zionism expected the vast majority of Jews to emigrate to Palestine, and later Israel, but as this did not happen, the parting of the ways is now, nearly six generations later, inevitable.

NOTES

* I wish to thank Gavin Kitching and Saul Newman for their very useful and constructive comments.

1. 'You do not like my ideas too much, those "strange" ideas that are put into the youngsters' heads in the humanities. Those ideas that neither you nor the relatives can fully take on board, that distance you from the old and decayed tribal sentiment, that integrate you with others in one form or another. With the others who, according to you (and the uncles and aunties), must remain apart, while many, a great many of them (of the others) think that it is us who must remain apart. Those ideas that lead you to believe that if Israel destroys a school in Egypt or a whole village in Lebanon it is an aggressive people. But that you cannot express during meal times because there is always an auntie that will tell you with dignity, disdain and in an ominous tone: *Di vist an indischer anti semit* [Yiddish in the original: You are a Jewish anti-Semite].' (My own translation from Spanish.)

2. Herbert C. Kelman (1998) *Israel in Transition from Zionism to Post-Zionism*, Annals, AAPSS, January, p. 49.

3. The term 'organised' Jews refers to those who are affiliated to Jewish organisations as distinct from those of Jewish background who affirm their Jewish identity but are not affiliated to Jewish organisations.

4. Yoram Hazony (2000) *The Jewish State, The Struggle for Israel's Soul*, New York, Basic

Books, p. xxviii. This book sustains the implausible argument that post-Zionism results from the machinations of a handful of academics in the 1950s and earlier at the Hebrew University in Jerusalem! The argument about the lack of Jewish support for the Zionist cause is developed from a different perspective in Thomas A. Kolsky (1990) *Jews Against Zionism, The American Council for Judaism, 1942–48*, Philadelphia, Temple University Press, p. 16.

5. This does not apply to Orthodox religious Jews whose identity is constructed through religious devices impervious to mundane concerns. However, Orthodox Jews are only a small minority of diaspora Jews.

6. The former Israeli minister and senior labour politician Yossi Beilin has disproved the mainstream diaspora Zionist organisations' argument that financial contributions of diaspora Jews have a decisive impact on the well-being of the State of Israel. Beilin argues that total Jewish contributions are less than 1 per cent of Israel's total budget. See Yossi Beilin (1999) *Moto shel hadod me'amerika, iehudim bameah ha-21* (The Death of the American Uncle, Jews in the 21st Century), Tel Aviv, Miskal, Yedioth Aharonot and Chemed Books. English translation: Yossi Beilin (2000) *His Brother's Keeper*, New York, Schoken Books. All references are to the Hebrew original because of the not uncommon tendency of contemporary Israeli leaders to modify arguments when translating into English.

7. For an interesting but somewhat exaggerated impact of the pragmatic changes made by the Zionist leadership in the wake of pressure from US Jewry see Charles Liebman (1997) *Pressure Without Sanctions*, New Jersey, Associated University Presses. See below for the differences between the terms 'diaspora' (Hebrew: *T'futsoth*) and 'exile' (Hebrew: *Golah*).

8. Among others, the Jewish anti-Zionist socialist organisation Bund in Russia, Poland and Lithuania proposed a programme on national–cultural autonomy modelled on the work of Bauer and Renner; see Otto Bauer (2000) *The Question of Nationalities and Social Democracy*, with an introduction by Ephraim Nimni, Minneapolis, University of Minnesota Press. On the fascinating history of the Bund, see Henry J. Tobias (1989) *Jewish Bund in Russia from Its Origins to 1905*, Stanford, Stanford University Press; Jack L. Jacobs (ed.) (2001) *Jewish Politics in Eastern Europe: The Bund at 100*, New York, New York University Press; and, from a non-socialist perspective, the influential Jewish historian Simon Dubnow proposed a similar programme for non-territorial national autonomy for Jews, devoid of the Bund's socialist connotations: see Simon Dubnow (1970) *Nationalism and History: essays on old and new Judaism*, New York, Atheneum.

9. Martin Buber (1947) 'The Bi-National Approach to Zionism,' in M. Buber, J.L. Magnes and E. Simon (eds) *Towards a Union in Palestine*, Jerusalem, Union Association, p. 10 (emphasis added).

10. Judah Magnes, 'A Solution Through Force?' in Buber, Magnes and Simon (eds) *Towards a Union*, p. 20.

11. Hazoni, *The Jewish State*, part III, pp. 157–264.

12. Ahad Ha'am (2000), 'Truth from the Land of Israel' [1891], trans. Alan Dowty, in *Israel Studies*, vol. 5, no. 2, Autumn, pp. 161–2. He writes: 'From abroad, we are accustomed to believe that Eretz Israel is presently almost totally desolate, an uncultivated desert, and that anyone wishing to buy land there can come and buy all he wants. But in truth it is not so. In the entire land, it is hard to find tillable land that is not already tilled… From abroad we are accustomed to believing that the Arabs are all desert savages, like donkeys, who neither see nor understand what goes on around them. But this is a big mistake. The Arab, like all (Semites) children of Shem [*sic*], has a sharp intellect and is very cunning. The cities of Syria and Eretz Israel are full of Arab merchants who also know how to exploit the public and to proceed furtively with all those with whom they deal, exactly as in Europe. The Arabs, and especially those in the cities, understand our deeds and our desires in Eretz Israel, but they

keep quiet and pretend not to understand, since they do not see our present activities as a threat to their future. ... However, if the time comes when the life of our people in Eretz Israel develops to the point of encroaching upon the native population, they will not easily yield their place.' Ahad Ha'am's criticisms of the Zionist leadership are also found in 'Lo zu Haderekh' (This is not the way).

13. For an interesting comparison between political Zionism and Serbian nationalism, see David MacDonald (1998) 'Political Zionism and the "Nebeski Narodniks": Towards an Understanding of the Serbian National Self', in *Slovo*, vol. 10, pp. 91–113. There are intriguing similarities between the Serbian image of Kosovo and the Zionist image of 'Judea' and 'Samaria' (West Bank).

14. D. Howarth, A. Norval and Y. Stavrakakis (2000) *Discourse Theory and Political Analysis*, Manchester, Manchester University Press, p. 8.

15. Ernesto Laclau and Chantal Mouffe (1985) *Hegemony and Socialist Strategy*, London, Verso, p. 69.

16. Ernest Gellner (1983) *Nations and Nationalism*, London, Blackwell, p. 1.

17. John Stuart Mill (1995) 'Of Nationality as connected with Representative Government', chapter 16 of *Considerations on Representative Government*, in Omar Dahbour and Michelime Ishay, *The Nationalism Reader*, Atlantic Highlands, NJ, Humanities Press, p. 99.

18. See A. von Chamisso, *Peter Schlemihl's Remarkable Story*, the story of a man who sells his shadow to the devil for a full wallet. This brings wealth to Peter Schlemihl, but his lack of a shadow brings him exclusion from society. The metaphor about Jews and other diaspora minorities is clear.

19. Gellner, *Nations and Nationalism*, p. 6.

20. Leon Pisker, in *Auto-Emancipation* (1882), argues: 'Judeophobia, together with other symbols, superstitions and idiosyncrasies, has acquired legitimacy of a phobia among all the peoples of the earth with whom the Jews had intercourse. Judeophobia is a variety of demonopathy with the distinction that it is not peculiar to particular races but is common to the whole of mankind, and that this ghost is not disembodied like other ghosts but partakes of flesh and blood, must endure pain inflicted by the fearful mob who imagines itself endangered. Judeophobia is a psychic aberration. As a psychic aberration it is hereditary, and as a disease transmitted for two thousand years it is incurable.' Source: *http://www.us-israel.org/jsource/Zionism/pinsker.html*, accessed 8 January 2002. This argument became, after 1967, one of the cornerstones of what Finkelstein calls 'The Holocaust Industry'. See footnote 41 below.

21. Nathan Birnbaum later reneged on the goals of political Zionism and aimed for Jewish autonomy instead. The term anti-Semitism was first coined by Wilhelm Marr in 1879 in Germany. He subsequently founded the League of anti-Semites (Antisemiten-Liga). See relevant entries in the *Encyclopaedia Judaica*.

22. *Ha'aretz*, 22 June 2000. While the numbers here must be treated with some caution as they side-track the unanswerable question of who is (and who is not) a Jew, they nevertheless reveal a trend that is important for our argument.

23. Ibid.

24. Charles Taylor (1994) 'The Politics of Recognition', in Amy Guttman (ed.) *Multiculturalism, Examining the Politics of Recognition*, Princeton, Princeton University Press, pp. 60–61.

25. For a discussion of these matters, see the thought-provoking work by Bhikhu Parekh (2000) *Rethinking Multiculturalism, Cultural Diversity and Political Theory*, London, Macmillan, p. 262.

26. This is an involved and complex debate, and cannot be entered into here. See Taylor, 'The Politics of Recognition'; E. Nimni (1999) 'Nationalist Multiculturalism in late Imperial

Austria as a Critique of Contemporary Liberalism, the case of Bauer and Renner', in the *Journal of Political Ideologies*, vol. 4, no. 3; Parekh, *Rethinking Multiculturalism*; Will Kymlicka (1995) *Multicultural Citizenship*, Oxford, Oxford University Press; Sasja Tempelman (1999) 'Constructions of Cultural Identity: Multiculturalism and Exclusion', in *Political Studies*, vol. 48, pp. 17–31.

27. Beilin, *Moto shel hadod*, p. 12.

28. Ibid., p. 43. What surprises and angers, in Beilin's book, is his lack of reference to Arab and Sephardic Jews, whose descendants are, after all, the majority of Israelis.

29. Ibid., p. 51. English translation, p. 23.

30. See the Blaustein–Ben-Gurion exchange, in which Jacob Blaustein, President of the American Jewish Committee in the 1950s, told the prime Minister of Israel, David Ben-Gurion, through the Israeli ambassador in the US, Eliyahu Elat, that Israel must not 'agitate among American Jews in the interests of a World Jewish Nationalist Philosophy' (Liebman, *Pressure without Sanctions*, p. 121). Ben-Gurion was forced to reply with what is an extra-ordinary statement for a fundamentalist Zionist Leader: 'The Jews of the United States, as a community and as individuals, have only one political attachment and that is to the USA. They owe no political allegiance to Israel' (Beilin, *Moto shel hadod*, p. 229; English transla-tion, p. 172). As Beilin argues, this exchange is inconceivable nowadays, when Zionist hegemony over organised US Jews is almost complete.

31. Will Kymlicka and Christine Straehle (1999) 'Cosmopolitanism, Nation-States and Minority Nationalism: A Critical Review of Recent Literature', in the *European Journal of Philosophy*, vol. 7, no. 1, April, p. 76; Tamir Yael (1995) *Liberal Nationalism*, Princeton, Princeton University Press.

32. The events and Zionist images projected around the 1967 war cannot be discussed here in detail.

33. 'Vedam vaesh yehuda nafal uvedam vaesh yehuda takum', slogan of Betar, the youth movement of the Herut party, a leading component of the contemporary Likud coalition, and the Herut-affiliated terrorist organisations Irgun Zva'i Le'umi, led by Menachem Begin, and Lochamei Herut Yisra'el, led by Yitzhak Shamir, both former Israeli prime ministers. The slogan originates from the anthem of the Brit Habiryonim (Union of Zealots [*sic*]) – which was the first terrorist movement in Palestine. Its leader, Abba Ahimeir, denounced democracy and parliamentarism and advocated corporatist politics. It fought against British rule, Communists, Arabs, the Zionist left, and reluctantly, the Nazis. In one of their publications they argued that apart from their anti-Semitism the Nazis had 'good ideas'. The group was suspected of assassinating Dr Hayim Arlosorov, a Labour Party and Jewish Agency leader. Professor Ben-Zion Netanyahu, the father of former prime minister Binyamin Netanyahu, was an activist in Brit Habiryonim. 'Biryonim' in contemporary Hebrew means thugs. See Mitchell Cohen (1987) *Zion and State*, Oxford, Blackwell, pp. 154, 172; Tom Segev (2000) *The Seventh Million*, New York, Holt & Company, p. 23.

34. Albert Einstein, quoted by Mordechai Richler (1996) *This Year in Jerusalem*, London, Vintage books, p. 1.

35. Israel Shahak (1994) *Jewish History, Jewish Religion, The Weight of Three Thousand Years*, London, Pluto Press.

36. Benjamin Beit-Hallahmi (1992) *Original Sins, Reflections on the History of Zionism and Israel*, London, Pluto Press, p. 22.

37. Idit Zertal summarises her unsettling account of Israeli testimonies on the Holocaust during the first years of the state in the following way: 'So effective and successful was the genera-tion-long prevailing Zionist concept and ideology of the "negation of the Diaspora", that few among the first Zionist envoys to the survivors could express genuine and generous

compassion towards the surviving ultimate victims of the Nazis ...'. Idit Zertal (1998) 'The Bearers and the Burdens: Holocaust Survivors in the Discourse of Zionism', in *Constellations*, vol. 5, no. 2, p. 284.

38. The argument was well understood in Hannah Arendt (1965) *Eichmann in Jerusalem*, New York, Viking; Segev, *The Seventh Million*, p. 358, presents the following account of Arendt's position: 'In her opinion, [Eichmann's] murder of Jews should have been termed a crime against humanity. ... The trial was only a medium, and Eichmann's role was simply to be there, in a glass booth; the real purpose of the trial was to give voice to the Jewish people, for whom Israel claimed to speak in the ideological spirit of Zionism. The state did not aspire to speak in the name of humanity: Israel, in fact, rejected efforts to categorize the Holocaust as a universal crime, seeing them as attempts to diminish the significance of the Final Solution and to deny the Jewish people's unique right to demand the support of other nations. Arendt couldn't accept that position ...'. In the following pages, Segev presents what he calls, with some justification, the 'hysteric' reactions in Israel to Arendt's critical stance.

39. Michael Warschawski (1995) 'Misappropriating the Mantle of the Slain', in *News From Within*, vol. 10, no. 6, June.

40. See Sarid's introduction to Marcel Zohar (1990) *Schlach et ami laazazel, begidah be kahol laban* (Let my people go to hell, treachery in blue and white), with an introduction by Yossi Sarid, Tel Aviv, Citrin, 1990. Zohar meticulously documents the cases of Argentinian Jews who were refused protection by Israel and were abandoned to torture and death in the hands of what Sarid calls the 'Nazi-style' dictators. Enigmatically, this important book has been translated neither into English nor into Spanish.

41. Norman G. Finkelstein (2000) *The Holocaust Industry: Reflections on the Exploitation of Jewish Suffering*, London and New York, Verso, p. 3. While Finkelstein advances an important and serious argument, the over-polemical style of the book, particularly the argument about abuse of compensation, unfortunately undermines its credibility. Finkelstein should have concentrated on the manipulation of the Jewish holocaust by political Zionism. What is paradoxical about this new 'Holocaust Industry' is that Zionists in mandatory Palestine and the early years of Israel, through the ideology of 'negation of the diaspora', often made offensive and disparaging remarks about holocaust Survivors. See Zertal, 'The Bearers and the Burdens', pp. 283–95.

42. The goal is not to forget the Jewish holocaust; on the contrary it must be remembered and taught as a powerful symbol of universal inhumanity. The argument here is simply to stop using it to instil fear for the future of the diaspora and as an argument for deflecting criticism of Israel's inhumane treatment of Palestinians. The US attitude to holocaust deniers exemplifies how liberal democracies show insensitivity to ethnic minorities. Jewish holocaust deniers defame, vilify and hurt Jews as a community, yet they are afforded the protection of freedom of speech.

43. Beilin, *Moto shel hadod*, chapter 3. See also the detailed roundtable on Yossi Beilin's *The Death of the American Uncle* in Israel Studies, vol. 5, no. 1, 2000.

44. Shahak, *Jewish History*, p. 32.

45. The term was traditionally used to refer to the classical deterritorialised minorities in Europe (Armenians, Jews, Roma and, to some extent, Greeks). Since the 1960s, there has been a phenomenal expansion in the use of the idea of diaspora to describe an array of ethnic and national minorities that traverse the homogeneity of the nation-state. See Kachig Tölöyan (1991) 'The Nation-State and its others', in *Diaspora*, no. 1, p. 4.

46. According to the Oxford English Dictionary, the term originates from the Septuagint, the Greek translation of the Bible, Deuteronomy xxviii,. v. 25: 'Thou shalt be a Diaspora (or

dispersion) in all kingdoms of the earth'. However, the Hebrew version, ('Devarim khaf chet, samach dalet', Deuteronomy xxviii, v. 64), states: 'V'hefitze'cha Adonai bkhol hamim mikze haharetz ve-ad kze haaretz' (you will be scattered among the nations, from one end of the Earth to the other). The Hebrew phrase is *v'hefitze'cha* (you will be scattered). The original term is therefore directly related to '*T'futsoth*' (dispersions), the modern Hebrew term for diaspora, and much less to *Galut* (exile). This last term is preferred by Zionist ideologues, because, unlike *T'futsoth*, it underpins the exile and alienation of Jews in the diaspora. For an interesting comment, see Michael Galchinsky (1998) 'Scattered Seeds', in D. Biale, M. Galchinsky and S. Heschel, *Insider/Outsider, American Jews and Multiculturalism*, Berkeley, University of California Press, p. 194.

47. For an interesting discussion of the term, see Jon Stratton (1997) '(Dis)placing the Jews: Historicizing the Idea of Diaspora', in *Diaspora*, vol. 6, no. 3, pp. 310–15.

48. Arnold M. Eisen (1986) *Galut*, Bloomington, Indiana University Press, p. 64.

49. A more contemporary example of this *Haskalah* rejection of the term '*Golah*' can be found in the Blaustein–Ben-Gurion exchange. Here Blaustein argued that 'American Jews vigorously repudiate any suggestion that they are in exile (*Golah*). American Jews ... are profoundly attached to America ... Under America's free institutions they and their children have achieved that sense of security unknown for long centuries'. See Beilin, *Moto shel hadod*, p. 126. English translation, p. 59.

50. Israeli Hebrew speakers are not always aware of the considerable conceptual difference between *Golah* and *T'futsoth*.

51. Joseph De Maistre (1974) 'Of the Divine Influence in Political Constitutions', chapter 6 of *Considerations on France*, trans. Richard A. Lebrun, Montreal, McGill–Queen's University Press.

52. David Sorkin (1999) 'Emancipation, Haskalah and Reform: The Contribution of Amos Funkestein', in *Jewish Social Studies*, vol. 6, no. 1, p. 101.

53. The Blaustein–Ben-Gurion exchange is ample evidence of this. For an extensive discussion of this debate see Liebman, *Pressure without Sanctions*, pp. 118–31; Charles Liebman (1974) 'Diaspora Influence on Israel: The Ben-Gurion–Blaustein Exchange', in *Jewish Social Studies*, vol. 36, nos. 3–4, pp. 271–80; Beilin, *Moto shel hadod*, Appendix A.

54. The issue is nicely explained by Professor Daniel J. Elazar: 'The Israeli position, fully supported by the Zionist movement, was that Jews who were permitted to leave the USSR because they requested to immigrate to Israel as part of the reunification of families scheme (the formal reason why the Soviets let them go) should be required to complete the journey. At the very least, if they drop out they should not be eligible for assistance from other Jewish sources. The Diaspora position, most prominent among the American Jewish leadership, was that the issue is one of rescuing Jews, which is a Jewish responsibility under any circumstances, and the destination of any Jews so rescued should be their personal choice.' Daniel J. Elazar, *Reinventing World Jewry: How to Design the World Jewish Polity*, The Jerusalem Center for Public Affairs (http://www.jcpa.org/dje/articles3/rwj6.htm).

55. For a stimulating discussion of the needs for collective rights for minorities, see Parekh, *Rethinking Multiculturalism*.

56. Ibid., p. 197.

57. Ibid., p. 262.

58. The Bund (*Algemeyner Yidisher Arbeter Bund in Lite, Poylin un Rusland* – General Jewish Workers' Union in Lithuania, Poland, and Russia) was an anti-Zionist socialist party that advocated national–cultural autonomy for Jews in the countries mentioned above. Simon Dubnow was a famous Jewish historian who also advocated national–cultural autonomy for Jews in the diaspora, but devoid of the socialist connotations of the Bund. Chaim

Zhitlowsky was a Russian social revolutionary theoretician and an advocate of Jewish autonomism, but, in contrast to the *Haskalah*, he was a strong defender of Yiddish as the Jewish language.

59. See Nimni, 'Nationalist Multiculturalism in Late Imperial Austria', pp. 289–314.

60. In a recent very provocative book, Baruch Kimmerling argues that the Ashkenazi-dominated set of alliances that kept the elite in power are reaching their political exhaustion. The '*Ahuselim*' (acronym for Ashkenazi, socialist, secular, established nationalists) is short-hand for the Israeli political elite. While Kimmerling's erudite discussion of Israeli society contains, as usual, many thought-provoking insights, the secular ethnocultural construct (*israeliut*) is more versatile and cannot be so neatly encapsulated. See Baruch Kimmerling (2001) *Ketz Shilton ha-Ahuselim*, ('The end of Ashkenazi Hegemony') Jerusalem, Keter.

61. The term '*edot hamizrach*' is used by mainstream Israeli sociology to refer to Jews of Sephardic and Arab background. The term is unsatisfactory as it is an unwarranted generalisation of what are diverse communities, and it has a pejorative geographical connotation (occident = good, orient = bad). I prefer to use the term 'Jews of Sephardic and Arab background'.

62. Sammy Smooha (1992) *Arabs and Jews in Israel*, Boulder, Colo., Westview Press; (1978) *Israel, pluralism and conflict*, London, Routledge and Kegan Paul; Shlomo Swirski (1989) *Lo nechshalim ela menuchshalim*, translated as *Israel, the Oriental Majority*, London and New York, Zed Books; Ella Shohat (1988) 'Sephardim in Israel: Zionism from the Standpoint of its Jewish Victims', in *Social Text*, nos. 19/20, to quote just a few.

63. See the moving accounts of this dilemma in Yosefa Loshintzky (1996) 'Authenticity in crisis: *Shur* and new Israeli forms of Ethnicity', in *Media, Culture & Society*, vol. 18, pp. 87–103; and Henriette Dahan-Kalev, chapter 8 in this volume.

64. There are a few writings in English about this movement. For a pro-Zionist, unsympathetic view, see Yaacov Shavit (1987) *The New Hebrew Nation, a Study in Israeli Heresy and Fantasy*, London, Frank Cass. The conclusion reluctantly admits the impact and influence of the 'post-Canaanite' argument (p. 153). A more balanced discussion can be found in James Diamond (1986) *Homeland or Holy Land: the Canaanite Critique of Israel*, Bloomington, Indiana University Press; L. Silberstein (1999) *The Post-Zionist Debates*, London, Routledge, pp. 67–88; Dan Laor (2000) 'American Literature and Israeli Culture: The Case of the Canaanites', in *Israel Studies*, vol. 5, no. 1, pp. 287–98.

65. Uri Avnery (1968) *Milchement Hayom Hashvii*, ('The Seventh Day War'), translated as *Israel Without Zionism*, London, MacMillan.

66. Steven Gold (1997) 'Transnationalism and Vocabularies of Motives in International Migration: The case of Israelis in the United States', in *Sociological Perspectives*, no. 40, pp. 408–37.

67. Rina Cohen (1999) 'From Ethnonational Enclave to Diasporic Community: The mainstreaming of Israeli Jewish Migrants in Toronto', in *Diaspora*, vol. 8, no. 2, pp. 121–36; Rina Cohen and Gerald Gold (1997) 'Constructing Ethnicity: Myth of Return and Modes of Exclusion among Israelis in Toronto', in *International Migration*, vol. 35, no. 3, pp. 373–92.

68. Cohen, 'From Ethnonational Enclave', p. 121.

69. Ibid., p. 123.

70. Ibid., p. 128.

7 ◎ Post-Zionist Discourse in Alternative Voices

A Feminist Perspective

Hanna Herzog

The post-Zionist perception has taken shape within public and academic discourse in Israel, touching and intermingling with post-modernist discourse. The term 'post-Zionism', like post-modernism, has been defined and applied in various ways. Both concepts are the subject of controversy as to their meaning, and therefore the terms should be regarded more as generic names for a variety of manifestations. It needs to be recognised, moreover, that these perceptions are changing and developing.[1]

Definitions of the various 'post-' theories (post-modernism, post-structuralism, and so on) by their opponents have long since become an inseparable part of the phenomena themselves. Among the definitions that have taken hold among the Israeli public and in academic discourse on post-Zionism is the one that identifies post-Zionism with anti-Zionism. The present chapter argues that this is but one of many possible positions in the discourse, and not necessarily the most fruitful for understanding Israeli reality. In this chapter I assume that, just as post-modernism does not signify the end of modernity, but subsists rather in various diagnoses of the developments that emerged from modernity and which include radical critiques of it, so too the term post-Zionism is to be understood in a similar way. Just as post-modernism is a quest for broad corrections within modernity, so post-Zionism is a search for a better society within Israel.

Analytically, it is very important to differentiate between post-Zionism as a social condition and post-Zionism as a political claim. Post-Zionism is first and foremost a social condition stemming from the realization of the central ideas of Zionism: the establishment of the Jewish state and, even more than that, a deepening awareness among all the peoples in the region that the state of Israel is a fact of life and not a passing phenomenon, as some of its opponents had hoped and some of its supporters had feared. Different groups experienced the state in different ways; for some it was an empowering situation, for others (like Arabs, *Mizrahim* and women) it became a subordinating, marginalising experience. The various diagnoses of the developments ensuing from the institutionalisation of the state and of Zionism are what constitute the discourse of which a part is called 'post-Zionism'. From a sociological point of view, one should bear in mind that the conditions for post-Zionism also led to the emergence of various neo-nationalist and neo-orthodox discourses. As a social condition, post-Zionism gave rise to a debate and struggle over the social definition of boundaries, and the significance of the collective and the state. The struggle is found within academic discourse in its various disciplines, in public discourse, and in what passes between them. Current Israeli feminist claims should be engaged with against the background of the post-Zionist situation, and as part of that discourse.

Post-Zionism as a political claim has adopted two central concepts from the post-modernist discourse: that of the end of grand narratives, and that of subversive logic. These two concepts have opened up a public space for various critical voices, including those of women. Even though these voices include anti-Zionist ones, there are also some that call for a different interpretation of Zionism. To these, women have added the feminist discourse or, more precisely, feminist discourses.

The central argument of my paper is that, in the course of confronting the dominant Zionist discourse, various views of women are making themselves heard. There is not just one feminine voice, and certainly no single organised body that represents all women. The voices emanate from the academic and public discourse alike, with a blurring of the boundary between the two. These voices challenge the dominant order, but at the same time they compete with and criticise one another. From a 'modernistic' perspective, the absence of political integration or mobilisation around a unifying identity adversely affects the ability to bring about social change. But I would suggest that the multiplicity of voices have a cumulative effect, which assaults the dominant agenda from various angles and eventually compels the creation of a new, diversified agenda. The new discourse criticises the different location of women in institutionalised Zionist society. While in Zionist discourse gender loyalties became subordinate to national loyalties, post-Zionist discourse makes claims for alternative politics and agendas. While the masculine discourse focuses upon the public sphere and matters of state, boundaries and identity, the post-

Zionist feminine discourse adds a discussion of everyday life. While the post-Zionist discourse does speak of a change in the place of the individual in relation to the collective, it is only feminine post-Zionist discourse that translates this demand into concrete language.

Zionism, post-Zionism, and modernity – several background comments

'Post-Zionism' cannot be understood as a social phenomenon and a social stance without taking note, at least roughly and generally, of the social, political, and cultural processes that led to the emergence and realisation of Zionism and of the problems created by that realisation.

As indicated earlier, post-Zionism must be examined as a growing, changing phenomenon, and the background to its emergence must be considered. I wish to argue that the solutions offered by Zionism for the problems of the Jewish collective in Europe in the age of modernity created a situation that, with time, became the problem of collective living in Israel, and thereby became the basis of the post-Zionist condition and thought.

Just as Zionism is part of modern existence and of modern discourse, so post-Zionism is part of post-modern reality, even if not all thinkers who speak in its name consider themselves active participants in post-modernist discourse.

Zionism was one of a number of solutions that arose during the second half of the nineteenth century in response to the existential problems that confronted Jewish communities in Europe, especially Central and Eastern Europe. Emancipation, democratisation, the accelerated development of capitalism, processes of secularisation within Jewish society and in the society around it – all these opened up new options that brought with them personal and collective dilemmas. Numerous solutions were propounded, among them socialism, communism, citizens of the Mosaic persuasion, assimilation, nationalism, and retrenchment within the world of religion (ultra-orthodoxy). Each of these solutions had its own social carriers. Most or all drew boundaries of belonging and meaning and defined themselves and their identity, while excluding 'others'.

Even the migration to Palestine (Eretz Israel) at the end of the nineteenth century was constructed in different ways. At the beginning of the 1880s, the number of those emigrating to Israel who defined themselves as Zionists was minuscule compared with the number drawn by religious motives. Ultra-orthodoxy deepened its roots in Eretz–Israel during the very years that the Zionist project began: both were responses to the existential conditions of the modern era.

Zionism – no matter whether one interprets it as a national movement, in the spirit of the Zionist discourse, or as a colonial movement – was part and parcel of the experience and discourse of the modern world. The state and nationalism are projects of modern times. The nation-state was perceived and represented as progress, as a solution to the communal, economic, and social problems of national groups. This was so for the Jewish State, and it is also how the Palestinian struggle, with its demand for the recognition of Palestinian rights to self-determination and statehood, should be understood.

The nation-state stands at the centre of Zionist activity. As noted, it was one of the options that were implemented in answer to the existential problems of European Jews, and this was undoubtedly the case after the holocaust. However, with the establishment of the state, that state itself became the existential problem for many other groups as well, both within it and around it. Therefore, a central concern of post-Zionist discourse is the state, its identity, its relations with its citizens, and its political, economic and social relations with other communities and states undergoing the globalisation process.

It should be noted that until the end of the 1960s the character of the state, and the Zionist perception put into practice within it, were dictated by the labour movement. When speaking of Zionist hegemony, the first meaning is the hegemony of the socialistic streams of Zionism. This fact is of great importance, since in the process of building up Zionist hegemony in its pragmatic–socialistic form, various nationalist Zionist groups were shunted to the sidelines along with non-Zionist groups. Collective goals and collective loyalty were emphasised and given primacy over the rights and welfare of the individual.

Among the more prominent groups for whom the process of building a nation and establishing a state created existential conditions of marginality and exclusion are, first and foremost, the Palestinians. But other groups were also relegated to the margins by the mechanism of Zionist hegemony. This was the fate of Jews originating in Arab countries (whose numbers grew significantly during the first decade of the state's existence), various right-wing groups, and religious Jews, especially the ultra-orthodox. The place of women was also determined by the rules of the dominant discourse. The post-Zionist discourse, then, has emerged from the confrontation with the hegemony. It questions the way in which various groups were pushed off the stage of history, but it is also mobilised to tell a different story, the story of the 'other'. The following analysis is an attempt to unveil the genderised character of Zionist discourse by means of a number of examples, of which the common denominator is their clash with that discourse, but which simultaneously lay the foundations for alternative discourses.

We too have a share in Zionist history

The end of the 1980s saw the beginnings of a process of revising Zionist history in an attempt to establish women as participants in the story of building the nation. While the dominant discourse had assumed a total identity between male actions and the process of nation-building, gender research turned its attention to the part played by women in that process. One of the most notable examples is the story of women's struggle for the right to vote.[2] In this new historiographic writing, women are represented as active partners in laying the foundations of Israeli democracy. But even more important is the uncovering of the mechanisms by which women were ousted from the dominant historiography, and the methods by which their voices were silenced.

The book *Pioneers and Homemakers,* edited by Bernstein,[3] is an example of the insertion of women into the history of nation-building. It includes articles that recount the roles of women in small towns, in kibbutzim, in urban collectives, in literature and in cultural creativity, in social and political initiatives, in the spheres of welfare, health and education. From this historiographical work, one learns not only that women were present at the same places as were the men, but also that they made unique contributions and had other avenues through which they experienced the process of nation-building. Even though some will argue, with considerable justification, that a study of this kind reproduces Zionist discourse,[4] one cannot ignore the subversive aspects, which challenge its dominance and contribute to the process of its breakdown.

The feminine experience of the *Yishuv* era ruptures the uniform collective voice. Feminine writing and poetry juxtapose the private and personal with the public and collective. The experiences of women that are brought to the surface by research and in various artistic expressions reveal difficulties ignored by the male narrative. They lay the foundations for exposing the myth of equality between the genders constructed by the Labour–Zionist hegemony.

Mothers of the nation

A large and growing number of studies adopt a critical approach to Zionist historiography in the spirit of Foucauldian critique. They argue that Zionism has created a regime of knowledge operating through the pastoral power of identification with the collective, and that this regime has produced the feminine Zionist subject, including women as the mothers of the nation, but at the same time shunting them off to the sidelines and denying them access to various positions of power. The foundations for these studies were laid by Nira Yuval-Davis, who preceded the post-Zionist era in Israel with a series of studies whose thrust is today being expanded and intensified. Growing up in *Matzpen*, the avowed Marxist, non-Zionist movement, Yuval-Davis indicated how the condition of women in Israel is a product of religious legislation that presumes and reproduces the women as bearers of the collective and its boundaries.[5]

A decade later, several studies criticise the way women have been incorporated into the nation. 'Imagining the nation as woman-mother in the establishing of the imagined nation conceals and covers up the fact that we are talking about arrangements between men – a totally male history', claims Orly Lubin.[6] According to her analysis, the nationalist discourse has allowed little space for women. Hever supports this claim through his analysis of the political process involved in the canonization of Hebrew literature.[7] The Hebrew literary canon constructed a normative national subject, identity and culture grounded in Zionist discourse by marginalising the 'others' and silencing them. This discourse is built on taken-for-granted assumptions of binaries, hierarchies and power relations constructed around gender differences.[8]

Even the first two laws that aimed to include women as equal citizens – the 1949 Defense Service Law and the 1951 Women's Equal Rights Law – were bounded by the perception of women as the mothers of the nation. In her analysis of these two laws, Berkovitch shows how the Jewish– Israeli woman is constructed first and foremost as mother and wife, and not as individual or citizen.[9] Motherhood is defined as a public role that carries national significance. It is via this notion of 'motherhood as a national mission' that women are incorporated into the collective.

The unveiling of the relations between national identity and gender led to studies dealing with the influence of the Israeli–Arab conflict upon the status of Jewish and Palestinian women in Israel. In the name of the conflict, the two communities are led to reinforce the distinctions between the private and the public, and the traditional division of roles between men and women.[10] The studies I refer to confront the world of men with that of women, calling attention to the similarity of the experiences of Jewish and Palestinian women. In other words, they point to existential problems created by the Zionist experience that are common to women and that cut across national boundaries. While the dominant discourse puts Jewish and Palestinian women on opposite sides of the barricades, gendered post-Zionist analysis sets them on the same side, opposite the men, and thereby suggests a different political agenda.

Women's positionings as subversive logic

Uncovering the mechanisms by which the feminine Zionist subject has been constituted has also paved the way for raising other voices. The common denominator of these voices has been the call to feminise political discourse.

Since the 1980s, there has been a growing use of the discourse of motherhood, mounted by women from both right and left wings as strategies for political participation.[11] The better-known examples are: *Mothers against Silence*, *Mothers for Withdrawal from Lebanon*, *Four Mothers* on the left, and *Women in Green* and *The Rachelim Women* on the right. Though opposed in their political views, both discourses challenge the dominant civic discourse, which is based on male rational discourse positioned in the public sphere. Excluded from the political sphere, women – from both left and right – used the family's centrality in national-Zionist discourse in a subversive way. They invoked the mother's voice, considered to be legitimate in the private sphere, in order to promote political messages. By using mothers' voices and motherhood practices in the public arena, women appropriated the men's dominance of political action. By subverting the characteristic of motherhood as an exclusively private voice, they blurred the distinction between the private and public spheres. In both cases, women who were excluded from politics became autonomous, independent political actors challenging the general rules of the game, and particularly those of their own communities.

Alongside motherhood as subversive logic stands the alternative feminist logic that refuses to see every woman as being a mother, either real or potential. For example, in their study of the protest vigils, 'Women in Black', Hellman and Rappaport found that the women emphasised that they were demonstrating as women, not as mothers.[12] In the mode of their protest, they constituted a symbolic new type of political woman. The struggle of the Women in Black for a place in the political realm was defined not in terms of their domestic identity, nor in terms of the male normative political definition of political activity, but rather in terms of who they were within the context of the event itself. Challenging and subverting the political and social categories which relegate women to marginality, they offered new ways to define women and politics.

State apparatuses as gendering apparatuses

Criticism of the army and of militarism is perhaps one of the more striking manifestations of post-Zionist reality. Within the Zionist discourse, the army has been a vehicle for the expression of identification with the Jewish collective and with the state. According to the Zionist ethos, army service accords the right of civil participation. This is also one of the bases for the rationale of recruiting Jewish women to the Israeli Defence Forces (IDF). Military service is constructed in terms of a community that both embodies and shapes 'Israeliness', and that mediates between the individual and the national society.[13] This constructed 'Israeliness' is based on male modes of behaviour, with masculinity as the normative subject. Not only is the military a deeply gendered institution but the IDF is also one of the most powerful apparatuses that gender the social order.[14]

Another state apparatus that has gained attention is that of the committees for terminating pregnancy, committees which have turned into educational bodies. By their attitude towards the women applying for approval of an abortion, they have become a force constituting the marginal Israeli woman, whose non-normative status is suited to her non-normative behaviour in the realms of sexuality, childbearing, and family relations. Through their work, the committees contribute to the constitution of the normative Israeli woman, who is, by contrast, married, responsible (uses contraceptives and does not become unintentionally pregnant), committed (accepts her pregnancy from the moment it exists, even if it was unintentional), and astute (capable of weighing prospects and dangers, does not let herself become pregnant as a result of 'problematic' relations – that is, outside marriage or at an unsuitable age).[15]

Other studies are concerned with the welfare state,[16] and with the institutions dealing with rape cases,[17] and so on. Even though treatments such as these take place within the general feminist discourse, their presence in the dialogue with the state in its present dominant Zionist form contributes to the diversification and gendering of post-Zionist criticisms.

Every woman has her own room and her own voice

Feminism's stance produces to a critique of the dominant male Zionist discourse, and seeks to re-examine national history and aspirations, focusing on controlling and oppressive relationships: as such, it is situated at the heart of post-Zionist discourse and is an integral part of it. By introducing the gendered dimension to analyses of the social order, it deepens criticism of the dominant social order.

Post-Zionist feminist discourse challenges the universalistic perception of woman, including the Zionist woman, and an effort is being made to uncover the various positionings of women and their interpretations of reality: *Mizrahi* women,[18] national religious,[19] ultra-orthodox,[20] secular, single-parent, lesbian,[21] poor, bourgeois, Palestinian,[22] and so forth. Moreover, much research work is being done on the processes of subordination and subjection of women to other women: Palestinian women to Jewish, *Mizrahi* women to Ashkenazi, immigrants to established veterans, the poor to the bourgeois, and so on.[23]

There is growing acceptance in academic and public discourse that, in Israeli society, deprivation and marginalisation on an ethnic and national basis are inseparable from the emergence of gendered identity.[24] Women react differently to the experience of war and occupation, as shown in studies of women settlers[25] and women peace activists.[26] However, women members of peace organisations who are drawn from different national, religious and ethnic backgrounds also experience and interpret the battle for peace differently.[27] Religious women do not constitute a single category, and they cope in different ways with the world of higher education, which is barred to them, as shown in research into *haredi* women[28] and Religious Zionist women.[29]

This short and superficial survey reveals an abundance of positions within the critical feminine discourse. Feminism in its first, liberal, stage was part of modernist discourse; it tried to establish a single category of women and to construct an imaginary feminine community with a common past and a common future. However, acceptance of post-modernism and the demand for reflexivity very quickly created a polyphonic discourse. In the Israeli context, the feminist confrontation with the dominant Zionist discourse has resulted in the dismantling of the category of 'feminist women' even before that category could become entrenched.

Not only do the voices that are heard challenge the dominant order, they simultaneously compete with and criticise one another. From a 'modernistic' point of view, there is therefore an absence of a mobilising and unifying power and of a common identity that would enable relating a common story in order to build a different future.

This dilemma is not just a theoretical issue, it has obvious political implications. Is there a shared basis for *Mizrahi*, Palestinian, and Ashkenazi women to act? Can poor women and rich women share common ground? What kind of politics can and should be conducted when not all women share the same characteristics, the same life experience, and the same objectives? Feminist attempts to answer these questions in theoretical and practical terms are nurturing post-Zionist feminist discourse, and propose a range of solutions and challenges to that discourse.

Post-Zionist discourse and gender relations

Most of the men who speak in post-Zionist discourse are part of academic institutions that are centres of power and which control learning. While they do indeed attack the academic establishment, if they were critical of themselves to the same extent that they criticise the ruling groups, they would discover that they too often apply the same means and mechanisms as the subject of their criticism. They build retinues, institutionalise schools of thought, and devote time and effort to self-canonisation. It is enough to read issue number 8 of *Theory and Criticism*,[30] which is devoted to the discourse of the new historians, as well as a number of articles published by academics in the daily press, in order to discover where the boundaries of post-Zionist discourse lie and who are recognised as its official spokespeople. Women are included in this discourse, as in the dominant discourse, in niches; that is, in special issues.[31] In his book on post-Zionist discourse, Silberstein[32] supports this trend of canonisation by locating the journal *Theory and Criticism* as the key site of current post-Zionist discourse, thus ignoring almost any other writing, mainly that of women.

As Silberstein rightly claims, there is no essential post-Zionism.[33] A growing number of scholars are writing in the critical spirit of post-Zionism and/or from a post-Zionist position, and there are many others who wrote in that spirit before the labelling of 'a school' emerged,[34] but many of them are not part of the emerging canon. Post-Zionist discourse is a hybrid phenomenon, nourished by different theoretical schools and various academic disciplines as well as by variegated public discourse. I wish to warn of the tendency to appropriate the exclusive right to be defined as 'post-' and as 'critical' on the part of a group whose members apparently read mostly what is written by other members of their own circle, to judge by their citations. If the struggles over post-Zionism are struggles for the control of cultural space and social inclusion, the social carriers of post-Zionist discourse should be sufficiently aware of the exclusionary work they may be performing in their own realm.

Post-Zionist discourse should learn a lesson from the feminist experience. Feminist discourse began by challenging the mainstream male-biased discourse: on its way to institutionalisation, the dominant feminist discourse was challenged by women of various ethnic, racial, national and class origins with a demand for reflexivity and inclusiveness. Israeli feminist discourse took the same path, and it is still open to such criticism. The *Mizrahi* and Palestinian feminists criticise the dominant discourse, with reason, for being elitist and Ashkenazi. In recent years, awareness has grown among female speakers concerning the female 'others', as can be learned from the feminist journal *Noga*, in the special issues devoted to gender in scientific journals such as *Zmanim* [Times] (which published an issue called *Zman-Nashim* [Women's Times] and from the two issues of *Israel Social Science Research*[35] devoted to women in Israel, and the text book, *Sex, Gender, Politics*.[36] Moreover, in post-Zionist feminist discourse, the boundary between academic and public discourse is deliberately blurred for ideological reasons. For example, in a book edited by Barbara Swirski and Marilyn Safir titled *Calling Equality's Bluff*,[37] chapters based upon research appear alongside personal testimonies that represent a broad spectrum of Jewish and Palestinian women's voices. This variety is also in evidence among women's organizations, especially women's peace organizations. At the end of 2001, the Annual Conference on Women and Gender Studies and Feminist Theories was held at Tel-Aviv University, in conjunction with the Israeli Forum for Feminist Studies and Gender Research. It aimed to bring together in a single framework as many varied feminist voices as possible. Moreover, the conference, which was titled 'War and Peace – Feminist Perspectives', served as a praiseworthy example of attempts to blur the boundaries between academic and public discourse. In the sessions, researchers presented their studies together with field activists who presented the experience they have gained in applied work. It was a riveting attempt to bring together research and practice, and social change theory with social change practice and involvement. However, just as feminist discourse still has a long way to go, so does post-Zionist discourse. As a hybrid phenomenon, post-Zionist discourse must by definition apply an all-inclusive, multicultural, and multi-voiced approach.

Post-Zionist society from a feminist perspective

The profusion of feminist voices has a cumulative effect which assails the dominant agenda from a variety of perspectives, and eventually makes inevitable the emergence of a new and varied agenda.[38] Although it is not unified and univocal, it does have a common denominator. This agenda would have gender relations at its centre; it would include the personal and the domestic and what lies between them.

The feminist perspective contains explicit alternative trajectories that are trying to define themselves as post-Zionist. However, many feminist endeavours are not necessarily driven by declared or intentional post-Zionist ideology. My central argument is that redefinitions of the worlds of political content and the changing forms of political action, as reflected in feminist discourse, are becoming pivotal motives in the civil-ising of Israeli society and in its breaking away from subordination to the state-national perception. By deconstructing gendered ethno-national structures and in demanding inclusive citizenship, such feminist voices find themselves at the heart of post-Zionist endeavours.

New Profile is an example of a movement with a feminist post-Zionist awareness that seeks to advance a civil agenda. It is a feminist movement whose members are women, men, and young people working together. The movement's objective is to transform Israeli society from a militaristic to a civil one. It strives to change the military thinking prevalent in Israeli society, which sets in motion one war after another. It aims to promote education towards building peace instead of militaristic education, to annul compulsory conscription, to acknowledge the right to be a conscientious objector, to end the occupation, and to facilitate and safeguard life in an egalitarian, humane society.

However, the civil agenda in Israel is informed by multiple feminist perspectives that challenge the dominant Zionist discourse from various sources. This agenda calls for a fresh perspective on politics and political struggle. According to this perspective the struggle for social change is not limited solely to the corridors of the Knesset, though this is an important arena. Politics, in this perspective, takes place in quotidian efforts, by challenging the predominant definition of power concomitantly with constantly revealing control and gendering principles. Waging battles against inequality in the educational domain, in the workplace, against domestic violence and sexual harassment, querying speech patterns used towards and about women, combating insensitive advertising, contributing to the debate over abortion, health policy, surrogate motherhood, the feminisation of poverty, sexual abuse, women's wages and family law, defining alternative options for family and sexual patterns — all of these are arenas where women are present and where they encounter, and respond to, the gendered structure. They do so not with a single voice, nor with a uniform voice. All these struggles combine to broaden the definition of politics, a broadening that inherently constitutes political action, in more meanings than one. It also implies taking part in shaping social reality, a participation that is the very epicentre of the political process, and also of broadening the arenas of political struggle, and defining the rules of the political game. Here, feminist discourse and feminist practice interlink in a wider process that is taking place in post-modern society — the process of decentralising power. As part of the process, different patterns for exerting power and making political endeavours are being created. Forms of organising are included in those patterns, but so is the critical analysis that lays bare exclusionary and oppressive mechanisms of the state, the nation, and ethnic groups. Alongside a critical analysis, patterns of protest and subversion are spotlit as, equally, are the survival strategies that are being implemented. Critical analysis shows us that accepting the existing situation without reacting is no less a political action than applying a survival strategy, and the latter is preferable as it is conscious and proactive. If one analyses power from this point of view, then the disintegration taking place in feminist discourse signifies not the loss of political power, but changes in the ways that power is being applied. Political effort has become diffuse not only in terms of the issues it addresses but also in terms of the diversity of those making it. This is not a political movement in the accepted sense of the term, but it is clear that political power is present here, with tremendous potential for generating social change. The prime issue is the civil-ising of Israeli society from a feminist perspective.

NOTES

1. Ilan Pappé (1995) 'The New History of Zionism: The Academic and Public Confrontation', in *Kivvunim: A Journal of Zionism & Judaism*, vol. 8, pp. 39–48 [Hebrew]; Uri Ram (1996) 'The Historical Recognition in Israel: Between Neo-Zionism and Post-Zionism, A Sociological Viewpoint', in *Gesher*, vol. 42, pp. 93–7 [Hebrew]; Eliezer Schweid (1995) 'Towards the Understanding of Essence and the Background of "Post-Zionism"', in *Gesher*, vol. 41, pp. 18–27 [Hebrew]; Laurence J. Silberstein (1999), *Postzionism Debates: Knowledge and Power in Israeli Culture*, New York and London, Routledge.
2. Sylvie Fogiel-Bijaoui (1992) 'The Struggle for Women's Suffrage in Israel: 1917–1926', in D. S. Bernstein (ed.) *Pioneers and Homemakers: Jewish Women in Prestate Israeli Society*,

Albany, NY, State University of New York Press, pp. 275–302: Hanna Herzog (1992) 'The Fringes of the Margin: Women's Organizations in the Civic Sector at the Time of the *Yishuv*', in Bernstein (1992) *Pioneers and Homemakers*, pp. 283–304.

3. Bernstein, *Pioneers and Homemakers*.

4. For example, Silberstein, *Postzionism Debates*, p. 192.

5. Dina Hecht and Nira Yuval-Davis (1978) 'Ideology Without Revolution: Jewish Women in Israel', in *Khamsin*, vol. 6, pp. 179–205.

6. Orly Lubin (1995) 'Trifles from Nehama's Kitchen: An Alternative Nationalism in Devora Baron's Novel *The Exiles*', in *Theory and Criticism: An Israeli Forum*, vol. 7, p. 164 [Hebrew].

7. Hannan Hever (1994) 'The struggle over the Canon in Hebrew Literature', in *Theory and Criticism: An Israeli Forum*, vol. 4, pp. 99–123 [Hebrew].

8. Silberstein, *Postzionism Debates*, pp. 191–206.

9. Nitza Berkovitch (1999) 'Women of Valor: Women and Citizenship in Israel', in *Israeli Sociology*, vol. 2, pp. 277–318 [Hebrew].

10. Hanna Herzog (1998) 'Homefront and Battlefront and the Status of Jewish and Palestinian Women in Israel', in *Israeli Studies*, vol. 3, pp. 61–84; Ronit Lentin (1997) 'Women, War, and Peace in a Culture of Violence: The Middle East and Northen Ireland', in R. Boric and K. Biljana (eds), *Women and the Politics of Peace*, Zagreb; Simona Sharoni (1995) *Gender and the Israeli–Palestinian Conflict – The Politics of Women's Resistance*, Syracuse, NY, Syracuse University Press.

11. Yael Azmon (1997) 'War, Mothers, and Girls with Braids: Involvement of Mothers' Peace Movements in the National Discourse in Israel', in *Israel Social Science Review*, vol. 12, pp. 109–28: Tamar El-Or and Gideon Aran (1995) 'Giving Birth to Settlement: Maternal Thinking and Political Action of Jewish Women on the West Bank', in *Gender and Society*, vol. 9, pp. 60–78; Nurit Gilath (1991) 'Women against War: Parents against Silence', in Barbara Swirski and Marilyn P. Safir (eds) *Calling the Equality Bluff: Women in Israel*, New York, Pergamon Press, pp. 142–6.

12. Sara Helman and Tamar Rappaport (1997) 'Women in Black: Challenging Israel's Gender and Socio-Political Orders', in *British Journal of Sociology*, vol. 48, pp. 682–700.

13. Sara Helman (1997) 'Militarism and the Construction of Community', in *Journal of Political and Military Sociology*, vol. 25, pp. 305–32.

14. Dafna N. Izraeli (1997) 'Gendering Military Service in Israeli Defense Forces', in *Israel Social Science Research*, vol. 12, pp. 129–66.

15. Delila Amir (1994) 'The Israeli Woman as Responsible, Accountable and Sensible', in *Women Studies International Forum*; Delila Amir and Orly Benyamin (1992) 'The Abortion Committees: Educating and Controlling Women', in C. Feinman (ed.), *The Criminalization of a Woman's Body*, New York, Haworth Press, pp. 5–25.

16. Esther Hertzog (1996) 'Who Benefits from the Welfare State?' in *Theory and Criticism – An Israeli Forum*, vol. 9, pp. 81–104 [Hebrew].

17. Esther Eillam (1994) *Rape Survivors, Rape Crimes and Authorities*, Jerusalem, The Jerusalem Institute for Israel Studies [Hebrew].

18. Pnina Motzafi-Haller (1977) 'You have an Authentic Voice: Anthropology and the Politics of Representation' in *Theory and Criticism – An Israeli Forum*, vol. 11, pp. 81–98 [Hebrew]; Vicki Shiran (1991) 'Feminist Identity vs. Oriental Identity', in Swirski and Safir (eds), *Calling the Equality Bluff*, pp. 303–11; Ella Shohat (1979) *Israeli Cinema East/West and the Politics of Representation*, Austin, University of Texas Press.

19. El-Or and Aran (1995) 'Giving Birth'; Tamar Rappaport, A. Penso and Y. Garb (1994) 'Contribution to the Collective by Religious Zionist Adolescent Girls', in *British Journal of Sociology of Education*, vol. 15, pp. 375–88.

20. Tamar El-Or (1994) *Educated and Ignorant: Ultraorthodox Jewish Women and Their World*, Boulder, Colo. and London, Lynne Rienner Publishers.

21. Jo Oppenheimer (1991) 'The Pressure to Be Heterosexual', in Swirski and Safir (eds) *Calling the Equality Bluff*, pp. 108–14.

22. Manar Hasan (1994) 'Murder of Women for "Family Honour" in Palestinian Society and the Factors Promoting its Continuation in the State of Israel', MA dissertation, Gender and Ethnic Studies, University of Greenwich, England; Hanna Herzog (1999) 'A Space of Their Own: Social–Civil Discourses among Palestinian Israeli women in Peace Organizations', in *Social Politics: International Studies of Gender, State and Society*, vol. 6, pp. 344–69; Nadera Shalhoub-Kevorkian (1997) 'Wife Abuse: A Method of Social Control', in *Israel Social Science Research*, vol. 12, pp. 59–72.

23. For example, Henriette Dahan-Kalev (1997) 'The Oppression of Women by Other Women: Relations and Struggle between Mizrahi and Ashkenazi Women in Israel', in *Israel Social Science Research*, vol. 12, pp. 31–44; Ayala Emmett (1996) *Our Sisters' Promised Land: Women, Politics, and Israeli–Palestinian Coexistence*, Ann Arbor, University of Michigan Press.

24. Nabila Espanioly (1994) 'Palestinian Women in Israel: Identity in Light of Occupation', in T. Mayer (ed.) *Women and the Israeli Occupation – The Politics of Change*, London and New York, Routledge, pp. 106–20; Vicki Shiran (1991) 'Feminist Identity'.

25. El-Or and Aran (1992) 'Giving Birth'.

26. Helman and Rappaport (1997) 'Women in Black'.

27. Emmett (1996) *Our Sisters' Promised Land*.

28. El-Or (1994) *Educated and Ignorant*.

29. Tamar El-Or (1998) *New Pessach: Literary Identity of Young Religious Zionist Women*, Tel Aviv, Am Oved [Hebrew].

30. *Theory and Criticism – An Israeli Forum* (1996) vol. 8 [Hebrew].

31. See, for example, *Theory and Society* (1995) vol. 7 [Hebrew].

32. Silberstein, *Postzionism Debates*.

33. Ibid., p. 7.

34. For example, Ella Shohat (1988) 'Sephardim in Israel: Zionism from the Standpoint of Its Jewish Victims', in *Social Text*, vol. 19–20, pp. 1–34.

35. *Israel Social Science Research* (1997).

36. Dafna Izraeli, Ariela Friedman, Henriette Dahan-Kalev, Sylvie Fogiel-Bijoui, Hanna Herzog, Manar Hasan and Hannah Naveh (1999) *Sex, Gender, Politics – Women in Israel*, Tel Aviv, Hakibbutz Hameuchad [Hebrew].

37. Swirski and Safir (eds) (1991) *Calling the Equality Bluff*.

38. Hanna Herzog (ed.) (2000) 'Knowledge, Power and Feminist Politics', in *Fifty Years – Society in Reflection*, Tel Aviv, Ramot [Hebrew].

8 ◎ 'You're so Pretty – You Don't Look Moroccan'

Henriette Dahan-Kalev

*You're so pretty – you don't look Moroccan.** I grew up hearing this sentence from the time my parents brought me from Morocco to Israel in 1949, to the immigrant camp *Sha'ar Aliyah* and to the *Ma'abara* (transit camp) *Pardes Chana*. I heard it from the white-uniformed white nurse, who came to our tent in the immigrant camp to tell my mother how she should raise me, my sister, and my baby brother, who was born in that tent. This nurse spoke of 'raising children' as if it was something Zionists invented. The tall silver-haired *Yekke* (German Jew) kindergarten teacher also used this sentence. This teacher then took my name – Henriette – from me and gave me in its place the awful name 'Ahuva'. She did this 'because Henriette is difficult to pronounce – both for me and the other children'.

I continued to hear the sentence from neighbours and their children, and throughout my adolescence when, upon meeting people for the first time, special attention was given to my looks. Today, as an adult, when wrinkles have begun to carve my face, the sentence has been replaced by 'Really? You don't look it.' My so-called non-Moroccan appearance helped me more than once to become an invisible person, who can see but is not seen. Hence, I often still hear opinions about Moroccans spoken among non-Moroccans who take me for one of them. This has enabled me throughout my life to learn a great deal about inclusion and exclusion, superiors and inferiors, in Israeli society from the 1950s until today.

As early as the age of 4, hearing the sentence provoked in me vague, incomprehensible feelings; there seemed to be some tension between the green colour of my eyes, my relatively light complexion, and my origin. Only later on did I understand that these feelings were the conscious side of the unconscious subtext: 'I am lucky that I don't look Moroccan'. But as a young child, I understood very early that there was an apparent conflict between aesthetic value and being Moroccan. This experience was exemplified when my mother came to my teacher to complain about the hostility shown toward me by other children in the class. The response of the teacher was that my mother was behaving like a pushy Moroccan street peddler, and that there was 'no room for such vulgarity and primitivism in our school'. The teacher completely ignored the content of my mother's complaint. My father transferred me to a 'better' school in Holon, named after a great Zionist thinker – Moshe Hess. His ambition for his children was that they should be absorbed quickly and efficiently. This school was 'better' because it was populated largely by the children of veteran immigrants (the so called 'pioneers') who were mostly Ashkenazi (of European origin). Most of the children participated in extra-curricular enrichment programmes such as ballet, piano, and violin. They included the children of artists and politicians. I, too, attended an enrichment programme: I 'took' a drawing class out in the sand dunes of Holon by myself. I loved to draw, and apparently showed some talent, but my father let me know in no uncertain terms that 'you'd be better off reading a book than wasting time out in the dunes'.

At this time in my life, I felt what I later realised was a deep sense of alienation. The axle around which this turned was the dissonance between the knowledge of who I was and what people took me to be: I don't look Moroccan and this is why I am 'lucky', but I am 'very lucky' that I look just like an Ashkenazi. Trapped between who I was – a Moroccan girl – and who people thought I was – an Ashkenazi girl – my world-view crystallised according to a clear dichotomy of what was good and what was bad, which derived ultimately from notions of where people came from.

When I was 10, my parents moved again, this time to Jerusalem (owing to my father's promotion at work). This gave me the opportunity to open a new page in my life. I told my new Jerusalem friends that I had been born in France. In order to be convincing I consciously eliminated my distinctive Arab accent when pronouncing the letters *Khet* and *Ayin,* and trained myself to adopt the typical Ashkenazi accent of *Chet* and *Ain.* Obviously, I did not invite any of my friends home; I could not risk their discovering my lie. I was afraid that, if they came home with me, they would hear my mother speak to me in Arabic. I forbade her absolutely to speak Arabic when outside the house. It was from this time that I was busy constructing (and protecting) the child I wanted to be – the French child, whom I believed other people thought I was. Soon I began to believe my own deceptive tales, as, little by little, I constructed a desirable identity for myself. I milked my parents for bits of information about French history, culture, and language. My parents had knowledge about things French, since they had studied at the Alliance Israelite French colonial school back in Morocco. It was from them that I first heard of Zola, Hugo and *Les Misérables*, about Rousseau and the Revolution, about Napoleon and his battles, and about General Lyotée. My mother told me the history of France long before I began to study it in general history classes in school.

All of this I incorporated into the identity that I was constructing for myself, to which I added further biographical details that were meant to ensure my acceptance amongst the children in my class. For example, I claimed that I went to fine art classes after school. Later, I added that I also studied dance. People believed what I said, since I possessed some natural ability in these areas. I even survived the tests I was put to; for example, once, during a youth training course, I was asked to perform a 'piece'. I made something up; later I found out that this was called 'improvisation' – and it went down very well.

As the reality gap faced by the child I was at home and the child I was at school grew wider, my tales developed and became more involved. This was difficult to do, so I also cushioned my world with soft, fluffy, happy imaginative thoughts. I outdid myself when I bragged to my teacher at the vocational high school that I had been chosen to participate in the Habima Youth (Habima is the Israeli national theatre company). Habima Youth was an organisation that existed only in my imagination; I added that it was meant to promote talented young actors. The teacher believed me, and even permitted me to leave class early every Tuesday. It is apparent that the common denominator to all my tales, whether or not I was conscious of it at the time, was Ashkenazi, Western culture. This was not a problem for my friends, and was only of benefit to my self-image.

Only of benefit? To whom? To my self? Which self was my self? The self of that imaginative girl? The real me I hated, and tried to wish out of existence; the Moroccan me, the non-French immigrant who did not participate in extra-curricular enrichment programmes like the other kids, who did no more than her very annoying schoolwork. At school I had to read and memorise entire books about me and the Jewish people through-out the world (meaning Eastern Europe); about my ancestors in the *Shtetl* (East European Jewish villages); the 'Family of Fighters' who broke through to besieged Jerusalem, and took part in the *Choma u Migdal* (building the walls and towers of new kibbutzim). In vain I searched, but never found the real me, nor my father, in these books. In despair I stopped studying, and became more certain that I should hold on to the identity of that imaginary French girl. *Mikra'ot Yisrael* and *Historia shel Am Yisrael* (obligatory elementary school texts on Israeli literature and history) provided background for the invented European girl, and only reinforced my belief that the other girl – the real me – did not deserve to exist.

Once, when I finally found something on the real me, I discovered that I was a Mizrahi (Oriental), the term used in Israel to define non-Western Jews, those of African or Asian origin. In these texts I was described as dirty, poor, riddled with contagious or infectious diseases, spiritually impotent, lacking in moral capacity, ignorant, violent, and lazy.[1] In the best of cases, my parents were described as 'having fallen into an historical coma'.[2] In the worst of cases, my parents and I were accused of bringing about the cultural demise of the *Yishuv* due to our so-called inferiority complex over belonging to undesirable tribes and *Edot* (*Edot* being the term used to refer to something just short of 'ethnicities', lest it be known that Jews do not constitute a singular 'ethnic' group).[3] By then I had sufficiently convincing evidence to justify my extermination of that hated girl, since even the history books said that she was bad, and who wanted to be primitive and dirty anyway?

Once I found myself leafing through a children's book, *Rumiah, The Little Nanny*.[4] The author of this book, Levin Kipnis, received the Israel Prize for his life's work and contribution to children's literature. The book tells the story of a 12-year-old Yemenite girl, 'a dirty and starving new immigrant'.[5] She is brought to a veteran settler's house by her father, who wants to hire her out as a nanny for the settler's son. At the settler's house, she goes through a metamorphosis. First, they change her name to the more Hebraicised 'Moriah'. Then they bathe her, clean her, and comb her hair. They believe, Kipnis tells us, that in a very short time she will become a real human being ready to learn some manners. Rumiah had two very important attributes in the eyes of the veterans: one, her father did not ask for much money in exchange for her work; and, two, she was considered better than an Ashkenazi girl, for she ate little and worked a lot. When selling Rumiah to the child's mother, the 'matchmaker' or 'go-between' (a woman herself) explains that all Rumiah requires is a stick and a belt, 'without which one cannot get her moving'.[6]

I found this book in 1991 at the National Book Fair in Jerusalem, when I was searching the children's literature counter for books for my own son. While holding this book in my hands, it occurred to me that the feelings of alienation, contempt and self-hatred that I had experienced, and which developed during my childhood, had been based on knowledge that I had absorbed from my social and educational environment. As a reader of this sort of literature, I believed every word. All that is Mizrahi is retarded, degenerate and primitive, and therefore I had to choose the Ashkenazi alternative – I had to 'Ashkenazify' myself (become 'white'). For me this meant establishing a modern, progressive, clean identity, and destroying, down to the roots, the identity that my parents gave me. This meant rejecting everything: their past, their language, their values, their loves, their hates, their pains and their joys.

My Ashkenazification was quite successful. I knew about Stockhausen's avant-garde music as well as about *a cappella* singing. I was familiar with Mozart and his biography long before the movie *Amadeus* came out, and I could identify many of his pieces by their Köchel number. I was also familiar with the Wimbledon tennis championships and could answer most of the questions on Shmuel Rosen's radio quiz show, and I could solve the *Ha'aretz* crossword puzzle with ease. My father was proud. I knew about *Yalkut Hakzavim* (local Israeli folkloric tales) and I became an expert teller of *Chizbat* (one kind of folkloric Israeli tales), as if I had heard them from my own grandmother. Those who showed some knowledge of these tales were assumed to belong to the families of pioneers and fighters who had been in Israel for many years. I worked extremely hard to make this knowledge mine, and in acquiring it I invested all of my energies. But I did it as a thief in the night. I looked out of the corner of my eye to see what other kids ate, how they played, and what they wore. I listened to their conversations about cello lessons, messy rooms, and the punishments they received from their mothers. I visited their homes and paid special attention to how their rooms were furnished. I saw their 'little radios' and how they listened to *Hamasach Oleh* (high-culture theatrical broadcasts). I aspired to be like them, to speak like them, to be considered one of them. Nothing that was mine (the real me) seemed appropriate to share in exchange, which is why I concentrated on imitating the look and the form, on refining the costume. While they ('my friends') were succeeding in acquiring the 'real thing' – in-depth study of the formal curriculum – I was failing. The teacher told my mother 'she could succeed and achieve if she only wanted to', and my mother was sure to repeat this to me often. I truly wanted to succeed, but there was a limit to my capacity to absorb both the canon and the entire context in which it was rooted. I was held back a grade and then sent to a vocational school to become a good cook. I was expelled from there as well.

I was a failure in their eyes and mine. Later, in the army – another Israeli melting pot – I also failed the course. I was left imprisoned in an inner world built of shattered bits and pieces of my identities; like a room full of mirrors – a fictive reflection of an Israeli, a despised Moroccan, and an imaginary French girl.

Spiritually breathless, I continued to chase after this body of knowledge. I discovered that Kipnis and Shmuely were 'mere' teachers. The foundations upon which they based their work were laid for them by the intellectual leaders of their generation. My failure in school was but proof of the elaborate theses regarding my backwardness, theses that flourished in the ivory towers of The Hebrew University of Jerusalem. The frameworks for research into Israeli society were established by the intellectual elite, who constructed a picture of the desirable Israeli, a picture that matched the parameters set by the ideology of the Labour Zionist movement. It was only later that I realized that my conceptions of what was desirable and detestable were based on these 'scientific' cornerstones.

These philosophers inspected and scrutinised me like a scientific object – a laboratory rat – and postulated the following:

> the results these youth have reached during systematic examination, point to intellectual development retardation. Various non-verbal examinations conducted prove retardation of one to two years, and very often even more, in comparison with youth of similar age in Europe. Are we to interpret this as biological inferiority and to see their difficulties as an expression of lack of intellectual abilities and limitations in psycho-physiological activity?

This is what was written about me by Karl Fuerstein and M. Richel in their book *The Children of the Melah: The Cultural Retardation among Moroccan Children and Its Meaning in Education*.[7] What followed was an attempt by these philosophers to offer practical advice for the educators faced with the task of the re-education of my brother, my sister, and myself. They promised to conquer all the social and cultural factors that influenced my 'dysfunctional development'.[8]

I also found out that the authors had decided not only that I was retarded, but that I lacked curiosity. What is more, no one around me was capable of arousing my curiosity: I showed no interest in observation, and I was unable to differentiate between the real and the imaginary, the natural and the supernatural.[9] They did not bother to ask me whether I lived in an imaginary world of my own choosing; they simply decided that I was incapable of doing otherwise. They entered the innards of my consciousness.

Without consulting me, Fuerstein and Richel decided on the following instructions for my teachers: they should avoid showing disrespect for my traditions and beliefs, *even though they are superstitions*. Teachers would face resistance because I was incapable of grasping abstract explanations.[10] Moreover, beneath 'the religious problem' lay my problematic relationship with the father figure.[11] My educators were forewarned that my presence in a group of children could be dangerous due to my lax sexual morality, as informed by my North African way of life, and should be conditional on the professional opinion of a psychologist.

Contrary to Fuerstein, Karl Frankenstein was busy addressing the question of what should be done in order to change the ethnic character of my parents.[12] As the ethnic character of my father and mother was rooted in their unconscious, Frankenstein asserted that it could not be changed by conscious instruction.[13] 'Only forces directed at the unconscious are likely to change [their] ethnic character'.[14] Therefore, my parents and I were to struggle actively with our ethnic character.[15]

My parents believed him, and so did I. I actively struggled, even at the tender age of 6, both on the individual and the collective level, just as he recommended.[16] I invented the French girl from scraps of information taken from my mother, because that girl's chances of acceptance by the Frankensteins of my new country were greater. My world was tailored according to his measurements, but all in vain. For, despite his recommendations, Frankenstein declared himself sceptical of my ability to change, and, like Fuerstein and Richel, he thought that my intelligence and ability to think abstractly were deficient. Thus I was not blessed with the ability to think causally, to understand the ways of the world, to distinguish between the essential and the non-essential, to relate to situations that 'require comprehending reasons, rules, and the essence of things, and to adapt to new conditions which require quick observation of the common and the different'.[17] In his article 'On the Concept of Primitivism', Frankenstein analyses the different kinds of primitivism known to him – that of the child, that of the retarded, that of the mentally ill, and that of the backward primitive and his or her deficient self-consciousness.[18] All these 'constitute only an introduction to our main subject – the analysis of the primitive mentality of the Mizrahi Jews who come to us from culturally backward regions'.[19] '[W]e said that the primitive person lacks a self and that his world is beyond the personal'; to which he added that, in this world, what indicates degenerate primitivism is 'an inflated self [narcissism], ... narrow egotism, and a lack of understanding of extra-individual values'.[20] From my educators, who hungrily consumed his writings, I learned that my self lacked all functional content (whatever that means). He also claimed that I was incapable of abstractly conceptualising the 'other' as having a 'self' of his or her own![21]

What all this meant for me as an individual was of no concern to either Frankenstein or his colleagues. What mattered to them was 'the big picture' – they were concerned with 'the fate of the People of Israel'. Frankenstein's opinions infuriated Akiva Ernest Simon, another member of the club, who was the one to etch the term 'primitivism' into this body of work.[22] From here on, the debate became increasingly detached from reality and entirely scholastic. My parents and I became abstract entities in this discourse; we were looked upon as guinea pigs on which the argument was to be tested. '[T]he anthropocentric position [as opposed to religious, social, or national positions] calls for extreme caution and moderate pacing, if any possible changes are to take place in the social lives of those same immigrants [meaning my social life and that of my parents]'.[23] '[W]e have found that there are two fronts: the absorbers and the absorbed, the directors and the directed, the culturally developed and the culturally more primitive'.[24] This claim caused Nathan Rotenstreich (yet another member of the club) to state angrily that there is a basic methodological problem regarding the question, 'to what extent is it possible and/or permissible to draw a line distinguishing between the different sides ... [of the pair of terms used in the previous sentence]'.[25] Rotenstreich's words did not fall on deaf ears. They influenced leading figures such as David Ben-Gurion, who claimed that the unity of Israeli society was dependent upon common conceptions of collective objectives and the means for achieving them. Rotenstreich asked the rhetorical question: 'Is there hope that such unity can be reached upon the background of the present reality of the veteran settlers? ... [A return to fundamentals is necessary] in order to merge into the lifestyle founded on the ideas of Israeli society'.[26]

Who was I to doubt these truths? In a sense, I did not exist, whereas these fictitious truths did exist – they had been propounded by the members of the intellectual elite of society. How could I not believe that these philosophers knew what they were talking about? I conformed. Over the years I have come to see that this discourse functioned as a massive system of exclusion, filtering out those of us who failed the Ashkenazification test, a system essentially fertilised by philosophical, literary, ethical and educational authorities. This discourse stimulated the minds of subsequent thinkers, all of whom, in turn, nurtured the myth of primitivity versus modernity.

Astonished, I watched them fuel the fire of this discourse, and tried with all my might to digest the perverted ideas they had cooked up for me.

Once that generation's leading thinkers had established their polemical positions and documented them in public lectures, at conferences, in books, and in journals, a solid infrastructure existed upon which Ben-Gurion could base his characterisation of me as morally deficient. The educational system in which my brother, my sister and I were processed was based entirely upon these judgments, not unlike the superstructure of Israeli sociology, a sociology whose primary purpose was, during its first years, to serve the governmental authorities in absorbing the mass immigration of 'oriental' Jews.[27] The ideological and emotional proximity of the founders of Israeli sociology to the Zionist project blurred the distinction between the academic and the political.[28] Even in instances of ideological disagreement, the aggressive Zionist belief in the establishment and subsequent fortification of the state forged a common emotional and conceptual consensus among politicians and sociologists.

In all of his research, Eisenstadt preserved the distinction between pioneers and *Olim* (immigrants). My parents, who had arrived after the establishment of the state, could not be considered pioneers by his definition. Moreover, in his view, they possessed no national identity, since they were neither secular nor modern enough. They were the antithesis of pioneers, and even a danger to the Zionist enterprise, for they were traditionally religious.[29] According to him, my parents were incapable of consciously transforming their economic and employment patterns or their social and cultural lives.[30] My father, who had been a senior bank officer in Morocco, did change his 'employment pattern' – he went to work in a cement factory and the citrus harvest for several years – yet he was still not suitable enough for absorption according to Eisenstadt's thesis. My father had to go through 'something' metaphysical – which Eisenstadt termed 'de-socialization' – to be followed by 're-socialization'.[31] In any event, this entire process, according to Eisenstadt, related to how the members of the *Olim* groups 'acquired new social values and attitudes ... required for gradual change'.[32] This laid the responsibility for my father's failure on his own shoulders.

According to Eisenstadt's classification, my father was uneducated, despite his professional experience in banking, and my mother, a *cum laude* graduate of the Alliance Israelite, was but 'another one of the illiterate Mizrahi immigrants'. The fact that both of them had experienced Western culture in the colonial city of Casablanca, and the French education they had received at the Alliance was of no value in his eyes. Eisenstadt attributed my parents' failure to be absorbed to their being 'unripe', that is, unready to enjoy the privileges of Israeli citizenship and utilise it for their 'upward employment mobilization'.[33] As a result, my mother worked as a maid in the Ashkenazi house of Yitzhak Ben Zvi (the second President of Israel), and was fired after only two days for being Moroccan rather than Yemenite! In another Ashkenazi house she discovered that they did not keep *kashrut* (the Jewish dietary laws). In shock, she came home and exclaimed, 'they're not Jews!' This was the point at which she discovered that a deep chasm separated her from *Eretz Israel*. This was not the society into which she wanted to be absorbed. Unlike my father, my mother chose to 'fail' at her social absorption. Caught in this chasm, I finally made my choice in favour of the rich, successful and strong (winning) side – Ashkenazification. The price I paid for this effort was full alienation from myself and my identity, not to mention the contempt I felt for my parents' helplessness in this process.

The story of our absorption was no more than an abstract analysis in Eisenstadt's terms of pioneers versus immigrants – two groups, two worlds, the former positive, the latter a danger to the former. In his evaluation of absorption policy, Eisenstadt deemed it mostly appropriate, and saw the mistakes made along the way as a reasonable price for Israeli society to pay to learn a lesson.[34] He put it this way in general terms, as if the whole of Israeli society paid the price for this lesson. But in fact it was I, Eisenstadt's object of research, who was the one who paid, and is still paying, this price. Not he, or Ben-Gurion, or their families, or the honourable liberator of Jerusalem, Yitzhak Rabin, or the members of Knesset Naomi Hazan, Yael Dayan, Amnon Rubinstein and Dan Meridor.

The Wadi Salib riots of 1959 were the outcome of a steadily growing correlation between low socio-economic status and Middle Eastern origin. The oppression had reached such a critical point that it could not but backfire in the faces of the hegemonic Ashkenazi elite. Who, among others, was appointed to the governmental committee to investigate the cause of the riots? Shmuel Noah Eisenstadt, who concluded that the entire affair was no more than an outburst by a gang of thugs, who, he assumed, represented neither my parents nor me.[35]

The scientific conceptualisation and description of all our defects in the spirit of structural–functional theory not only constituted the basis of official policy, it formed the contours of Israeli sociology as well. The Education and Social Work departments in Israeli universities based all their research and definitions of backwardness, social gaps and disadvantaged communities

on these scientific conceptualisations. Programmes were written introducing me and my parents to my Ashkenazi friends upon this basis. The
pioneer's child, whom I envied, was defined as 'an ancient Hebrew who has
already shed his Diaspora qualities and has renewed himself in his land'.[36]
After this, the story goes, my parents and I arrived, bringing with us our
negative values – a dislike of physical labour, conservatism and an inclination
to violence, all of which constituted a threat to Zionism. Then again, our
Arabised way of living was seen as a threat to the Zionist project and so had
to be disposed of by all means possible. My own experiences made it clear to
me that it did not matter what I did or did not do – my Ashkenazi friends
had to reject me. So I Ashkenazified. This Ashkenazification still runs
through my bones to this day – an Ashkenazi skeleton in my closet.

Today, in the new millennium, I hear people saying that the Mizrahi–
Ashkenazi tension does not exist anymore; instead there are Power Rangers,
Coca Cola and other such cultural diseases that have Americanised us all.
Then again, a student of mine of Arab Jewish origin expressed his being fed
up with the issue: 'Hey, look at me – I reached university, and have never
experienced discrimination. Whoever wants to can make it. I don't want to
deal with your problems, your parents' problems, and not even my own
parents' problems – all of that is irrelevant to me'. It is I, and maybe one or
two others like me, who spoil reality for this student and cloud the Israeli
consensus that, in the new century, is prepared, at most, to admit that once
upon time there was an ethnic problem in Israel ('and anyway, mixed
marriages are on the rise'). A number of years ago Dorit Rabinian, a second-
generation Iranian Israeli, defined herself as a 'Nouveau *Frank*' (*Frank* being
the pejorative term used to describe Moroccan Jews). She wrote:

> Any good Ashkenazi boy knows that – 'love shmove' – it's still better to marry
> 'one of ours' [an Ashkenazi] … [as opposed to the Ashkenazified Mizrahi boy
> who 'jokes' with 'the real thing' and asserts], 'I don't have a gold chain [a
> Moroccan sign], I don't curse in Arabic, and my Benetton shirt is buttoned all the
> way up!' Any minute, he thinks, his face will pale in identification with the other
> side.[37]

What are the Ashkenazified Mizrahim supposed to do? Return to the
past? Romanticise the culture in nostalgia? What culture? That of Kurdistan,
Morocco? That of today, of yesterday? I speak Yiddish–Hebrew, think
according to European cultural patterns, I inhale Zionist ideology and
exhale the *Reut* song (the semi-formal national hymn) at a dizzying pace,
and hurt in 'integration' terms (educational reform meant to achieve the

'melting pot' ethos). Therefore, all of this is still relevant. It is relevant because the vast majority of children's literature written today is the project of people of European origin, the same people who, literature researcher Adir Cohen found, are also responsible for the stereotypes that represent the Arab child as inferior and monstrous. It is relevant because students of education are still exposed to the texts that I have quoted here.[38] It is there that the students find the sources that define who is disadvantaged and who is backward, and why. It is in their libraries, compiled according to Ashkenazi priorities and belief structures, that I found the books and articles I referred to earlier on.

Today, I wonder whether Frankenstein himself was not too primitive to be able to recognize me as the 'other' – that is, in terms other than negative, and as having a 'self of my own'. Were I to send Fuerstein to the Tudra Dunes (a village in the Atlas Mountains where the geology, weather, and dangerous conditions of the wild world make physical life very difficult) with no knowledge of the language and with no skills for contending with such a way of life, would he have survived the intellectual and physical tests of such a situation? What did those researchers know about me as an 'other' anyway? Why did they find it necessary to project on to me all of this psychologism? I, the research object, ask today as a subject who became a researcher.

In her book *A Critique of Postcolonial Reason*,[39] Gayatri Chakravorty Spivak suggests that I re-examine the Freudian fiction, based on the Oedipal story, according to which my identity was constructed, the fiction upon which my educators leaned. Postcolonial women, in her opinion, do not necessarily have a European story versus a traditional one. She provides me with the explanation that I am caught between two worlds. I feel that my story is one primarily of oppression: traditional European oppression, colonial oppression, Western oppression, and Zionist oppression. Inside all of this lies a shattered, confused identity that is fighting a Sisyphean struggle for control over my consciousness, my values, my feelings, my passions, and my will. I am trapped in a world of mirrors.

This is a process whose nature and power I am still largely unable to comprehend. It is not a return to my roots, nor a rehabilitation or reconstruction of identity. These are suspicious and dangerous words to my ears. One thing though is clear to me: whether I am conscious of it or not, I am a product of an educational, intellectual and economic steamroller that squashed everything and left no room for any self-development outside of that of a distorting Ashkenazi, Zionist, Israeli, European hegemony.

NOTES

* This paper started life as a lecture I gave in Hebrew a long time ago. Rachel Jones translated it into English, and the translation was edited by Haim Marantz, who adopted several suggestions made by Natan Aridan. I would like to thank Haim Marantz for convincing me to publish it

1. See Ruth Firer (1986) 'The Image of the Mizrahi *Edot*,' *Iyyunim beKhinuch*, no. 45, pp. 23–33, especially p. 28 [Hebrew].

2. Eliezer Shmuely (1970) *Toldot Amenu BaZman HaChadash* [The History of Our People in the Modern Era], vol. 7, Tel Aviv, p. 268 [Hebrew].

3. Ibid., p. 414.

4. Levin Kipnis (1981) *Rumiah, The Little Nanny*, Tel Aviv, p. 12 [Hebrew].

5. Ibid.

6. Ibid.

7. Karl Fuerstein and M. Richel (1953) *The Children of the Melah – The Cultural Retardation among Moroccan Children and Its Meaning in Education*, published by the Henrietta Szold Institute and the Jewish Agency, Jerusalem, p. 17 [Hebrew].

8. Ibid.

9. Ibid., pp. 17, 101, 185.

10. Ibid., p. 194.

11. Ibid., p. 195.

12. Karl Frankenstein (1951) 'On Ethnic Differences,' *Megamot*, B3, pp. 261–76 [Hebrew].

13. Ibid., p. 270.

14. Ibid.

15. Ibid., p. 272.

16. Ibid., p. 292.

17. Ibid.

18. Karl Frankenstein (1951) 'On the Concept of Primitivity,' *Megamot*, B4, pp. 342, 344, 347 [Hebrew].

19. Ibid., p. 352.

20. Ibid., p. 353.

21. Ibid., p. 352.

22. Akiva Ernest Simon (1951) 'On the Meaning of the Concept Primitivity,' *Megamot*, B3, p. 227 [Hebrew].

23. Ibid.

24. Ibid.

25 Ibid., p. 335.

26. Ibid., p. 338.

27. Henriette Dahan-Kalev (1992) 'Self Organizing Systems: Wadi Salib and The Black Panthers – Implications for Israeli Society', Ph.D. thesis, Department of Political Science, The Hebrew University of Jerusalem, pp. 37–42 [Hebrew]; see also Uri Ram (1995) *The Changing Agenda of Israeli Sociology*, New York, especially chapter 3, pp. 23–46.

28. Shmuel Noah Eisenstadt (1951) 'Immigration Absorption', MA thesis, Department of Sociology, The Hebrew University of Jerusalem [Hebrew].

29. Shmuel Noah Eisenstadt (1967) *Israel, A Society in the Making*, Jerusalem [Hebrew].

30. Ibid.

31. For further discussion, see Dahan-Kalev, 'Self Organizing Systems', especially. pp. 37–40, 73–96.

32. Shmuel Noah Eisenstadt (1953) 'Leadership Problems among the "*Olim*",' *Megamot*, no.

32, pp. 182–91 [Hebrew].

33. Ibid., p. 44.
34. Ibid., p. 152.
35. Ibid., p. 263. For an extended account of the Wadi Salib Riots and an analysis of the responses to it, see Dahan-Kalev, 'Self Organizing Systems'.
36. Firer, 'The Image of the Mizrahi *Edot*', pp. 25, 28–9.
37. Dorit Rabinian (1993) 'Nuvo Frenkit', *Ha'Ir*, 29 September, p. 43.
38. That these ideas are still current can be seen in the fact that they are still repeated today by Israeli educational experts. See, for example, Shoshana Keiny (1999) 'Response to "Human Rights in History and Civic Text Books: The Case of Israel",' in *Curriculum Inquiry*, vol. 29, no. 4, pp. 513–21, especially pp. 518–19. See also Ruth Firer (1998) 'Human Rights in History and Civic Text Books: The Case of Israel', in *Curriculum Inquiry*, vol. 28, no. 2, pp. 195–208.
39. Gayatri Chakravorty Spivak (1990) *A Critique of Postcolonial Reason*, New Haven, Yale University Press.

9 ◎ Conclusion

Some Thoughts on Post-Zionism and the Construction of the Zionist Project

Nira Yuval-Davis

Writing a conclusion to a book on post-Zionism in June 2002 requires a large measure of Gramscian 'pessimism of the intellect, optimism of the will', and it is the second half of the prescription that is the more difficult to adhere to.*

And yet to do so would be to follow in the footsteps of the courageous contingent of Israeli – and even more courageous Palestinian – leftists and feminists, who even these days have not given in to cynicism and bitterness, let alone fear and despair. They are continuing to struggle for democracy and human rights, protesting against the occupation and the accumulating humiliations, oppressions and war crimes taking place within it. At the same time they are also persisting in conducting a dialogue across borders in a quest for a positive solution beyond communal schisms. These schisms have always existed, but after the disappointment of the 'Oslo process', they have widened into what often seem bottomless gulfs.

When this book was first conceived and when I agreed to write the conclusion for it, the 'post-Zionism' trend was becoming, if not the hegemonic academic discourse in Israel, then a major contesting one. It was crowned as the most exciting 'avant-garde' discourse, on a par with the latest developments in Western social sciences. As such it was confronting, if not actually slaughtering, some of the sacred cows of Zionism, thus enabling some invisible chapters (at least invisible to most Israelis) in the his-(and her-) story of the Zionist settlement society to come to light.

At the time of writing, post-Zionist discourse has lost much of its 'trendy' glitter – the backlash is gathering strength. Some 250 academic teaching staff who signed a declaration supporting the rights of their students to refuse to serve in the Occupied Territories were accused of incitement and threatened with legal action. One of the major advocates of the post-Zionist message, Dr Ilan Pappé (see chapter 3), has had his tenured job threatened, and others who have not yet gained tenure have found their pathways strewn with many new obstacles. In a more endemic way, the actual message of 'post-Zionism' has been challenged. Given Sharon's political project and the overwhelming support he has had from the Israeli public, to describe these days as belonging to the 'post-Zionist' epoch requires a very specific reading of the Zionist project.

As Ephraim Nimni writes in his introduction, and several other contributors reiterate in different ways in their chapters, as well as other people who have written on the subject,[1] the concept of post-Zionism has been used in the literature and in public discourse alike in many different and confusing ways. Adding my own view, I would argue that one can distinguish three major uses of the term 'post-Zionism': one relating to specific methodological, analytical and normative approaches in the Israeli social sciences, especially history and sociology; one identifying as such specific political trends and forces within contemporary Israel; and one that identifies a particular period/project of the Israeli polity/society as a whole as post-Zionist. As we can see in the contributions to this book, these three different usages can slide and collapse into each other. This can only add to the general confusion.

My main interest here is in the third usage of the term and the attempt to characterize Israel of the 1990s as having been gradually, and in a contested way, transformed into a post-Zionist society. In such a construction, post-Zionism is closely related to global developments in the post-cold-war period, globalization and post-modernity. In the Middle Eastern context it is closely related to the so-called 'Oslo process'. My main argument is that such a usage of the term can be highly misleading in any attempt to understand Israeli society, and especially the Israeli–Palestinian conflict.

Any attempt to define the Israeli state and society as post-Zionist is closely related to the ways in which Zionism itself is being analysed. In the following pages I shall offer a framework for such an analysis.

As many have commented in this volume and elsewhere, the Zionist movement, more than almost any other national movement, has been Janus-faced.[2] On the one hand it saw itself as a national liberation movement of oppressed and persecuted Jews from all over the world. On the other hand, its mode of organisation and development has been that of a settler colonial state, oppressing, exploiting and excluding the indigenous population of Palestine from its project.

There is no space here to get into the details of Zionist history.[3] The Zionist movement has been just one response – and for a long time a minority response – to the crisis of 'classical' Jewish existence[4] in Europe, when, with the rise of modernity, capitalism and nationalism, the traditional Jewish mode of existence could no longer survive. Hasidism and Jewish orthodoxy on the one hand and reform and liberal Judaism on the other hand have been the major religious movements that emerged as another reaction. Secularisation and assimilation, of both a liberal and a socialist character, have been two other popular reactions, as have individual and communal immigration to various countries in the 'new world' – settler societies developed by European empires.

The Zionist movement was one of two Jewish political movements that attempted to solve the 'Jewish question' as a national question. The Bund, which was the dominant Jewish national movement in Eastern Europe before the Second World War,[5] saw the Jews there as constituting an autonomous national collectivity, with its own language (Yiddish) and cultural tradition. They aspired for a multinational state structure in Eastern Europe, in which the Jews, like all other national minorities, would have national and cultural autonomy.

The Zionist movement aspired for the 'normalisation' of the Jewish people by establishing a Jewish society and state in an independent territory in which, ideally, all Jews would eventually settle. In contrast, the case of the Jewish Bund, the boundaries of the Jewish collectivity as constructed by the Zionist movement encompassed not only Eastern Europe or even Europe as a whole (although it was mostly people originating from Europe who have controlled the Zionist movement and the Israeli state throughout their history). The Zionist boundaries of the Jewish people encompassed the Jews from all over the world, although the question of 'who is a Jew' has been a controversial and divisive one in Israel since its inception. Accordingly, the 'Jewish language' promoted by the Zionists has been not Yiddish but Hebrew – used traditionally in the various Jewish communities as mostly a religious language. After long debates and the proposal of various alternative locations, it was decided that Palestine, which in the Jewish tradition had been the 'Land of the Fathers' and the 'Promised Land', would be the territorial basis for the state.

The accusations against the Zionist movement that came, in its early history,[6] from the Left were mainly against its utopian character, which was seen as distracting the Jewish masses from fighting against anti-semitism wherever they lived. It was also accused of divisiveness, concentrating on the few who could afford to emigrate and settle in Palestine as a result of their class position, age and gender (the early Zionist 'pioneers' were mostly single young men of petit-bourgeois origin), rather than offering a solution for the whole Jewish community. Such accusations, in somewhat different form and by different social agents, were directed against the leadership of the Zionist movement also in a later period of the Second World War, when they were accused of prioritising the interests of the Zionist settlement in Palestine, the *Yishuv*, over saving a maximum number of Jews from the Nazis. It was only after the establishment of the Israeli state, and especially after the rise to political power and legitimacy of international anti-colonial and Third World movements, that critiques of Zionism and Israel started to emerge, primarily aimed at its settler colonial character.[7]

The Jewish holocaust in the Second World War has been a major legitimator of the establishment of the Israeli state in the international community, although its establishment also fitted the interests of the rising imperial powers in the Middle East at the time – the USA and also, for a short period, the USSR. They used the establishment of the Israeli state as leverage against the waning influence of the older imperial powers in the region – the British and French. Establishing the State of Israel, and directing most of the post-war refugees there, enabled the US and other Western countries to appear to support the Jewish victims of Nazism without bearing a major cost in terms of absorbing too large a number of Jewish refugees. Such support also helped to mask their relative lack of support before and during the war. For many Jews, the holocaust was a major factor in their coming to support Zionism and Israel. It became some kind of 'insurance policy' – a Jewish haven to which they could escape with no immigration controls, if a new Holocaust ever threatened.

Other Jews, who remained anti-Zionist and diaspora-oriented,[8] felt differently, although with the years, especially from 1967 until recently, theirs was very much a minority position. They pointed out that, first, it was not Zionism that saved the Jews in the *Yishuv* from a similar fate to that of other Jewish communities, but rather the historical accident of the British victory over the Nazis in North Africa before they arrived in Palestine. Second, some argued that the Zionist idea of 'gathering the exiles' and convening all Jews in one place would make it easier, not more difficult, to kill all Jews. The place where Jews face the highest physical danger to their existence in the world over the last fifty years has been Israel. Third, given Israel's financial and political dependence on colluding diasporic Jewish communities and their political lobbies, there is no guarantee that Israel would actually be able to save them if the need arose. An additional related question is what percentage of Israeli Jews arrived there not as a result of active Zionist persuasion of at least one member of the family, but as an effect of the Zionist project itself. The mass immigration of Jewish communities from the Arab world into Israel in the 1950s, for instance, was to a great extent a consequence of the deterioration in their situation as a result of the Israeli–Arab conflict.[9]

What does it mean for Israel to become post-Zionist from this point of view? To the extent that Zionism's task has been to establish a Jewish state to which all Jews could immigrate and get automatic citizenship, it could be argued that we have been living in post-Zionist Israel since the establishment of the Israeli state, with the Law of Return as one of its major constitutional laws.

To the extent that the Zionist task has been to 'gather' all the Jews in the world into Israel – by whatever means – there has been a partial success. It is still the case that only a minority of world Jewry lives in Israel, but the percentage is growing. This is a result both of assimilatory processes and low birth rate in diasporic Jewish communities, which have caused their numbers to decline. But it is also a result of massive Jewish immigration to Israel, the largest of which in recent years has been from the post-Soviet Eastern European countries, especially Russia. As Nimni mentions in his article, quoting Pergola, Israel is likely to have the majority of the world's Jews within the next 30 years even without a major influx of new immigrants.[10] It could be argued that it would not be until then that Israel can begin to pass into its post-Zionist phase.

Paradoxically, however, most of the discussion on post-Zionism, in this volume and elsewheret, does not refer to post-Zionism as the era after the most important or basic goals of the Zionist movement have been achieved (although Uri Avnery and other Israeli radicals used to describe themselves as post-Zionist in the 1960s in similar terms). The discussion on post-Zionist Israel in the 1990s and the beginning of the twenty-first century is linked to an opposite phenomenon – the partial breakdown of the Zionist character of the state and the hegemonic Israeli–Jewishness as it has been constructed by what Uri Ram calls 'classical Zionism' and Baruch Kimmerling calls the '*Ahuselim*'.[11]

This is because, of course, post-Zionism in this discourse is primarily constructed not in relation to the 'Jewish question', which constituted the basic internal political problematic of Zionist discourse. Rather, post-Zionism is constructed here in relation to the social and political reality of the Israeli state and society, which includes also the non-Jewish and/or non-Zionist citizens of the Israeli state. It also includes reference to the 1.2 million Palestinians who are ruled and controlled by the Israeli state but have no citizenship rights whatsoever. In other words, such post-Zionist discourse draws attention to the other Janus-face of Zionism – not the national liberation movement but the colonial settler society.

To characterise Israel as a settler society and state seems obvious on one level. There is no descriptive history of, first, the '*Yishuv*',[12] and then of the State of Israel that can ignore the fact that Israel is a society of immigrants who settled in the country in the name of a political movement that claimed political sovereignty of the state. As in other settler states, the indigenous people of the country were excluded partly or completely from the new society and polity that were established in the settled territory.

In spite of the obviousness of this process, central to the Zionist movement, it was not read as such internally in Israel. The hegemonic political discourse in Israel, including the sociological one for many years, saw this process of settlement via the national gaze, as a 'gathering of the exiles' and a 'return' to the traditional homeland of the Jewish people 'after 2000 years'. The Jewish immigrants were construed not as moving from one country to settle in another country but as 'rising' from what was considered a semi-human condition of living in the diaspora into full and dignified new independent life in the homeland.[13] Any comparative analysis that did take place in the literature for many years compared Israel to other western-style nation-states rather than to other settler societies. Interestingly enough, such a tendency can be seen even in a 'post-Zionist' volume such as this one, in the introduction and in some of the other contributions.

However, analysing Israel purely in nationalist terms cannot explain some of the basic interdependent exclusions and racialisation processes that have taken place in Israeli society, nor some of the facets of the Israeli–Palestinian conflict.

In the introduction to our book *Unsettling Settler Societies*,[14] Daiva Stasiulis and I defined settler societies (p. 3) as 'societies in which Europeans have settled, where their descendants have remained (at least for major parts of that society's history) politically dominant over indigenous peoples, and where a heterogeneous society has developed in class, ethnic and racial terms'. As such, 'settler societies' must be seen as falling along a continuum rather than between clear and fixed boundaries, and have to be seen as sharing many characteristics with other (colonial, post-colonial or metropolitan societies), especially given that the circuits and relations of power are vastly more complicated, both globally and in specific locations, than any binary division allows. Moreover, the extent to which a society is a 'settler society' is contested by the decolonising movements of various ethno-national groups within.

A variety of exclusionary and inclusionary mechanisms – political, economic, social and legal – operates in settler societies for constructing and deconstructing boundaries between collectivities. Crucial mechanisms for exclusion/inclusion have been those of immigration control and citizenship policies towards both indigenous and migrant groupings. While different settler societies in different historical periods have varied in their immigration policies, what seems to be common is the need to balance ideological pressures for encouraging 'desirable' immigrants – that is, those of the hegemonic ethnicity – to settle in the country and to block entry to the 'undesirable' ones, especially those from racialised collectivities. Because of the central importance of the demographic dimension in settler society projects ('populate or perish' used to be the rallying cry of the Australian settler project, for instance), migration policies and relations with the indigenous population need to be analysed as mutually dependent and interrelated. A lot, of course, depends on the relative numbers of people within the indigenous and settler communities, as well as on other specific features and historical contexts of the different settler-society projects.

As Adam has claimed, 'settler societies' have complicated the neat dichotomy between Europe and the rest of the world insofar as they are distinct from 'colonies of exploitation'.[15]

In every settler society project, the country is perceived by the settlers, at least to some extent, as a 'new world', available not only for immigration but also for establishing a 'new and better society' (often called, by Christian religious refugees in particular, 'the New Jerusalem'). In the specific nature of the Zionist project this new society was perceived to be, at the same time, a rehabilitation of an old one – the biblical Judaic state – and the 'New Jerusalem' was going to be built in the land of the 'Old Jerusalem'.[16] Theodor Herzl, the 'father' of the Zionist movement, wrote a utopian book that was supposed to describe the desired Jewish state. He called it 'Altneuland' – the old/new country. Thus even before the establishment of the Israeli state, the Zionist project claimed essential indigenous status for the Jews in Palestine, constructed as 'the Land of Israel'.

In hegemonic Zionist vision, history virtually stopped in the 'Land of Israel' since the Jews were exiled 2000 years ago. In such a vision, the indigenous population could be seen not only as part of the local exotic 'natural' environment – as the populations of other colonial societies were often perceived – but also as part of the orientalist vision of biblical times.[17] Zionism has constructed the myth of Palestine as sparsely populated: 'land without people for a people without land'. First uttered by Israel Zangwill, a Zionist and contemporary of Herzl in 1901, this myth became the predominant ideology of the Zionist settler movement, penetrating much of its cultural fabric.[18]

However, between a vision constructed in Europe and the reality developing on the ground, the difference is vast. The Zionist settler project in Palestine, while unique in its structure, objectives and goals, was not less colonialist than other settler projects. Palestine was not sparsely populated and the indigenous Palestinians were resentful of Zionist settlement. Since the crumbling of the Ottoman Empire in the late nineteenth century, Arab nationalism in the Mashreq and particularly in Greater Syria, which included Palestine, Lebanon and Syria, was developing. And while the Zionists in Europe were engaged in constructing their ideology of the 'new–old world', indigenous Palestinians were struggling for their national independence. On their national agenda, especially after the Balfour Declaration of 1917, was resistance to the very project of Zionist settlement.[19]

Like all major social and political movements, the Zionist movement was not homogeneous. Ehrlich, in chapter 4 of this volume, describes some of the main different strands of Zionism. For all its heterogeneity, however, the main thrust of the Zionist settlement project for most of its history has been to dispossess and then to exclude the Palestinians whenever possible from control over the various resources of the country and the state. There are many significant signposts throughout Zionist history of this process. The two most crucial are, first, the 1948 *nakba* (disaster), when the Palestinians in the area that became the territory of the Israeli state became refugees or a minority in their own country under military government, and, second, the 1967 war, when Israel conquered and then occupied the rest of historic Palestine, rendering its inhabitants stateless. The nature and character of Zionism evolved from a minority political movement into a powerful state in the region. The goals of the conquest of land *(Kibbush Ha'aretz)* and, in more partial and contested ways, the conquest of labour *(Kibbush Ha'avoda)* and the conquest of the market *(Totzeret Ha'aretz)*, have been pursued before and since the establishment of the state.

However, it is precisely because of the settler-society nature of the Zionist project that one needs to look at the relationships among the settlers themselves and not just between them and the indigenous population. While some non- and 'post'-Zionist scholars analysed the particular nature and history of the Zionist settlement project in relation to the Palestinians, and how it was influenced by other settlement movements, for instance German ones,[20] others looked at the ways in which the veteran Ashkenazi settlers benefited from the ways in which the Mizrahi Jews were incorporated into the Israeli labour market and political structure as part of the settlement process, especially after the establishment of the state.[21] One also has to remember that a large portion of the Jews who immigrated into Israel did this not primarily or at all from Zionist motivation but because they could not migrate to any other country. Nonetheless they helped to reproduce and fortify the Zionist settlement project. The interdependence between migration and the position of the indigenous people has not been limited to Jewish migration. Since the late 1980s, when it was considered of primary national interest to exclude Palestinian labour to a large extent from the Occupied Territories, non-Jewish migrant workers were recruited to replace them, although the terms of their migration were aimed at minimising the chance of their becoming a permanent settled community inside Israeli society.[22]

Another analytical dimension in which the *Yishuv* and Israeli society have been studied has been by feminist scholars. They examined the effect that the settlement project dynamic has had on gender relations in the *Yishuv* and Israeli society, in areas of the labour market, the military, demographic policies and national reproduction.[23]

The epoch of post-Zionism in Israel, as especially the chapters by Ram, Pappé and Herzog in this volume emphasise, is assigned to the time since the naturalising and homogenising effect of hegemonic Zionist discourse started to crumble. This happened under the pressure of changing demographic relations, new immigrations, new economic and technological developments, new regional and global contexts and the changes in internal political and religious contestations. While social and political diversity always existed in Israel, and the hegemony of the *Ahuselim* was always resisted to a certain degree, it is only in the 1990s that it has seriously destabilized. Ephraim Nimni describes this change as the transformation of Israeli society into a multicultural society.

Multiculturalism is a highly controversial ideology and policy, which has been challenged from both right and left. I do not have space here to discuss most aspects of the phenomenon, either generally or in Israel.[24] Multiculturalism has, however, often been described as a particular mode of reforming the welfare state and accommodating it to the mass settlement of immigrants and refugees from ex-colonial countries.[25] Applying the notion of multiculturalism to Israel in the 1990s constructs it as as a similarly pluralist society with a progressive social-democratic state.

Indigenous people usually oppose multiculturalism. They perceive the policy as co-opting them into one more ethnic minority, no different in their entitlements from all the other ethnic communities among the settlers, who are for them – to use an Australian aboriginal expression – all part of the 'imposing society'. It is only from the perspective of the settlers that the indigenous population could not possibly have more rights and claims on the country than other ethnic collectivities in the population (that is, once they have come to accept them as visible, entitled citizens at all – a situation that most often does not obtain in the early stages of settlement). The ability of the indigenous people to resist being co-opted into such a multiculturalist social order, however, depends on the particular demographic and political nature of the settler society.

There are at least four specific characteristic of the Zionist settler project that differentiate it from other settler-society projects and might affect the long-term resolution between the settlers and the indigenous population.

First, as mentioned above, in the Zionist case the settled territory and the settler society have not been constructed simply in terms of a new homeland and the building of a new nation, bound together around a myth of common destiny. 'Zion', 'the Land of Israel' and the Jewish people have been constructed as organically bonded together around a myth of common origin and belonging, while effective bonds to countries of origin have often been repressed. Moreover, as Nimni alludes to in chapter 6, because of the after-effects of the Nazi holocaust, and the hegemony of Zionism among most diasporic Jewish communities, Israel has been constructed as a post-factum 'homeland' not only to the Israeli Jews but also to many Jews who have never lived in Israel nor have any familial connection with any Israelis. At the same time, the 'chasms' between secular and religious Israeli Jews, Ashkenazim and Mizrahim, veterans and newcomers, as well as Jewish and non-Jewish (Palestinian, immigrants and migrants) citizens and residents of the state, point, as several contributions to the book have shown, to the highly partial and contested nature of the hegemonic Hebrew national collectivity that has been constructed in Israel.

Second, as Ehrlich points out, the Zionist settler project has been supported throughout its history mostly by the hegemonic imperial powers in the region, who saw the settlers as their natural allies in such a sensitive strategic global zone. At the same time, the Zionist movement was never an official colony of any empire. It was an autonomous international movement and then a state, a junior ally, rather than the product or puppet of any superpower. In contrast to the case of Algeria, for instance, (but as in the case of South Africa), no other state but that of the settler society can come to an effective agreement and resolution of the conflict with the indigenous people.

Third, unlike in most other settler societies, there is no clear majority either of indigenous people or of the members of the settler society. This makes the mode of resolution of the conflict between the settlers and indigenous people less predictable and predetermined. It probably protracts the time and suffering of the people before a stable resolution is achieved. It also makes demographic policies of immigration, emigration, other population movements and 'transfer', as well as the bearing of children (see Herzog's chapter 7) of even more central strategic importance in this conflict than in many others.

Fourth, the Israeli–Palestinian conflict has not only national, strategic and demographic dimensions but also a highly explosive religious one. The Jewish 'Promised Land' is also the Christian 'Holy Land', and was at the centre of the medieval 'clash of civilisations' between the Christian and Muslim worlds at the time of the Crusades. Palestine was always a central icon in the Pan-Arabic movement, but with the Islamisation of political resistance movements in and beyond the Arab world, Palestine (and especially, of course, the Muslim holy site in Jerusalem) has acquired such a symbolic status in a much wider constituency. At the same time, the growing political power of Christian evangelists in the USA who believe that Jewish possession and domination of the 'Holy Land' is vital for the return of Christ has a devastating effect on US foreign policy. Many of them support the Israeli right and especially the ethno-religious zealots who have been at the forefront of the settlement movement in the post-1967 Occupied Territories, particularly the West Bank, in which most of the Jewish holy sites are located.

Describing Israeli society in the 1990s, let alone now, as a post-Zionist or multicultural society does not allow space to consider these factors. As can be seen, especially in the chapters by Uri Ram and Ilan Pappé, there has been a move from describing Israeli society as post-Zionist to describing certain Israeli political trends as post-Zionist. They therefore added 'neo-Zionism' as a political trend contending with post-Zionism, both of which contest, if not replace, 'classical Zionism' as the dominating political power in contemporary Israel.

However, as some analyses, – such as those of Ehrlich and Ghanem in chapters 4 and 5 of this volume, and especially that of Oren Yiftachel,[26] who developed the notion of Israel as an ethnocracy – have shown, such a radical break with the 'classical Zionist' past has never taken place. The changes have been much more gradual and partial, and the Zionist project has continued to be active throughout its history in its mission to Judaise Palestine. This has had a profound effect on the nature of Israeli citizenship and democracy, as Yiftachel argued in a recent article:

> Israel has ruptured, by its own actions, the geography of statehood, and maintained a caste-like system of ethnic–religious–class classification. Without an inclusive geography and universal citizenship, Israel has created a colonial setting, held through violent control and a softening illusion of a nation-state and democratic citizenship'.[27]

This is an important warning against a certain complacency that sometimes appears when analysing Israel as a post-Zionist, liberal, multiculturalist society and/or even as an ethnic democracy.[28] In the latter description the ethnic domination of the Jewish collectivity in the Israeli state is constructed as 'normal' and as compatible with the construction of Israel as a democratic state.

Such complacency helped to foster the illusion during the so-called 'Oslo process' that the Israeli–Palestinian conflict is basically a conflict on borders between two neighbouring nations, each with its own distinct homeland, rather than a conflict between an ethno-settler project and a resisting indigenous population; or, rather, that the difference between these two analytical models is not crucial.[29] I would argue that ignoring or marginalising the construction of Israel as a settler society, with its own specific characteristics, prevents most Israelis, both emotionally and analytically, from understanding some epistemological and ontological aspects of the Israeli–Palestinian conflict. Such blindness can be found even in Nimni's introduction to this book, which in so many other ways is excellent, when he engages with Edward Said's and Perry Anderson's critiques of the politics of some post-Zionist scholars.

Moreover, I would argue that such an understanding is vital for any possible transversal dialogue[30] between the conflicting sides that goes beyond the manipulative simulation games of conflict resolution models that have occupied such a central place in the Oslo negotiations in a most 'postmodernist' manner. It does not necessarily make the solution of the conflict easier – especially given regional and global developments as well as local ones. But it establishes political and moral clarity, which can be used as a first stepping-stone in the long haul towards any resolution of the conflict and any process of reconciliation that would involve some measure of dignity and justice. It would also help to maintain the distinction between anti-semitism and anti-Zionism, which Israel is doing its best to blur, and might help in the long run to combat some of the possible devastating results of Jews as well as Palestinians paying a horrendous price for being caught between the warring blocs of the 'clash of civilizations'.

Contemplating all this, I can only go back to Gramsci, trying to retain my 'optimism of the will' alongside my extreme 'pessimism of the intellect'. Perhaps it is better yet to adhere to Noam Chomsky's words that have been circulating recently in email peace lists:[31]

> If you assume that there's no hope, you guarantee that there will be no hope. If you assume that there is an instinct for freedom, that there are opportunities to change things, there's a chance you may contribute to making a better world.

Amen to that.

NOTES

- I would like to thank Oren Yiftachel, Avishai Ehrlich and Ephraim Nimni for their helpful feedback to the first draft of this paper.

1. E.g. Lawrence J. Silberstein (1999) *Postzionism debates: Knowledge & Power in Israeli Culture*, New York and London, Routledge; Ner Livne, 'The rise and fall of post-zionism', in *Ha'aretz*, 21 September 2001.

2. Tom Nairn (1977) *The Breakup of Britain*, London, Verso. His observation is about nationalism in general.

3. E.g. Arie Bober (ed. for Matzpen) (1972) *The Other Israel: The Radical Case Against Zionism*, New York, Doubleday; Simha Flapan (1987) *The Birth of Israel: Myths and Realities*, New York, Pantheon Books; Baruch Kimmerling (1983) *Zionism and Territory*, Berkeley, University of California Press; Zeev Sternhell (1995) *Nation-Building or Reform of Society*, Tel-Aviv, Am-Overd [Hebrew].

4. Israel Shahak (1981) 'The Jewish religion and its attitude to non-Jews', *Khamsin* 9, London, Ithaca Press, pp. 3–49.

5. E.g. N. Levin (1977) *While Messiah tarried: Jewish socialist movements 1871–1917*, New York, Schocken Books; Y. Peled (1989) *Class and ethnicity in the pale: the political economy of Jewish workers' nationalism in late Imperial Russia*, New York, St Martin's Press; see also Nira Yuval-Davis (1987) 'Marxism and Jewish nationalism', *History Workshop Journal*, no. 24, pp. 82–110; A.K. Wildman (1973) *Russian and Jewish social democracy*, Bloomington, Indiana University Press.

6. E.g. V.I. Lenin (1976) *Critical Remarks on the National Question*, Moscow, Progressive Publishers; S. Eisendstadt (1929) *History of the Jewish Workers Movement*, Tel Aviv, Hakibutz Ha'artzi [Hebrew]; Leon Trotsky (1967) *History of the Russian Revolution*, vol. 2, p. 42.

7. Dov Ber Borochov, the leader of the Marxist Zionists, used the anti-colonial argment to

object to Zionist settlement in Uganda but did not see it as a factor in the settlement in Palestine because of what he saw as its particular social and economic characteristics, which he believed would bring the eventual assimilation of the Palestinians into the settler society. Dov Ber Borochov (1972) *Nationalism and Class Struggle*, American Zionist Youth Foundation Booklet, pp. 7–38.

8. E.g. Elmer Berger (1942) *Why I am a Non-Zionist*, New York; Jonathan Boyarin and Daniel Boyarin (2002) *The Power of Diaspora*, University of Minnesota Press; R. Tekiner, Abed Rabbo and Norton Mezvinsky (eds), *Anti-Zionist Analytical Reflections*, Rattleboro, Vermont, Amana.

9. See, for example, Shlomo Swirsky (1989) *Israel: The Oriental Majority*, London, Zed Books; Ella Shohat (1988) 'Sephardim in Israel: Zionism from the standpoint of its Jewish victims', *Social Text* 19–20, pp. 1–34.

10. Although Nimni may not have considered the possibility of major Israeli emigration in the event that the current state of conflict continues much longer.

11. The *Ahusalim* are the Israeli equivalent of the WASPs in the USA – in this case Ashkenazi [Western], secular, veteran settlers, socialists and Zionist/nationalist Israeli Jews.

12. *Yishuv* actually means settlement and is the Hebrew name of the Zionist settler society in Palestine before the establishment of the Israeli state in 1948.

13. The word used for the act of migrating to Palestine/Israel by Jews is '*aliya*', 'rising' – the same term used when Jewish men come up to the stage in synagogues to read from the Torah. In other words, the act of migration has been constructed as a sacred – if not actually religious – task.

14. Daiva Stasiulis and Nira Yuval-Davis (eds) (1995) *Unsettling Settler Societies, articulations of gender, race, ethnicity and class*, London, Sage.

15. Heribert Adam (1972) *Modernizing Racial Domination*, Berkeley, University of California Press, p. 17.

16. See Nahla Abdo and Nira Yuval-Davis (1995) 'Palestine, Israel and the Zionist Settler Project', in Stasiulis and Yuval-Davis, *Unsettling Settler Societies*, pp. 291–322.

17. Ella Shohat (1991) 'Making the silences speak in the Israeli cinema', in Barbara Swirski and Marilyn P. Safir (eds), *Calling the Equality Bluff: Women in Israel*, New York, Pergamon Press, pp. 31–40.

18. Shlomo Finkel and Shimshon Bichler (1984) *The Desperate: The Money Aristocracy in Israel*, Tel Aviv, Kadima [Hebrew].

19. See, for example, George Antonius (1939) *The Arab Awakening: The Story of the Arab National Movement*, Philadelphia, Lippincott; Gerard Chaliand (1972) *The Palestinian Resistance*, Harmondsworth, Penguin Books; Albert Hourani (1946) *Syria and Lebanon: A Political Essay*, London.

20. See, for example, Gershon Sahfir (1989) *Land, Labour and the Origins of the Israeli–Palestinian Conflict 1882–1914*, Cambridge, Cambridge University Press; Benny Morris (1991) *The Birth of the Palestinian Refugee Problem 1947–1949*, Tel Aviv, Am Oved [Hebrew].

21. See endnote 10, and Dahan-Kalev's chapter in this volume.

22. In the July 2002 issue of the newsletter of Kav Laoved (The Workers' Hot-line), an NGO dedicated to defending the rights of workers in Israel, it was reported that there are about 300,000 migrant workers in Israel, from countries as diverse as, for example, China and Somalia. Most work under conditions of indenture and bond. According to the Israeli Minister of Labour, Shlomo Binizri, trade in migrant workers is 'the most profitable business in Israel, estimated at about [US]$3 billion'.

23. See, for example, Debra Bernstein (1987) *A Woman in the Land of Israel*, Tel Aviv, Hotza'at Hapoalim; Hanna Herzog (1998) 'Homefront and Battlefront and the Status of Jewish and

Palestinian Women in Israel', in *Israeli Studies*, 3, pp. 61–84, and chapter 7 in this volume; Nira Yuval-Davis (1982) *Israeli Women and Men: Divisions Behind The Unity*, London, Change Publications.

24. For my position on multiculturalism, see the introductory chapter of Nira Yuval-Davis and G. Sahgal (1992) *Refusing Holy Orders*, London, Virago; also chapter 3 of Nira Yuval-Davis (1997) *Gender and Nation*, London, Sage.

25. Karl-Ulrik Scheirup (1995) 'Multiculturalism and universalism in the USA and EU', paper for the workshop Nationalism and Ethnicity, Berne, March; John Rex (1995) 'Ethnic identity and the nation-state: the political sociology of multicultural societies', *Social Identities*, 1 (1).

26. E.g. O. Yiftachel (1997) 'Israeli Society and Jewish–Palestinian Reconciliation: Ethnocracy and Its Territorial Contradictions', *Middle East Journal*, vol. 51, no. 4, pp. 505–19; A. Ghanem, N. Rouhana and O. Yiftachel (1998) 'Questioning Ethnic Democracy', in *Israel Studies*, vol. 3, no. 2, pp. 253–68; O. Yiftachel (1999) '"Ethnocracy": the Politics of Judaising Israel/Palestine', *Constellations: International Journal of Critical and Democratic Theory*, vol. 6, no. 3, pp. 364–90.

27. O. Yiftachel (2002) 'The shrinking space of citizenship: Ethnocratic politics in Israel', in *Middle East Report*, no. 223, summer.

28. E.g. Shafir Gershon and Yoav Peled (eds) (2000) *The New Israel: Peacemaking and Liberalization*, Boulder, Colo., Westview; Sammy Smooha (1997) 'Ethnic Democracy: Israel as an archetype', in *Israel Studies*, vol. 2, no. 2, pp. 198–241.

29. Even the notion of ethnocracy – as it is not specific to settler societies and is a model of ethnically divided states with one hegemonic ethnic collectivity, which has been spreading in post-colonial and especially post-Soviet countries – can blur this difference, unless it is seen as complementary rather than alternative to the settler society model.

30. See, for example, 'Soundings' (1999) *Transversal Politics* (Special Issue), no. 12; Nira Yuval-Davis (1994) 'Women, Ethnicity and Empowerment', in *Feminism and Psychology*, vol. 4, no. 1, pp. 179–98; and the final chapter of Yuval-Davis (1997) *Gender and Nation*.

31. I myself saw this quote in a mailing on 4 Sept 2002, without specific reference to any of Chomsky's writings, in a circular of the e-mail list of WICZNET (the international research network on Women in Conflict Zones).

◎ Appendix

What follows is an account by Edward Said of a public meeting that took place in Paris between three Palestinian intellectuals (including himself) and three Israeli intellectuals in 1998 (referred to in the introduction to this book). Said's reflections about the 'new historians' and Palestinian history are interesting for the immediate implications they have for the preceding discussion on post-Zionism, as the debate is not about historical events (on which there was remarkable agreement between most participants) but on what contemporary conclusions should be drawn from those historical events.

New History, Old Ideas*

Edward Said

The French monthly *Le Monde Diplomatique* together with the *Revue d'études palestiniennes*, a quarterly journal published in Paris by the Institute of Palestine Studies, held a conference last week which I attended and participated in. Although it was announced as the first time that the so-called 'new' Israeli historians and their Palestinian counterparts had exchanged ideas in public, it was actually the third or fourth time; yet what made the Paris meeting so novel was that this was certainly the first time that a prolonged exchange between them was possible.

On the Palestinian side there were Elie Sambar, Nur Masalha and myself; on the Israeli side Benny Morris, Ilan Pappé, Itamar Rabinowitch (who is not really a new historian, but a former Labour Party adviser, Israeli ambassador to the United States, professor of history at Tel Aviv University, and an expert on Syria, but whose views seem to be changing), and finally, Zeev Sternhell, an Israeli historian of right-wing European mass movements, professor at the Hebrew University, author of a very important recent book on the myths of Israeli society (the main ones of which – that it is a liberal, socialist, democratic state – he demolished completely in an extraordinarily detailed analysis of its illiberal, quasi-fascist, and profoundly anti-socialist character as evidenced by the Labour Party generally, and the Histadrut in particular).

Because it was not well advertised, the conference attracted rather small audiences on the whole, but because of the quality of the material presented and the fact that sessions went on for several hours, it was a very valuable exercise, despite the unevenness of some of the contributions. One very powerful impression I had was that whereas the Israeli participants – who

* From *Al Ahram Weekly*, no. 378, 21–27 May 1998.

were by no means of the same political persuasion – often spoke of the need for detachment, critical distance, and reflective calm as important for historical study, the Palestinian side was much more urgent, more severe and even emotional in its insistence on the need for new history. The reason is of course that Israel, and consequently most Israelis, are the dominant party in the conflict: they hold all the territory, have all the military power, and can therefore take the time, and have the luxury to sit back and let the debate unfold calmly. Only Ilan Pappé, an avowed socialist and anti-Zionist historian at Haifa University, was open in his espousal of the Palestinian point of view, and, in my opinion, provided the most iconoclastic and brilliant of the Israeli interventions. For the others in varying degree, Zionism was seen as a necessity for Jews. I was surprised, for instance, when Sternhell during the final session admitted that a grave injustice was committed against the Palestinians, and that the essence of Zionism was that it was a movement for conquest, then went on to say that it was a 'necessary' conquest.

One of the most remarkable things about the Israelis, again except for Pappé, is the profound contradiction, bordering on schizophrenia, that informs their work. Benny Morris, for example, ten years ago wrote the most important Israeli work on the birth of the Palestinian refugee problem. Using Haganah and Zionist archives he established beyond any reasonable doubt that there had been a forced exodus of Palestinians as a result of a specific policy of 'transfer' which had been adopted and approved by Ben-Gurion. Morris's meticulous work showed that in district after district commanders had been ordered to drive out Palestinians, burn villages, systematically take over their homes and property. Yet strangely enough, by the end of the book Morris seems reluctant to draw the inevitable conclusions from his own evidence. Instead of saying outright that the Palestinians were, in fact, driven out he says that they were partially driven out by Zionist forces, and partially 'left' as a result of war. It is as if he was still enough of a Zionist to believe the ideological version – that Palestinians left on their own without Israeli eviction – rather than completely to accept his own evidence, which is that Zionist policy dictated Palestinian exodus. Similarly, in his book Sternhell admits that the Zionists never considered the Arabs as a problem because if they did they would have openly admitted that the Zionist plan to establish a Jewish state could not have been realised without also getting rid of the Palestinians. But he still insisted during the conference in Paris that although it was morally wrong to expel Palestinians, it was necessary to do so.

Despite these discordances it is impressive that when pushed hard either by Pappé or by the Palestinians, both Morris and Sternhell appeared to hesitate. I take their changing views as symptomatic of a deeper change taking place inside Israel. The point here is that a significant change in the main lines of Zionist ideology cannot really occur within the hegemony of official politics, either Labour or Likud, but must take place outside that particular context, that is, where intellectuals are more free to ponder and reflect upon the unsettling realities of present-day Israel. The problem with other attempts by intellectuals on both sides to influence Netanyahu's policies, for instance, is that as in the case of the Copenhagen group they take place too close to governments who have a much narrower, much shorter-range view of things. If the years since 1993 have shown anything it is that no matter how enlightened or liberal, the official Zionist view of the conflict with the Palestinians (and this is as true of left Zionists like Meretz or centre left people like Shimon Peres) is prepared to live with the schizophrenia I referred to above. Yes, we want peace with the Palestinians, but no, there was nothing wrong with what we had to do in 1948. As far as real peace is concerned this basic contradiction is quite untenable, since it accepts the notion that Palestinians in their own land are secondary to Jews. Moreover, it also accepts the fundamental contradiction between Zionism and democracy (how can one have a democratic Jewish state and, as is now the case, one million non-Jews who are not equal in rights, land owning, or work to the Jews?). The great virtue of the new historians is that their work at least pushes the contradictions within Zionism to limits otherwise not apparent to most Israelis, and even many Arabs.

It is certainly true that the great political importance today of the new Israeli historians is that they have confirmed what generations of Palestinians, historians or otherwise, have been saying about what happened to us as a people at the hands of Israel. And of course they have done so as Israelis who in some measure speak for the conscience of their people and society. But here, speaking self-critically, I feel that as Arabs generally, and Palestinians in particular, we must also begin to explore our own histories, myths, and patriarchal ideas of the nation, something which, for obvious reasons we have not so far done. During the Paris colloquium Palestinians, including myself, were speaking with a great sense of urgency about the present since, in this present, the Palestinian *nakba* continues. Dispossession goes on, and the denial of our rights has taken new and more punishing forms. Nevertheless, as intellectuals and historians we have a duty to look at our history, the history of our leaderships, and of our institutions with a new critical eye. Is there something about those that can perhaps explain the difficulties as a people that we now find ourselves in? What about the conflict between the great families or *hamulas*, the fact that our leaders have traditionally not been elected democratically, and the fact, equally disastrous, that we seem to reproduce corruption and mediocrity in each new generation? These are serious, and even crucial matters, and they cannot either be left unanswered or postponed indefinitely under the guise of national defence and national unity. There is perhaps a start of critical self-awareness in Yezid Sayegh's new book on the history of Palestinian armed struggle, but we need more concretely political and critical works of that sort, works whose grasp of all the complexities and paradoxes of our history are not shied away from.

So far as I know neither the work of Morris, Pappé, or Sternhell has been translated into Arabic. This absence should be remedied forthwith. Just as important, I think, is the need for Arab intellectuals to interact directly with these historians by having them invited for discussions in Arab universities, cultural centres, and public fora. Similarly I believe it is our duty as Palestinian and yes, even Arab intellectuals to engage Israeli academic and intellectual audiences by lecturing at Israeli centres, openly, courageously, uncompromisingly. What have years of refusing to deal with Israel done for us? Nothing at all, except to weaken us and weaken our perception of our opponent. Politics since 1948 is now at an end, buried in the failures of the Oslo process of attempted separation between Israeli Jews and Palestinians. As part of the new politics I have been speaking about in these articles, a splendid opportunity presents itself in continued interaction with the new Israeli historians who, while a tiny minority, nevertheless represent a phenomenon of considerable importance. Their work, for instance, had a great influence on the 22-part film series, *Tekuma*, shown on Israeli television as a history of the state produced for its 50th year celebrations. They are greatly in demand in Israeli schools as lecturers, and their work has attracted the attention of historians and others in both Europe and the United States. It seems anomalous, not to say retrograde, that the one place they have not been fully heard is the Arab world, but we need to rid ourselves of our racial prejudices and ostrich-like attitudes and make the effort to change the situation. The time has come.

◎ Index